INTERPRETING THE PRECAUTIONARY PRINCIPLE

INTERPRETING THE PRECAUTIONARY PRINCIPLE

EDITED BY TIM O'RIORDAN
AND JAMES CAMERON

earthscan
from Routledge

First published in hardback in 1994 by Cameron May Ltd

First published in paperback by Earthscan 2009

A catalogue record for this book is available from the British Library
ISBN 13: 978-1-138-16648-6 (hbk)
ISBN 13: 978-1-85383-200-0 (pbk)

Typeset by Cameron May Ltd

For a full list of publications please contact:

Earthscan
2 Park Square, Milton Park, Abingdon, Oxfordshire OX14 4RN
Simultaneously published in the USA and Canada by Earthscan
711 Third Avenue, New York, NY 10017, USA

First issued in hardback 2017

Earthscan is an imprint of the Taylor & Francis Group, an informa business

Earthscan publishes in association with the International Institute for Environment and Development.

At Earthscan we strive to minimize our environmental impacts and carbon footprint through reducing waste, recycling and offsetting our CO_2 emissions, including those created through publication of this book.

CONTENTS

Foreword *6*

PART I - HISTORY AND CONTEXT OF THE PRECAUTIONARY PRINCIPLE

1 The History and contemporary significance of the precautionary principle *12*

2 The precautionary principle in Germany - enabling government *31*

PART II - IMPLICATIONS FOR SCIENCE

Editorial Introduction *62*

3 Precaution, science and the sin of hubris *69*

4 What if? versus If it ain't broke, don't fix it *102*

5 Taking care *108*

6 The social construction of precaution *117*

PART III - IMPLICATIONS FOR MANAGEMENT

Editorial Introduction *128*

7 The precautionary principle and economic anaysis *132*

8 The precautionary principle and moral values *152*

9 How the media respond to precaution *165*

10 The regulation of genetically modified organisms *172*

11 The precautionary principle in local government *183*

PART IV - THE INTERNATIONAL DIMENSION

Editorial Introduction *200*

12 The precautionary principle in US environmental law *203*

13 The introduction of precautionary principle in the UK *229*

14 The precautionary principle in Australia *252*

15 The staus of the precautionary principle in international law *262*

PART V - THE FUTURE

16 Seeping through the pores *292*

FOREWORD

by Lord Crickhowell - Chairman of the National Rivers Authority

It is curious that the concepts embraced in the Precautionary Principle have only been accorded their present significance for less than two decades because the need for such concepts seems so obvious that it is hard to conceive that anyone could omit them from any serious structured attempt to protect the environment. However, the fact that they were all too frequently omitted in the past has been painfully brought home to many Members of Lloyds, now ruined by asbestosis and clean-up liability claims, and is at the root of the problems now faced by governments and regulators who have to deal with the consequences of contaminated land and polluted aquifers.

Some environmentalists argue that so great are the dangers that there must be no discharges of any polluting or potentially polluting substances to air, land or water, regardless of quality, regardless of the diluting capacity of the receiving media, regardless of cost and regardless of social consequences. Such an approach that would take us back to a pre-industrial era and impose devastating costs is unrealistic. In the real world industry, governments, and regulators, have to attempt environmental impact assessments that seek to balance costs and benefits. In Britain an approach has been developed for the protection of the water environment based upon the application of environmental quality standards which define the needs for the protection of different uses identified for a given stretch of water. The approach has the advantage that it is sensitive not just to the effects of industrial discharge, but to the combined effects of the whole range of different discharges into a water body, and it enables an overall limit on levels of contaminants to be set according to the required uses of that water body. It is an approach however that may not be equally appropriate for all media, and it does not effectively deal with those substances that are persistent and have a tendency to build-up in the environment. For substances of this kind it is necessary to adopt a more precautionary approach and constrain the amounts permitted to be discharged by means of emission standards. This method of dealing with the problem has been formally introduced into British national legislation by the 1990 Environmental Protection Act. It is also the approach on which many E.C. Environmental Directives are based. Environmental policy in the United Kingdom will increasingly involve the integration of the two approaches and Integrated Pollution Control will eventually ensure that the entry of prescribed substances into the environment will be strictly controlled, and where it is thought desirable, eliminated.

Even if we avoid the economic and social consequences that would arise from an excessively restrictive application of the Precautionary Principle, governments and regulators may still be confronted with extremely difficult choices about the possible consequences for the environment itself of even a moderate approach; and quite often such decisions are taken because of political pressure rather than on the basis of strict scientific analysis. For example, a version of the Precautionary Principle was enshrined in the 1987 Ministerial Declaration over the North Sea, but it can be argued that the decision taken at the North Sea Conference to ban the dumping of sewage sludge at sea may on balance have been actually harmful to the environment. The costs have been very great and have prevented expenditure on other environmental priorities while the alternative means of disposal of sludge by incineration or its application to agricultural land, can themselves lead to significant environmental damage. A proper cost benefit appraisal might have led to the conclusion that different policies were appropriate for the deeper waters of the Atlantic than those judged necessary in the shallow and confined waters of the North Sea.

While those involved have been deliberating on such issues, substantial legal battles have been fought about the responsibilities and the liabilities that arise from actions taken long before the Precautionary Principle was established as a central concept in environmental management. In the civil liability case, Cambridge Water Company v. Eastern Counties Leather plc, which was argued before the House of Lords on Appeal in October 1993, Eastern Counties Leather was successful in overturning the 1992 Appeal Court ruling holding them liable for solvent contamination of groundwater, on the basis that the damage caused was not reasonably foreseeable. It seems clear that in future such cases will be judged on the basis of knowledge at the time that the actions that eventually led to damage took place, which will prevent many actions for historic pollutions. At about the same time a House of Lords Select Committee began examining whether there was a need for an European Union wide system of civil liability. The Committee recommended a strict civil liability regime for future pollution, and concluded that strict liability for past pollution is justified where the present owner or operator was responsible for the action that caused it and knew, or should have known, that the activities were potentially dangerous.

The Select Committee pointed out that the Precautionary Principle and the Polluter Pays Principle (both enshrined in article 130 (r), of the Maastricht Treaty) provide no more than general indications of what might be desirable policy and practice; and that difficult practical and political judgements need to be made about where in equity the costs and benefits should fall; and that the consequences of decisions may have trans-boundary economic social and environmental effects. The Committee suggested that a public debate on these complex issues is required if Member States and the Community policies are to command public understanding and support. Other equally complex and important questions are being widely debated as well, such as the impact of the Precautionary Principle on conventional cost-benefit analysis, and the danger that if the duty of environmental care is very strict, we could see a throttling of invention, innovation and growth. The way in which such questions are resolved has profound implications for industry, insurers, consumers who have to pay the costs, for society that benefits from modern processes and technology, for the sustainability of the environment, and for governments, regulators, and lawyers, who have to establish acceptable standards and enforce them, and where regulation has failed to apportion blame and responsibility.

These issues and others were examined at a Conference organised by the Centre for Social and Economic Research on the

Global Environment and Green College, Oxford, in April 1983. Those who took part agreed that there was no comprehensive text on the subject, especially as it applied to contemporary national and international developments in environmental policy. Apart from a few legal articles there is no adequate treatment of the subject in published form. This book attempts to remedy that deficiency and it brings together contributions from a number of contributors expert in their own particular fields. It was conceived with the idea that it might become an essential work of reference for national and international environmental research and management organisations and for students in environmental law, environmental science, and environmental management, but I believe that the subject is of such compelling interest and importance that it will be read by a very much wider circle than that.

INTERPRETING THE PRECAUTIONARY PRINCIPLE

Part I

History and Context of the Precautionary Principle

Chapter 1

The History and Contemporary Significance of the Precautionary Principle

Timothy O'Riordan and James Cameron

The precautionary principle is a culturally framed concept that takes its cue from changing social conceptions about the appropriate roles of science, economics, ethics, politics and the law in pro-active environmental protection and management. As this book will reveal, it is a rather shambolic concept, muddled in policy advice and subject to whims of international diplomacy and the unpredictable public mood over the true cost of sustainable living. Because of the insistence and persistence of the sustainability debate, largely as a result of the much analysed UN Conference on Environment and Development held in Rio de Janeiro in June 1992, precaution thrives in the flux of values and new organisational arrangements generated by the Rio meeting.

Above all, however, precaution continues to evolve because of the peculiar requirements of adjusting to global environmental stresses and strains. Humanity is in trouble: up to 10000 people die daily because of avoidable environmental foreclosure in their wretched lives. The earth itself is showing signs of wear and tear in terms of soil erosion, savage loss of land cover, potentially massive species loss, destruction of stratospheric ozone, and a huge gamble with future climate, to say little of ubiquitous toxification of ecosystems, excessive demands on water resources and mounting piles of waste materials. All these points are well covered in regular reports by the World Resources Institute (1993), Worldwatch Institute (1993), the UN Environment Progamme (1993), the World Bank (1992) and the Organisation for Economic Cooperation and Development (1991) together with thoughtful anthologies by Simmons (1989), Turner et al. (1991) and Myers (1993). Global environmental change stimulates the precautionary principle in three ways:

The requirement of collective action

The global "commons" is a life support system of intricate complexity. We are only just beginning to realise how unique and precious it is in the cosmos as a whole. More to the point we are slowly recognising how utterly vital it is for our survival as a civilised and wealth generating species. It is still incalculable how much it would cost us to replace by artificial means all of the services that natural systems provide in assimilating, buffering, cleansing and absorbing, to say nothing of their primary role, namely redistributing chemical and physical energy to renew life in every nook and cranny of the globe. Jim Lovelock in Chapter 5 makes a stab at the air conditioning value of tropical forests - one small point of a myriad of functions supplied by these mysterious ecosystems. He concludes they are at least worth the total value of annual wealth generated by humanity itself. He may be far out, who knows: but his analysis points to the crucial issue that we have for far too long taken these functions as not only free and accessible, but also indestructable.

To safeguard these critical life support processes requires collective action by every nation state and every global citizen. We do not know how far they are being stressed, though the consensus is that this stress is fairly massive. Nor do we know how close to breakdown any or all of these functions may be. Because everyone has to play their part, and because we must allow the earth room to breathe, so precaution adopts the mantle of earth protector and earth shop steward.

The requirement of burden sharing

Not all countries are equally in a position to play their part as protector or steward. So precaution has to enter the realm of broker and facilitator in devices to help the strong to assist the weak in the common cause of survival. The Rio Conference essentially failed to extract any commitment from the rich to the poor. But in its declaration 15 it did accept that the application of precaution should be handled by each country according to its capabilities. This opens up the scope for burden sharing by recognising that those whose greater wealth has in part been won at the expense of the poor and of environmental life support systems have a greater moral and public responsibility to help those unable in themselves to follow a precautionary and sustainable growth right now.

The rise of global citizenship

Global change naturally is time driven. Then full effects of current disruption will only be felt by the next two generations, and all of the second remain to be born. Global citizenship means taking care across both space and time, recognising that every individual act has implications not only for the household undertaking it, but for all households on the earth today, and the billion or so of new households that will be formed within 25 years. Each additional molecule of CO_2 or chlorofluorocarbons or methane remains active for at least 25 years, and usually over 50 years. An unknown number of our actions have incipient global and generational implications. Precaution captures this mood of a new self interest in collective "sacrifice", namely that good citizenship is both a life saver and a recognition of solidarity with creation. Only by <u>anticipating</u> possible catastrophe and by <u>taking care</u> over every daily practice can we imbue a precautionary sensitivity in ourselves and our offspring.

There are reasons enough for introducing a precautionary line of thinking into all human cultures. As the text that follows suggests, and as the editorial introductions to each of the three main sections of the book elaborate, three additional factors are shaping the evolution of the precautionary principle in modern environmentalism:

Extending science

Natural processes appear to operate in ways that are not fully understood by conventional scientific methods. Indeed much of the life support functions already described may act in an indeterminate, and hence act in a thoroughly unpredictable manner. The usual scientific approaches, dependent on observation, verification, falsification and replication coupled to prediction by reference to statistical inference, hypothesis testing and modelling may not be sufficient to instil confidence. Of crucial significance is that elusive zone where phase changes in such systems might occur. These would result in possible catastrophic convulsions in human use of the earth and huge costs of remediation or substitution. Society is terribly ambivalent about this matter. Catastrophe is truly too awesome to contemplate so is sidestepped. But natural resilience, though always profoundly impressive and humbling to contemplate, cannot be relied upon forever. This dilemma is well described by Simmons (1989).

Anticipatory action

International agreements covering global or regional environmental protection are increasingly based on proactive or preventative measures which encompass collective action and burden sharing. As a result signatories to major agreements have to give to significant changes in their economies and lifestyles ahead of scientific proof of the likely gains of making such sacrifices. This is one of the most awkward aspects of applying the precautionary principle in a democracy. Citizens like to be assured of the justification of pain and forebearance. When the cost benefit analysis look alarmingly loaded in favour of high initial expenditures for uncertain and distant gains, occurring well beyond present lifetimes of voting and taxpaying families, proaction in a self serving democracy becomes sorely tested.

Shifting the burden of proof

As evidence of life-threatening environmentl transformation accumulates, wealthy societies at least, and impoverished cultures if given the option, are becoming more risk averse. They expect better guarantees of zero discharges or strictly limited damage before allowing change to proceed. This is inevitably shifting the burden of proof onto those who propose to alter the status quo, rather than simply to expect victims subsequently to seek compensation. This is having a major effect on the common and statute law of liability with far greater emphasis on self insurance or shared compensation pools. Inevitably the protection of adequate statutory regulation backed by national and international cash safeguards will be required, but that is a little way off. It is of interest to note that bilateral and multilateral aid agencies are increasingly being required to ensure proactive safeguards to ensure that local inhabitants are not defenceless in any case of environmental liability (see Costanza and Cowell, 1992).

Definitions of the precautionary principle

As Sonja Boehmer Christiansen points out in the chapter that follows, the prcautionary principle evolved out of the German socio-legal tradition, created in the heyday of democratic socialism in the 1930s, centering on the concept of good household management. This was regarded as a constructive partnership between the individual, the economy and the state to manage change so as to improve the lot of both society and the natural world upon which it depended for survival. This invested the precautionary principle with a managerial or programmable quality, a purposeful role in guiding future political and regulatory action.

As Boehmer Christiansen argues, the German concept of Vörsorgeprinzip means much more than the rough English translation of foresight planning. It absorbs notions of risk prevention, cost effectiveness but in a looser economic framework, ethical responsibilities towards maintaining the integrity of natural systems, and the fallibility of human understanding. The right of nature means, in part, giving it room to accommodate to human interference, so precaution presumes that mistakes can be made. For the Germans, therefore, precaution is an interventionist measure, a justification of state involvement in the day to day lives of its länder and its citizenry in the name of good government. Social planning in the economy, in technology, in morality and in social initiatives all can be justified by a loose and open ended interpretation of precaution. As we shall see, it is precisely the unravellability that makes precaution both feared and welcomed.

Throughout the late 1970s and early 1980s these notions of care and wise practice have been extended to six basic concepts now enshrined in the precautionary principle.

(i) preventative anticipation: a willingness to take action in advance of scientific proof of evidence of the need for the proposed action on the grounds that further delay will prove ultimately most costly to society and nature, and, in the longer term, selfish and unfair to future generations.

(ii) safeguarding of ecological space or environmental room for manoeuvre as a recognition that margins of tolerance should not even be approached, let alone breached. This is sometimes known as widening the assimilative capacity of natural systems by deliberately holding back from possible but undesirable resource use.

(iii) proportionality of response or cost-effectiveness of mar gins of error to show that the selected degree of restraint is not unduly costly. This introduces a bias to conventional cost benefit analysis to include a weighting function of ignorance, and for the likely greater dangers for future generations if life support capacities are undermined when such risks could consciously be avoided.

(iv) duty of care, or onus of proof on those who propose change: this raises profound questions over the degree of freedom to take calculated risks, thereby to innovate, and to compensate for possible losses by building in ameliorative measures. Formal duties of environmental care, coupled to an extension of strict liability for any damage, no matter how unanticipated, could throttle invention, imagination and growth. Alternatively, when creatively deployed such strictures could encourage imagination and creativity in

technology, economic valuation, technological advance and unusual forms of ameliorative compensation. Hence the concept of proportionality can be regarded either as a deadweight or a touchstone for the visionary.

(v) promoting the cause of intrinsic natural rights: the legal notion of ecological harm is being widened to include the need to allow natural processes to function in such a manner as to maintain the essential support for all life on earth. The application of ecological buffers in future management gives a practical emphasis to the thorny ethical concept of intrinsic natural rights.

(vi) paying for past ecological debt: precaution is essentially forward looking but there are those who recognise that in the application of care, burden sharing, ecologically buffered cost effectiveness and shifting the burden of proof, there ought to be a penalty for not being cautious or caring in the past. This suggests that those who have created a large ecological burden already should be more "precautious" than those whose ecological footprints have to date been lighter. In a sense this is precaution put into reverse: compensating for past errors of judgement based on ignorance or an unwillingness to shoulder an unclearly stated sense of responsibility for the future. This element of the principle is still embryonic in law and practice, but the notion of "common but differentiated responsibility" enshrined in the UN Framework Convention on Climate Change, and the concept of conducting precaution "according to capabilities" as laid down in principle 15 of the Rio Declaration reflect to some extent these ideas.

By no means all of these interpretations are formally approved in international law and common practice. At present the line is to act prudently when there is sufficient scientific evidence and where action can be justified on reasonable judgements of cost effectiveness and where inaction could lead to potential irreversibility or demonstrate harm to the defenders and future generations. In substance, the application is usually derived for chemicals whose effects are potentially toxic, persistent or bioaccumulative (i.e. concentrating in the food chain from one predator to another), or where certain combinations or concentrations of chemicals could alter the physical and chemical state of soil or water. In this sense the notion in international affairs is mostly one of prevention, and justification of some action rather than to claim scientific uncertainty as a reason for delay.

Let us put precaution into both the sustainability perspective and that of proportionality, or economic-societal justification of possible adverse costs in favour of taking care. On the sustainability front, economists like to speak of weak and strong sustainability as a major distinction, with very weak and very strong variants on either side. The most accessible reference is Turner (1993). Very weak sustainability is based on the presumption that losses of environmental resources (natural capital) can be made up by innovation, ingenuity, imagination and adaptation. In Figure 1.1 rising damage costs spurs an interest in damage avoiding market prices, regulatory behaviour and technological substitution. Precaution has a place, mostly as a spur to innovation and managerial adaptation. So the line of precautionary action lies towards the upper left of the diagram, namely where the threat of irreversible damage is palpable, and the benefits of intervention are clear.

Weak sustainability places more emphasis on extended cost benefit analysis, that is in introducing firmer measures of the value of safeguarding ecological and biogeochemical processes that are irrecoverable if lost. These processes and their associated species mix are referred to as critical natural capital. The distinction between weak and strong sustainability lies in the degree to which the precautionary principle and its economic interpretation is applied to ensuring the protection of critical natural capital, including the creation of new critical capital by deliberate management. Note here that the curve of safeguard tends move towards the right, i.e. to ensure that plenty of life support systems remain intact. Both models of sustainability take a more sanguine view of inbuilt resilience of natural systems.

Very strong sustainability favours a more fundamentalist

mode of ecological solidarity with the earth. Here the line is to adapt to the frames set by natural systems, and to build precaution into an approach to living that is altogether more in empathy with the natural world. The amount of "ecological footprint" becomes progressively lighter, and the precautionary line drops to the lower right hand zone of the diagram, being triggered at the point of relatively little damage. Here, the bias of "proportionality" favours early action in the face of pessimism over the ability of the earth to cope with human intervention for the survival of the human species.

Figure 1.1 Precaution in the context of the sustainability debate. The diagram is based on one proposed by Turner et al. (1994, 59). The vertical represents increasing damage costs associated with human activity, leading to serious system instability in maintaining life support. The horizontal line represents the judgement by human actors of the room for manouevre. To the left, that "spree" becomes narrower and narrower for the precautious, but is still a matter of opportunism for the adventurous. The placing of lines therefore sets the limits for interpreting the precautionary principle in the context of the sustainability debate.

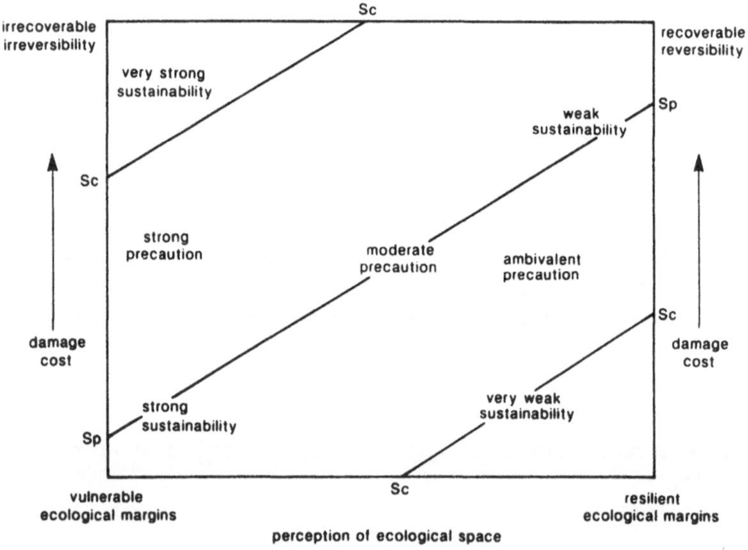

S_c is the line of the optimistic cornucopian in terms of global change

S_p is the more fuzzy line of the precautious environmentalist towards global change

S_e is the fundamentalist line of the deep ecologist against too much intervention

We can see how this applies to the principle of proportionality by looking at Figure 1.2. This point is discussed further by David Pearce in Chapter 7. Equating with the very strong sustainability position is a strong precautionary principle, when the costs of intervention outweigh obvious benefits. Clearly society places a premium on playing safe, so the benefits are loaded in favour of an assumption that critical thresholds are threatened. Strong sustainability equates more with the application of the very best technology and management practice, with still fairly loose controls over cost benefit analysis. Weak sustainability more formally applies the "not entailing excessive cost" principle of proportionality. This would imply more negotiation over the merits of playing sage, with greater social emphasis on a "wait and see" attitude. The very weak sustainability perspective would simply apply best guess economic environmental auditing to investments, allowing relatively modest room for buffering against ignorance.

These two diagrams are, of course, largely speculative and theoretical. But they serve to remind us that precaution is rather universally understood, not commonly interpreted. All of the perspectives offered on both the sustainability and proportionality fronts are part of the legitimate precaution debate. There is neither an agreed yardstick, nor a consensus as to how it should be applied. It is not the fault of the precautionary principle that it is in a muddle. The confusion is an inescapable part of the modern environmental dilemma.

All this should not surprise anyone when looking at how the precautionary principle varies greatly in its interpretation and application in various national cultures. The Americans and Japanese regard precaution as a threat to free markets and technological innovation. In international diplomatic circles they try to remove its influence by softening its significance and by introducing strict qualifications on usage. Thus any reference to burden sharing and shifting the burden of proof is strenuously resisted. Dan Bodansky in Chapter 12 suggests that despite the national political distaste for the principle, in fact various aspects of the principle operate in US administrative law on environmental protection, especially in risk prevention and waste minimisation statutes. Ironically the more stringent the congressional wording, the less willing are the regulatory agencies to interpret the principle too narrowly, such is the power of voter and individual backlash against excessive anticipation or too demanding protective edicts.

Figure 1.2 Precaution and the principle of proportionality. Proportionality applies to the application of costs and benefits, where part of the benefit is the avoidance of unnecessary risk by playing safe. The key to the principle of proportionality lies in individual, national and official attitudes to resilience, vulnerability and periodical irrversible thresholds. There are few yardsticks here: much depends on attitudes to science, expertise, international obligations, rights of nature and the fundamental responsibilities of humanity and earth.

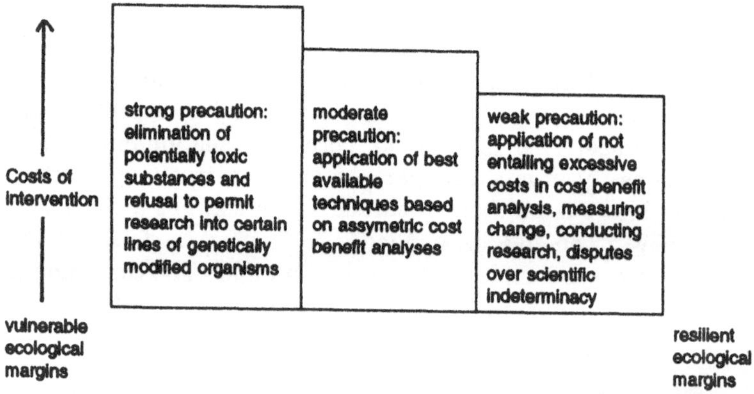

Nigel Haigh, in Chapter 13, indicates that the European Union is deeply ambivalent about precaution. At the environmental protection end, there is much sympathy for the principle, particularly because of the need for cross-border compliance. But at the "top" end of strategic policymaking there is far less enthusiasm with much greater emphasis on promoting growth and excessive stimulation in a recession-prone European economy. For instance the recent European Commission (1993) statement on growth, competitiveness and employment favoured more integration between environmental considerations and sectoral policies pertaining to regional development, industrial regeneration and transport. But EU leaders largely ignored the sustainability dimension in favour of promoting technological innovation, labour mobility and regional economic dynamism. The precautionary principle may be in the Maastrict Treaty, as it is in the Rio Declaration of Principles. But in both, its actual political influence remaining very marginal.

The Germans on the other hand see precaution not only as an excuse for greater federal participation in the social market economy. They also regard it as an entry point for stimulating fresh markets in low waste and environmentally restoring technologies aimed at conserving energy, reusing waste materials, cleaning up old waste dumps, restoring contaminated land and improving the monitoring of any changes in environmental conditions. This is potentially a very lucrative market, with over 200 billion ecu annually at stake so long as EU directives remain strong and politically supported in their enforcement.

The British by contrast, seek to protect the integrity of "sound science" as a basis for considered action. The line is to experiment to discover the reliability of data and models, and to move forward very slowly, monitoring carefully all the time, before committing massive action. Yet, as Nigel Haigh summarises in his chapter, the British have embraced both the risk aversion and the common responsibility aspects of anticipatory action. In so doing the British do distinguish more than most between precaution and prevention. Prevention is bound up with eliminating pollution at source, applying the polluter pays principle and establishing regulations based on avoiding harm both to humans and ecosystems. This is fairly standard

EU fare when it comes to environmental policy. Precaution applies to the more problematic area of uncertainty, possible irrversibility and collective environmental responsibility. Here the British position is a little looser, with a more generous attitude to cost benefit analysis, and a more forgiving willingness to err on the side of reasonable doubt. To quote the 1990 White Paper (HM Government 1990, para 1.88):

> "The precautionary principle applies particularly where there are good grounds for judging either that action taken promptly at comparatively low cost may avoid more costly damage later, or that irreversible effects may follow if damage is delayed."

Amongst this is also a little bit of moralising:

> "Just as we believe that it is irresponsible for Government to be extravagent with taxpayers money, so we see even stronger arguments against wasting the world's or this country's natural resources and bequeathing a burden of environmental debt tomorrow."

Here is an element of taking care, and, hopefully, listening to the citizens who will live in the residue of our actions. In this respect the Conservative administration's interest in opening up the private sector to a genuine partnership of voluntary self restraint fits in with an ethical stance that precaution, if soundly practiced, can only come about by informed mutual consent.

James Cameron in Chapter 15 emphasises how international environmental agreements are taking on more and more strands of the precautionary message. Conventions, protocols, institutional structures such as conferences of the parties and international commissions will all evolve to bind national governments into a greater sense of shared rsponsibility involving civic science (of which more in the introduction to section 1), global citizenship and good government in its modest sense. This is why the precautionary principle is both radical and enlightening.

This book will make clear that the precautionary principle is neither a single dimensional concept nor clearly defined even in its many features. It is entering the environmental arena in many ways, not all of which are obvious. Few of the openings contain traceable pathways suggesting where elements of precaution might lead. It is useful to contemplate the conditions through which precaution is likely to gain ground, and to envisage circumstances where it might be resisted. This discussion will be continued in the final chapter.

We suggest that the precautionary principle is most likely to be applied in the following circumstances:

(i) where new technologies are proposed in well regulated regimes and where public opinion is instinctively or knowledgeably risk averse. This will apply to certain aspects of biotechnology, genetic manipulation and the transfer of novel products to countries where natural products are displaced (i.e. synthetics for natural equiva lents).

(ii)where the principles of regulation allow for judgement as to what is socially tolerable. The emerging practices of best available techniques not entailing excessive cost (BATNEEC), environmental impact assessment (EIA), risk assessment (RA), environmental audits, life cycle analysis and critical load for pollution control all involve an increasing element of judgement of weighing incompatible advantages and costs over varying periods of time. It is very likely that the preventative, ecological space and onus of proof aspect of precaution will increasingly be brought to bear in the application of these techniques.

(iii) where there is a national culture of care for the less fortunate and the defenceless. This applies to the distribu tional aspects of environmental damage, where certain groups are disadvantaged simply because they have lower

income, fewer civil rights, fewer political defenders, or values that are not fully appreciated by the majority. The application of burden sharing and onus of proof will subtly shift the balance of power in favour of such interests.

(iv) where there is openness and accountability in policy formulation and decision-taking. This is a gratifyingly improving aspect of much of modern government in many countries both in the North and the South. As the political culture opens up, so the scope for effective participation should allow for a more constructive role for the precaution ary principle, notably around the application of care and responsiveness in management.

By contrast, the precautionary principle is less likely to evolve in regulatory regimes where environmental considerations do not yet figure prominently. This applies particularly to financial markets, national income accounting, corporate profit analysis, domestic household budgets, the hierarchical professions where established customs die hard (the law, accountancy, medicine, academia), and the media. Similarly in governing systems where care is not prized, where consultation is not welcomed, and where public interpretations of danger at odds with expert judgement are not accepted, so the precautionary principle will be resisted and treated with suspicion. It follows that day to day behaviour by individuals and households the world over is an amalgam of precaution and non-precaution. The great challenge is slowly but steadily to shift that bias towards a greater acceptance of precaution in the spirit of collective self interest.

Charting the text that follows

The reader will soon spot that we try to treat the analysis of the precautionary principle in a number of ways, so that we can bring the strands together in the final chapter. Our contention is that precaution will not explode onto the environmental stage sweeping out cost benefit analysis, risk assessment, strict liability and environmental impact assessment into heavily weighted antagonistic devices against development and change. Rather it will seep through the pores of decision-making institutions and the political consciousness of humanity by stealth. If this is the case, it will be because the tide of the times permits this permeation.

So we look first at the German experience, partly because it was the originator of the idea, and partly because German influence remains strongly felt in European Union environmental policymaking. It is not surprising that Germany has taken a lead in CO_2 removal and remains the strongest advocate of a unified carbon energy tax. Sonja Boehmer Christiansen charts the complexity of social and legal meanings attached to precaution to show how it has become closely linked to federal hegenomy over the lander, western dominance over the east, and technological innovation and economic prowess over the Union as a whole. Opportunistic as ever, the Germans have capitalised as a concept to transform it into their own brand of environmental-economic prowess. But as lander power grows in the new regional mood in Europe, as local agenda 21s begin to emerge as the guiding force in the sustainable transition, the Germans will have to reassess their approach to precaution to accommodate the new subregional politics of social identity. This will not be easy in political terms. In policy terms, precaution will have to be embraced by education and the media in ways that are still untried.

The second section on science is covered by our separate editorial introduction. We see this as an important zone of transition. Precaution is testing science, because global environmental change encompasses two highly indeterminate and complex systems, neither of which is manageable on its own. In combination the unmanageability becomes pervasive. We sense that precaution will be one of many devices to open up democracies to more creative search patterns for futures that will be forever self-defined, not given by experts or politicians.

The third section again is prefaced by an introduction which suggests that the management of precaution will require patience and forbearance. It would be most unwise to push precaution too far and too fast. The transformation of cost benefit analysis to incorporate proactive burden sharing will require transformation of regulatory and political institutions, again in a more negotiated participatory format. This should then allow economic valuation to be more closely associated with a fairer distrbution of power, and a wider understanding of likely futures. This places somewhat more of a premium on ethics within both valuation exercises and in political decision making procedures. So far that is a distant idea, partly because the ethical dimensions involved remain obscure. The regulation of genetically modified organisms offer the best hope for a good care study, and Julie Hill's contribution shows that here is an arena of some promise. The role of precaution in local government is probably one of the most exciting prospects: this brings full circle the discussion of the likely trends in Europe as a whole.

Finally we look to the international dimension to see what we can learn about the precautionary principle from other political cultures. This yields a rich vein of issues - common and statute law of risk aversion and proof bearing in the US, yet with little obvious radical effect on the order of things. A Europe still unsure of how far to trust the centre, so precaution becomes a cloak for testing the legal competence of a Commission suspiciously watched by national parliaments as well as its own parliament. An Australian study of power broking reminiscent of the German experience, but incorporating the all-important indigenous rights of the aboriginal peoples, and the grasping tentacles of international environmental law, where, arguably, precaution may still find its most comfortable home.

This is a story of exploration in settings that are more favourable to change than many realise, but where the overall objective is still shrouded in mist. Precaution is here to stay, but its success may lie in its modesty and its prepardness to be transformed into various facets of social and political change without worrying about losing its name.

References

Commission of the European Communities 1993. Growth, Competitiveness and Employment: The Challenges and the Ways Forward to the 21st Century. CEC, Brussels.

Costanza, R. and Cowell, P. 1992. The 4P approach to dealing with scientific uncertainty. Environment 34(9), 12-20, 42.

Dooge, T., de la Riviere, M., Goodman, G., O'Riordan, T. Marson-Lefevre, J. and Brennan, M. (eds). 1992. An Agenda for Science for Environment and Development. Cambridge University Press, Cambridge.

Myers, N. (ed). 1993. The Gaian Atlas of Planet Management. Gaia Books, Stroud, Glos.

Organisation for Economic Cooperation and Development 1991. The State of the Environment. OECD Paris.

Simmons, I.G. 1989. Changing the Face of the Earth: Culture, Environment, History. Basil Blackwell, Oxford.

Turner, R.K. (ed). 1993. Sustainable Environmental Economics and Management. Belhaven, London.

Turner, R.K., Pearce, D.W. and Bateman, I.J. 1994. Environmental Economics: An Elementary Introduction. Harvester Wheatsheaf, Hemel Hempstead.

Turner, W.L., Kates, R.W., Clark, W.B., Meyer, W. (eds). 1991. The Earth Transformed by Human Action. Cambridge University Press, Cambridge.

United Nations Environment Programme 1992. Environmental Data Report. Basil Blackwell, Oxford.World Bank 1992. Economy and Environment: World Development Report. Oxford University Press, Oxford.

World Resources Institute 1993. World Resources 1992-1993. Oxford University Press, Oxford.

Worldwatch Institute 1993. State of the World 1993. Earthscan, London.

Chapter 2

The Precautionary Principle in Germany - enabling Government

By Sonja Boehmer-Christiansen

Introduction

The precautionary principle is said to have made its way into English during the early 1980s as the translation of the German *Vorsorgeprinzip* (see von Moltke 1988). The *Vorsorge* concept has since become an ingredient of European and international environmental policy prescription (see chapters 13 and 15) as well as proving attractive to a number of academic disciplines and practitioners concerned with environmental management, (see chapters 3, 5, 10 and 16). It is therefore of some interest to discover what the principle means in German, how it has become enshrined in German law and applied in the practice of *Umweltschutz*, the protection, even defence, of the environment or literally the world around us. In the early 1990s, *Vorsorge* became a principle which not only supports calls for strict environmental protection but also for sustainable development.

This chapter explores the meaning, practical implementation and shortcomings of the *Vorsorge* approach in German environmental policy under five headings:

* Policy context

* Official definition and the tasks of government

* Meaning and usage of the term

* History and operationalisation with reference to air pollution and acid rain abatement

* Institutional and cultural dimensions

* Shortcomings

It deals primarily with the 1970s and 1980s when the principle became part of a much broader effort to initiate and justify a period of 'industrial restructuring and modernisation' which was to take place under official guidance. The hope that this process could readily be applied to East Germany and hence create prosperity there almost overnight has not, however, been fulfilled (Boehmer-Christiansen et al 1993). Both experiences hold lessons for potential 'importers' of the principle.

The dissemination of a concept from German to English is itself of interest, for the Germans had coined the term *Umwelt* for the English notion of 'environment' only a decade earlier. This was in response to the environmental debate in North America and Britain (Muller 1986). *Umwelt* came to replace *Natur* and refers primarily to the physical world - water, air, soil, climate, that is the *natürlichen Lebensgrundlagen* (the natural foundations of life). The *Umwelt* is assumed to be stressed, i.e. *belastet*, and hence needs to be protected by Vorsorge to prevent irreversible damage.

German policy statements therefore rarely refer to 'the environment' as such, but to *Umweltschutz*. The existence of a problem, and hence the *Schutz* (protection) tends to be assumed, so this requires solving rather than deeper understanding. An ambitious starting point is indicated by the notion of *Vorsorgeprinzip* as enabling government to take preventive action. *Umweltschutz* is now a constitutional obligation in several German states, the *Länder*. A recent attempt to make it a *Staatsziel*, a legally binding objective of the Federation as well, failed because of opposition from the major conservative parties. The political forces in charge of the German state in the early 1990s seemed afraid to accept the responsibilities they had so eagerly sought during the 1980s. Given the recession and the very costly restructuring of its eastern *Länder*, the German government cannot secure environmentally sound investments in the future unless more savings can be extracted through some form of taxation. This will require some reduction in consumption in order to maintain Germany as a leading nation of manufacturing and employment. This too will be a task of policy required by *Vorsorge*, especially as the government believes that organised proactive environmental planning can generate more jobs and technological innovation.

Policy context

The *Vorsorgeprinzip* is but one of five fundamental principles of German environmental policy. There are three principles commonly used in regulation, namely *Vorsorge*, *Verursacherprinzip* (polluter pays) and *Kooperation* (consensus), plus the principle of proportionality in cost and gain (*Wirtschaftliche Vertretbarkeit*) and the common burden principle (*Gemeinlast prinzip*). *Vorsorge* was adopted largely to counter the domination of one of these in the regulatory armoury that prevailed before 1974.

The *Verursacherprinzip* is usually translated as the polluter pays principle but literally means the principle of causation or responsibility. Co-operation requires that all interested parties, including industry, the trade unions and environmentalists, must be consulted and that policy should be based on consensus. The principle thus provides the basis of policy integration especially in the incorporation of environmental considerations in the main economic sectors of taxation, transport, industry, agriculture and trade. The parties that must be consulted are usually listed in the appropriate piece of legislation, weakening the discretion of the administration. The outcome, the 'concrete' action that is required by polluters, is therefore a result of bargaining as in most other administrative systems. If the state wishes to act with *Vorsorge* it may need to impose taxes or liability regimes on polluters. This is in keeping with traditional German concepts of state responsibility which allocates a strategic role to bureaucracy (see Johnson 1983 for a broad background to this theme).

Wirtschaftliche Vertretbarkeit or the principle of economic feasibility or tolerability enshrines the traditional restraints imposed by the courts. Making a business bankrupt is not usually the goal of environmental policy, least of all in Germany. A more recent version of the same concept argues that costs and benefits must be in proportion, i.e. *verhaltnismässig*, and this calculus may be applied to an entire branch of economic activity (such as the petrochemical industry) or even the national economy, the *Volkswirtschaft*, rather than individual firms. The principle is likely to be in the ascendancy when the capacity of the state to persuade and subsidise across the whole economy declines.

The Common Burden Principle, *Gemeinlast prinzip*, enables the state to overcome the unwanted consequences of inequality or incipient bankruptcy. The inability of polluter to pay or accept liability tends to legitimate subsidisation or compensation by public funds. The *Verursacher*, (it may well be the state) may require society as a whole to pay the bill. A desirable (or influential) firm or activity which is likely to fail if strictly regulated may become eligible for *Förderung*, i.e. uplifting help. Subsidies become public investments into the future and are justified with reference to *Vorsorge*. Problems then arise when the parties at which such legislative principles are directed, are required to translate these into 'concrete' measures.

Together, these principles ensure that all political actors bargain with each other on the basis of agreed ground rules rather than 'sound science'. Indeed, economic feasibility tends to win whenever the state withdraws as an important regulator and funding body. This issue is very much at the heart of the 1993 debate about the impact of environmental protection on the location of German industrial activity and hence the international competitiveness of products made in Germany employing a German workforce (DIW and RWIW 1993).

Since some of these other principles tend to counteract or even overrule precaution, it is a mistake to describe German environmental policy as purely precautionary. Rather, the policy outcome will reflect the balance of power of political forces and motivations at work in individual cases, for the state has many functions other than that of environmental protection. For example, the German Federal Government is by law obliged to promote 'counter-cyclical' investments and ensure that regulations with competitive impacts are uniform throughout the country. Regional inequalities are perceived as unfair and may indeed be politically destabilising in a federation.

Another fundamental question, therefore, is to discover whether the availability of the *Vorsorgeprinzip* in the conceptual tool kit of environmental management furthers the convergence of environmental goals with other aims of state - be these industrial policy, security, economic development, job creation or political stability. The Federal Ministry for the Environment (1993, 138), which does not speak for Government as a whole, nevertheless concluded recently that environmental protection is an investment in the future to secure sustainable development, i.e. *zur Sicherung einer langfristig tragbaren Entwicklung*. Precaution is therefore becoming entangled in the sustainable transition controversy, and is possibly being used by the environmental ministry as a point of leverage against the finance and industry ministries.

Towards a definition of Vorsorge and the tasks of government

The idea of Vorsorge applied to environmental policy can be traced to 1970 when the very first draft of new clean air legislation stated the intention *dem Enstehen schädlicher Umwelteinwirkungen vorzubeugen* - to prevent the development of harmful environmental effects (Wey 1993, 207). The literal meaning of *vorbeugen* is to bend beforehand and hence reduce the danger of being broken; the verb being commonly used in medicine. In the Federal Government *Umweltprogramm* of 1971, the same idea is expressed as *Umweltplanung auf lange Sicht*, i.e. long term planning for the environment. In brief, *Vorsorge* means state influenced planning and is therefore ideologically in conflict with free market doctrines. In 1971, the concept was particularly attractive to the ruling Social Democratic Administration determined to promote environmental policy as part of its aim to create a fairer society. *Vorsorge* helped to put environmental protection inside the Interior Ministry and Foreign Affairs. From a constitutional view *Vorsorge* promised to remove the legal constraints placed by the economic feasibility criteria on any policy prescriptions which demanded more than the repair of damage already done (Wey 1993, 204). The concept is closely related to that of *Gefahrenabwehr*, defence against dangers and threats. Clearly, the greater the threat, the greater the need for *Vorsorge* and hence powers by public authorities to ensure that society is defended.

In 1974 Parliament passed new clean air legislation. This legislation was prompted by the growing claim over the long term and possibly irreversible habitat damage associated with acid rain and photochemical smog. Of special worry was the then new and alarming prospect of *Waldsterben* or the death of the beloved and largely privately owned forests caused by acid rain. But waiting in the wings were the public health effects of smog, with its associated but unknown consequences for the toxification of natural habitats. The 1976 Act incorporated the *Vorsorgeprinzip* as a general guideline for administrators in their negotiations with certain polluters. By 1976 it had become a cornerstone of German environmental policy enshrined in legislation as a vague legal commandment, a *Gebot*. The policy implications became significant for German industry in the early 1980s, and a little later for Europe as a whole. The influential 1984 Report from the Government to the Federal Parliament on the Protection of Air Quality probably gives the fullest official definition of *Vorsorge*.

After asserting that:

> Responsibility towards future generations commands (*gebietet*) that the natural foundations of life (*natürliche Lebensgrundlagen*) are preserved (*bewahren*, a stronger if less militarist term than *schützen*) and that irreversible types of damage, such as the decline of forests, must be avoided.

Vorsorge was defined in approximate translation as follows:

> The principle of precaution commands that the damages done to the natural world (which surrounds us all) should be avoided *in advance* and in accordance with opportunity and possibility. Vorsorge further means the early detection of dangers to health and environment by comprehensive, synchronised (harmonised) research, in particular about cause and effect relationships..., it also means acting when conclusively ascertained understanding by science is not yet available. Precaution means to develop, in all sectors of the economy, technological processes that significantly reduce environmental burdens, especially those brought about by the introduction of harmful substances (BMI 1984, 53).

The large number of action verbs should be noted. The principles therefore empower the state to pursue environmental precaution by four types of action, the goal being that damage must be avoided. This is the *Gebot*, or moral requirement, as distinct from *Verbot*, or government command.

The actions which government is entitled to take under this rubric are:

* dangers must be detected early, hence research is essential;

* when irreversibility is feared, there should be action before there is full understanding, i.e. proof of damage is not required;

* technical developments to reduce current levels of dis charge of pollutants must be promoted, and

* the state must contribute to the introduction of cleaner processes/technologies into the private sector.

Research is needed for an early warning rather than for the evaluation of precise, cost effective targets or instruments. The role of science and the scientist is therefore more important in the earlier stages of policy-making, less so during implementation when the emphasis is on technology. What is considered harmful need not be *wissenschaftlich abgesichert* (scientifically proven); the suspicion of irreversible damage is sufficient. The issue of costs and benefit justification does not directly enter the definition of *Vorsorge*; rather the politician, industrialist, engineer and lawyer are invited to prepare for action. The potential for policy innovation is therefore large, for the decision criteria which are considered legitimate may be much wider than those defined by 'sound science'. This enables the pursuit of complementary goals without becoming subject to the accusation of irrationality. Precaution is therefore primarily an 'action principle', a guide for policy-makers and a means for persuading society to take the future into account.

Meaning and usage of Vorsorge

Vorsorge covers a territory of meaning that combines caution with caring for the future, as well as providing for it. Its literal meaning is 'beforehand or prior care and worry', the noun *Sorge* having a range of meanings which are best revealed by three verbs derived from the stem *sorg*: *sich sorgen um*, *sich sorgen über* (or *sich Sorgen machen*), and *besorgen*, meaning respectively: caring for or looking after, fretting or worrying about and obtaining provisions, or providing for. A squirrel storing nuts for winter, a factory taking out an accident insurance policy, a family saving for a rainy day would all be acting with *Vorsorge*, i.e. preparing for a future which is expected to be difficult. As environmentalists generally fear for the future of the natural world and want to care for its well-being, they tend to be fond of the precautionary principle.

Vorsorge demands more than care, it goes beyond *Sorgfaltspflicht*, which literally means duty to take care and does not require that the future is taken into account. *Vorsorge*, however, is readily linked to the concepts of investment and liability, and to the reversal of the burden of proof. It can be practised in many policy areas, for example in health and international relations, e.g. *Friedensvorsorge*, meaning pre-emptive action to avoid conflicts becoming violent. If wisdom and science combine to warn that current actions may lead to harm, government has the duty to change society by persuasion and regulation. This implies opportunities for state-dominant politics which have long been recognised by German politicians and civil servants, but creates difficulties for any administration subject to a political philosophy which sees a detailed state and a minimum of regulation as the way towards efficient 'competitiveness'.

German documents tend to appeal to *Vorsorge* in the early stages of the policy-formation process, i.e. when persuasion is important. For example, the first German *Enquete Kommission*, a parliament appointed body composed of legislators and scientists, set up to advise government on climate change between 1987 and 1990, was titled '*Vorsorge zum Schutz der Erdatmosphäre*'. An official German document translates this as 'Preventive measures to protect the earth's atmosphere'. The Commission concluded that action was needed 'as a precaution in our own interest and in the interest of future generations'. Once policy decisions had been taken, i.e. a general *Klimapolitik* had been defined, the second Commission simply concerned itself with 'Protecting the Earth's Atmosphere'. Environmental programmes tend to have no particular need for the word. *Vorsorge* is emphasised by politicians and their advisors when ambitious proposals face challenges either on the grounds of cost or insufficient science. It was therefore widely used to justify German responses to acid rain (Boehmer-Christiansen and Skea 1991).

When Konrad von Moltke (1988) studied the use of the term in German air pollution legislation for the benefit of the British government, he translated the word as precaution and foresight, implying good husbandry. However, when precaution is translated back into German, one tends to arrive at *Vorsicht* (literally before-sight, caution, attention) and *Verhutung* or *Vorbeuge* (as of conception and ill health), not *Vorsorge* which requires planning, not just taking care now. However, von Moltke (1991, 29) has since complained that the German Parliament translated the term wrongly as 'preventive policy'.

History and operationalisation of Vorsorgewith Reference to Air Pollution Control

Political motivations

Legal competence is the primary power possessed by the German Federal Government. Implementation and enforcement, as well as as considerable areas of legal competence, are left to the *Länder*. The struggle to wrest environmental competence from the latter and to encourage them to spend in times of recession dominated West German environmental politics in the 1970s and 1980s. To justify centralisation legally active principles were required, and Vorsorge was one of these. Under the German Constitution, uniformity of regulation can be required with reference to the *Länder* where transboundary impacts are involved. In every successful case the powers of central government are enhanced. The drive for change would initially lie in the hands of legal experts and their advisors. Environmental policy (*Umweltpolitik*) based on *Vorsorge* arrived relatively late in Germany and on the agenda of the political Left, yet it remained a focus of government attention during the 1980s when politics moved to the right. Nowadays its supporters are concerned about its fate in German democratic policy. Historical analysis of the acid rain dispute provides some clues.

New start after 1945

Germany emerged from the Second World War with little in the way of environmental controls apart from 19th century provisions and improved nature protection rules introduced during the Third Reich. Little had happened to alter the conceptual basis of pollution control, natural resource and landscape protection. For industrial pollution control this meant that the courts would only permit regulation that was subject to the principle of proportionality. The prevailing free market ideology discouraged regulation, most of which remained in the hands of the *Länder* or communes, with the latter perceiving themselves as the representatives not of the *Staat*, but of civil society which would compete with the former for competence.

The small but influential Interparliamentary Working Group for Nature-Appropriate Economic Activities (IPA), an all party committee of MPs, was formed in 1952 and became increasingly concerned about air pollution. It subscribed to principles which sound astonishingly modern today: concern about physical limits to economic growth, man's moral responsibility for the Earth, the importance of non-economic values and the need for ecological understanding. The group became the major challenger of German industry (acting through the Association of German Industry, BDI) throughout the 1960s, the task was later taken on by federal ministries.

Then as today, industry had its interests represented by the Federal Economic Affairs Ministry, the BMWi. The balance of power between 'hygiene and health' on the one hand, and industrial interests and the BMWi on the other, would therefore depend on the former gaining ministerial strength and support in Bonn, on the relative power of ministries and the alliances they could build, especially with the Chancellor, and on the persuasiveness of the arguments put to politicians and voters about how environmental protection would further their particular interests and concerns. Behind all parties would stand the prestigious engineering profession, organised through the *Verein Deutscher Ingineure* (VDI) which would offer advise on how to solve environmental problems by technology forcing. Neither the VDI nor the BDI had suffered much during the Third Reich, but represented powerful traditional institutional interests which government would have to use and, if necessary, reconcile.

The 1959 Clean Air Act

In 1959 pressure for national legislation (with the UK and legislation in Nord-Rhein-Westfalen as examples), created a new Federal 'Air Purity Law', *Luftereinhaltungsgesetz*. This was effectively an amendment to the 19th century Trade Regulations, the *Gewerbeordnung* (GWO) without replacing their underlying philosophy. Under paragraph 906 of the original GWO, emissions from a neighbouring plant had to be tolerated as long as these were 'customary in the location', i.e. established uses. Abatement measures demanded by the authorities had to be economically feasible and justifiable on health grounds only. In practice, this meant that emissions from a particular plant (as opposed to the general level of air quality) had to be demonstrated to be causing ill health.

The 1959 Act improved this unsatisfactory situation, though it contained little more than what German industry had already conceded in NRW. Nobody was required to act with *Vorsorge*, but the list of plants requiring permits was extended, the technical guidelines associated with the granting of authorisations were modernised and, importantly, the application of the principle of 'economic feasibility' was broadened to apply to sectors of industry not just to individual firms. Licensing authorities were empowered, for the first time, to require that new emitters were equipped with state of art emission control technology (*Stand der Technik*). Domestic and mobile sources were not covered by the Act, largely because of the vociferous opposition of the oil and gas industries. Not surprisingly, oil and gas became the first targets of environmental regulation in the 1970s.

What this meant in practical terms was left to the judgement of the *Länder* authorities. By now environmental groups were arguing that the prevailing regime of control based on air quality criteria was not working and that stringent emission standards were needed. In 1961, a Federal Health Ministry was set up and became responsible for 'the maintenance of pure air'. This was the first milestone towards the centralisation of environmental policy-formation (but not implementation). Yet it took until 1964 to implement the 1959 Act because of wrangling over the associated technical guidelines. The BDI was largely responsible for this long delay, primarily because it objected to the *Stand der Technik* criterion to which the IPA and the Federal Health Ministry wanted to give legal force. Once accepted, it would continue to be qualified however by the concept of 'economic feasibility'. With the administrative courts acting as the ultimate decision-makers, the legislators needed a new principle with which they could confront industry in the courts and win, if necessary with help of public opinion and green parties.

The Ruhr region remained polluted, giving the Social Democratic Party (SPD) a chance to turn pollution, and dirty air in particular, into an electoral issue. In 1961 Willy Brandt had failed to make 'blue skies over the Ruhr' a winning SPD slogan in the Federal elections. In 1969, however, his party won with a highly ambitious environmental programme and the promise of *Vorsorge.* Even then, the SPD could only govern with the help of the Free Democrats (FDP) and their leader, Hans Dietrich Genscher.

Reform euphoria

The environmental *Sofortprogramme* (immediate action programme) of the Federal Government was based on the party programme of the Social Democratic Party (SPD) to the extent that this had been mentioned by the FDP. The promise of Vorsorge was part of it.

The newly elected coalition government of SPD and FDP took a great interest in 'environmentalism' and recognised the opportunities for the management of the economy under the 'social market' doctrine. 'Reform euphoria' swept across Germany linked to the perceived economic and environmental crises of the time. The views and ideals of the North American environmental protest movement had struck a deep chord in German society. This allowed the state, and especially the *Bund* (federation) and its senior bureaucracy, to assert themselves in a new policy area, often by appealing to the Germanic fondness for future catastrophes (see Muller 1986 for a detailed history). The German government had also been strongly influenced by the 1972 Stockholm Conference and the opportunities it offered to a state emerging into the world international relations and environmental negotiations.

One of the first steps of the new Government was to add a paragraph to Article 74 of the Constitution. This centralised environmental policy-making by adding joint (concurrent, *Lander-Bund*) legislative competence for air, waste and noise to existing federal responsibilities for nuclear safety and radioactive waste management. In addition, environmental protection was removed from the Health Ministry and moved to the much more powerful Federal Interior Ministry (BMI) headed by Herr Genscher. New environmental institutions advising government were established, setting the stage for fierce interministerial bargaining, with BMI and BMWi as the major contestants. The BMI would have the duty of *Vorsorge* among its weaponry, with the Chancellor and a greening legal profession as supporters, while the BMWi would have to rely on economic feasibility.

The BMI immediately set to work to prepare new clean air legislation (see below). The basic assumption was that technical progress, economic growth and environmental protection could be achieved without 'trade-off', but would advance together, a belief which was, incidentally, shared by the East German Government. The environmental reform agenda and its conceptualisation were largely an achievement of the *Ministerialbürokratie* in the BMI, especially of Secretary of State, Dr Günther Hartkopf. Public opinion only began to play a role much later when government needed its support against industry. Hartkopf himself described these early years as consisting primarily of battles against industry (*'der Kampf gegen die Industrie'*) and its supporters, by whom he presumably meant the BMWi (Wey 1993, 203).

The inability of the SPD/FDP coalition to implement a great deal of this programme, especially after the resignation of Brandt, gave rise to the perception of a general 'implementation gap', a much studied phenomenon in German social science (Mayntz et al. 1978). This added to the subsequent disenchantment of voters and helps to explain the rise of Citizen Action Groups and green parties (Mayntz 1975). These came to form a genuine threat to German party politics and helped to move the entire party political spectrum into a greener direction (Langguth 1984).

The amended Constitution allowed the passing of the Federal Air Quality Protection Act, the *Bundes-immissions-schutz-gesetz, BImSchG*, its full title being the 'Law for Protection against Harmful Environmental Effects of Air Pollution, Noise, Vibrations and Similar Processes'. It potentially covered all sources of air pollution, stationary and mobile, and was 'to protect man as well as animals, plants and other matter from harmful environmental effects' and, as far as installations requiring authorisation were concerned, also from 'dangers, considerable disadvantages and considerable nuisances'.

The 1974 Act was inspired by the 1955 Atom Act, with one important difference. While nuclear safety was to be achieved by what was technologically possible in accordance with the latest scientific findings and without regard to cost, economic feasibility remained a component of the BImSchG. With reference to *Vorsorge* wealthy firms would became attractive targets for regulation. This would have desired impacts on energy policy and ensure that major investments stayed at home, were socially acceptable and politically useful (Koelke 1984). *Waldsterben* would provide the political energy and concern to promote an agenda developed long before the forest damage was officially acknowledged and measured.

BImSchG enabled the Federal Government to require owners of plant needing authorisations for emissions and discharges to act with precaution, i.e. take 'preventive action against the development and occurrence of harmful environmental effects' (Salzwedel and Preusker 1982). This was to be achieved by limiting emissions in accordance with the *Stand der Technik*, a term which would be defined later by federal ordinance, e.g. the Large Combustion Plant Ordinance of 1983. The issue of whether existing plants should also be compelled to comply with very stringent emission limits and timetables, however, remained undecided. The new concept of Vorsorge had been grafted onto an inherited one, namely that of 'state of art technology' or best practice. Because *Stand der Technik* is not defined in the enabling legislation, unless defined in law, it remains subject to negotiation between polluter and administrator, or between both and the courts. It is by no means confined to the best or latest technology or management practices. Rather it was closer to the UK concept of best practicable means, by providing a framework for progressive tightening of regulations as the state of technology improved.

The BImSchG enabled the Interior Ministry to draft ordinances which would be directly binding on polluters, as well as administrative directives (such as the *TA -Luft*) aimed at the administrations of Lander. It was the main product of the ambitious environment programme adopted in 1971 which also included the promise to reduce vehicle emissions by 90% by the end of the decade. This was not achieved until the early 1990s, for unlike stationary sources Germany did not dare to adopt unilateral measures on its all too important car industry.

There had been considerable initial opposition to the 1974 enabling legislation, especially by the southern Lander and NRW, all of which were at the time ruled by the Christian Democrats (CDU) and the Bavarian Christian Social Union (CSU), neither of them ideological adherents to economic liberalism. The Southern regions initially saw little need for clean air legislation, felt unable to implement it and were fundamentally opposed to national uniformity which implied a reduction of their own powers. They had not been active in air pollution abatement, but changed their minds rapidly when the public outcry over the forests led to a direct attack on the car industry and also offered the opportunity of giving nuclear power a greener image and hence weakening the Greens. *Vorsorge* was indeed called for on many grounds, only a few of which were either scientific or environmental. As most German forests and many nuclear utilities are located in the South, and political power had also shifted in this direction during the 1980s, the South 'greened' astonishingly quickly and accepted the notion of anticipatory action.

Green Keynsianism in the 1980s

As recession struck in the late 1970s, the SDP lost power and was replaced in 1981 by a CDU/CSU/FDP coalition led by Helmut Kohl, Herr Genscher, with Franz-Josef Strauss exerting his considerable conservative influence from his home base in Munich. The political need to be active in the environmental arena did not weaken for the Green Party entered the Brown Parliament for the first time. *Die Grunen*, it should be emphasised, did not create the precautionary principle, but helped with its implementation by strengthening a prevailing attitude of concern and anxiety about the future. Air pollution regulations were tightened to include existing power stations, and mobile source were cleaned up with the aid of the best available technology. Three way catalytic converters required cars to incorporate much profitable 'value-added' in the form of electronic components and the conversion to unleaded petrol. This took much longer than had been envisaged, but by early 1990, German policy on automobile emissions had become that of the European Community (Boehmer-Christiansen and Weidner 1992).

With reference to *Waldsterben, Vorsorge* and ecological modernisation, state intervention intensified in spite of political rhetoric favouring deregulation. While the phrase was not used, green Keynsianism was practised to ensure that the recession of the early 1980s was overcome by *Investionshilfen*, the aim being the 'positive development of markets for environmental protection plant, equipment and services' (BMU 1986). The raising of these funds was a responsibility of firms, communes and citizens, with the state giving *flankierende Hilfe*, such as loans and low interest credits specifically for environmental investments by smaller firms. In 1985, two such sources the *Kreditanstalt fur Wiederaufbau* and the *Deutsche Ausgleichsbank* alone co-financed environmental investments valued at over DM 9.5 billion. The former offered DM 3.5 billion under the 1974 Clean Air Act. This was enabled by a 1984 amendment of the Act which weakened the economic feasibility clause. These aids created, according to the BMU, almost half a million jobs. Unification has since altered the picture by reducing the capacity of the state to provide. But initially at least, a similar green cycle is expected to take place in the eastern *Länder*.

As the brief history of German environmental politics in the air quality realm suggests, Vorsorge is a politically framed concept. As such it can take many forms: the promotion of basic research and technological R&D, the setting up of liability and compensation regimes, forcing immediate investment into existing cleaner technology by regulation, and the use of economic measures, either state subsidies or taxation to 'internalise' externalities (or raise funds for government). This has not changed in recent years, though the ability of the state to force investments into the environmental technology sector declines during periods of economic difficulties.

Since subsidies tend to clash with *Verursacher* principles and may prevent industry from becoming more efficient, environmental taxes or 'contributions' (*Abgaben*) tend to be promoted by economists, but need to overcome more political obstacles, such as the arguments of regressive impacts on income and of reducing international competitiveness. The justification of state subsidies with reference to *Vorsorge*, while less dominant in the environmental area today, can still be heard. For example, a former German Federal Minister for agriculture and forestry, Herr Kiechle, was recently interviewed about his attitude to the Common Agricultural Policy. When asked why society needed a minister for agriculture and not one for pharmacy, as German pharmacists were also crying out for state protection, he replied:

> I can answer that one. You only need pills occasionally, but you need to eat every day. Where food is concerned, the state has a *Vorsorgepflicht*, (the state has the duty to act in order to prevent undesirable consequences) (quoted in Die Zeit 22 January 1993, 15).

A similar argument was used when the state had decided to create a new industrial branch and reduce unemployment. Precautionary action by the state need not, however, involve subsidies to private industry. Depending on the stage of the policy cycle, publicly funded research may be sufficient. For example, in response to any possible health impact of the precious metals released into the environment from auto-catalysts, the government recently justified new research being done as *Vorsorge*. The Waldsterben issue not only legitimated desired changes in energy policy, it also led to major investment in forestry research.

The German Government in the late 1980s/early 1990s was very keen to raise the price of energy for industry and consumers for a variety of reasons, and has long wanted to introduce a carbon/energy tax. This is justified with reference to *Vorsorge* and climate protection, though other goals, including revenue collection, the promotion of energy saving and efficiency (and hence the reduction of energy imports) are equally important. Germany is a major importer of fossil fuels and hopes to maintain a reasonably cost-effective nuclear sector. The response of industry, via the BDI, to this proposal is therefore of some interest.

German industry is currently engaged in a serious bout of bargaining against such a tax. By firmly opposing it, German industry (BDI, DIHT- Association of Chambers of Commerce, the Association of the gas and water industry and three electric utility organisations) nevertheless felt compelled to appeal to *Vorsorge*. They set up the 'Initiative of German Business for World-Wide Precautionary Action to Protect the Climate' (BDI 1993, 64) which argues that precaution requires all countries to be included in the effort to protect the climate 'with due respect to the cost benefit relationships', and that 'a precautionary policy confined to Europe will not do justice to the exigencies of climate protection'. A global approach is needed, which is of course precisely what government wants to preempt by forcing German industry to develop better technologies. For industry, however, the principal task 'must be to create a favourable investment climate with incentives for industry', i.e. to provide 'scope for the development of new and efficient technical processes'. Energy taxes, it is argued, would prevent investment by industry in more advanced technology.

This is sophistry: environmental economists have persuasively argued that ecotaxes would do precisely what it is claimed would not happen, namely promote R&D, stimulate resource use efficiency and incorporate social costs and valuations completely into the cost of doing business. *Vorsorge* need not be appealed to in order to impose ecotaxes, but it can be a particularly adroit ally when industry is aggressively antagonistic. According to German industry however, the EC should oppose regulatory and fiscal regimentation. Energy/carbon taxes, should they be adopted, should decline as CO_2 reduction targets are achieved.

Stand der technik

The approach generally adopted by the German bureaucracy has combined *Vorsorge* with the development and promotion of cleaner technologies, i.e. with engineering solutions. Professional engineers tend to see *Vorsorge* in terms of better emission and product standards, cleaner and less energy intensive processes, waste reduction and the development of new materials.

Inside the European Community the German interpretation of *Vorsorge* seems to have prevailed for industrial pollution control because of German political power and because the principle suited the political and economic ambitions of the Commission. For example, one of the Commission's administrators deeply involved in the drafting of the legislation associated with acid rain abatement, wrote in 1988:

> ...anticipatory standardisation (is) essential for the develop ment of new technologies which have infrastructural char acteristics so that companies will not invest against each other until one or more backs down.. (Narjes 1988)

In European legislation, *Vorsorge* has tended to become 'best available technology' (BAT), to which the unconvinced or technologically less ambitious have added 'not entailing excessive costs', giving us BATNEEC. This is a partial response to the principle of proportionality, and helps to explain why the phrase 'cost effective' usually appears in any international declaration favouring intervention ahead of proof.

The *Umwelt* in West Germany has become protected primarily by the *Stand der Technik*, or even the *beste Stand* wherever possible. This encourages investment and promotes technical change, as well as stimulating applied/industrial research and promising export markets. The convergence of environmental protection and other goals of state is enhanced, provided that the necessary investment funds and political motivation are available. Thus *Vorsorge* becomes a metaphor for a wide ranging industrial and economic strategy.

To achieve this linkage between metaphor and action three influential forces can be determined. Firstly, the number of political 'actors' participating in environmental debates is large, and long bouts of public bargaining are typical. The state itself is divided into political entities which compete and cooperate: the Länder, Federal Parliament and Federal Council, even the ministries which are not bound by the collective responsibility principle. Decision-makers, political parties and institutions of government, must agree on compromises because of competing ideologies and constituencies which are openly acknowledged. The federal nature of the German state itself, the dominance of coalition governments and the almost continuous assessment of politicians through elections, all tend to encourage ambitious rhetoric and programme development. The executive agencies find it difficult to implement at this regional and communal level where the real action powers lie.

Secondly it is the engineering profession and not natural scientists who dominate in the advisory process. Natural scientists tend to make their voice felt more from 'below' and through the media and green NGOs. Natural scientists do not enjoy a status superior to that of social scientists who therefore tend to get a more sympathetic hearing than they might elsewhere in Europe and North America. This relative weakness of natural science in government was part of the post-war settlement imposed on Germany and included the partial loss of a whole generation of natural scientists, especially physicists and chemists. Decision criteria additional to natural scientific or economic ones are promoted, especially those which relate to the innovation and application of new technology.

Thirdly, the courts play a major role in the interpretation and implementation of environmental regulation. So the administrative courts would decide disputes over *Stand der Technik* in specific cases, and whether precaution has been satisfied, unless that has been defined by federal ordinance. There are two current legal definitions of *Stand der Technik*, so in order to form an opinion the Court needs to take expert advice, i.e. from the VDI. Engineers working in research, government and industry tend to meet in the various working groups of the VDI in a neutral atmosphere to engage in 'prenegotiation'.

The outcome of this constellation of institutional and cultural factors has been a technology-led environmental policy justified less with reference to *Vorsorge* than by the rapid dissemination of best available technology. This is a policy orientation which would stress applied rather than pure research, much of it done in Fraunhofer Institutes and in the 'big', formerly nuclear research centres which began to diversify into environmental and social sciences during the 1980s. This does not necessarily apply elsewhere, and argues against the unquestioned export of the German recipe for *Vorsorge*.

Critics of the German approach

Three arguments are often heard against the German approach, coming from lawyers, scientists and economists. Fearing that the principle is becoming an international norm, one American legal theorist seems to have despaired of the principle altogether:

> the precautionary principle is too vague to serve as a regulatory standard because it does not specify how much caution should be taken (Bodansky 1991, 5).

I have tried to show that such a claim is made neither in German theory nor practice. Why should a principle also function as a standard? Rather, there should be a clear distinction between principle, measure and standard, with only the latter really possessing the precision needed by engineers. The reluctance of American lawyers to the principle may well have a political explanation. In the US environmental policy-making process apparently places the legal profession at the centre of controversy, thereby limiting the powers of the bureaucracy to make complex judgements and to rely on inexplicit criteria (see Vernon 1993). In Germany, this power relationship appears to be reversed, precaution giving discretionary powers to the bureaucracy rather than to lawyers, a development the American legal profession is not likely to welcome.

Others have argued that the principle stifles scientific research (Wynne and Mayer 1993). This is surely likely to be true only if science is funded because of its alleged policy relevance. It is not usually science that demands 'proof of damage', but the polluters or a government unwilling to act, with science tied to such demands and hence invited to act politically to promote the need for more 'findings'. A technology driven policy does not need continuous monitoring or ecological limits which are defined by effects in the environment and are difficult to understand and quantify.

Nevertheless, the view that the German approach undervalues science and weakens its essential role in policy formation cannot entirely be rejected. The question really is whether science ever plays a major role in defining policy. Basic science played a minor role even in final UK decisions on acid rain and became a major legitimation factor for inaction when government used scientific uncertainties to justify delay in emission abatement (Boehmer-Christiansen 1988). Science appears to function more as a provider of threat perceptions, and hence as legitimation for *Vorsorge*. These threats are then used in the political process which defines the decision criteria. For example, there has been a great amount of research carried out on 'critical loads' in defining abatement targets for SO_2 and NOx in Britain which has proved unable to influence subsequent policy effectively. Diagnostic science appears to play a powerful policy role in weak decision frameworks, i.e. at the intergovernmental level and in states opposed to specific environmental regulations.

German economists calculated enormous costs arising from 'acid rain', costs which natural scientists would rightly question because they assumed causality where none was as yet established (Wicke 1986). However, these large costs justified an expensive retrofitting programme which, over a ten year period, reduced the emissions of sulphur dioxide from large combustion plants in West Germany from 1.9 million tonnes to 0.3 mt, of nitrogen oxides from 0.96 to 0.25 mt, and of particulates from 0.1 to 0.02 mt (BMU 1993, 355). In German terms, the *Belastung* of the *Umwelt* has been significantly reduced. In addition, unemployment was reduced during a period of recession (1981-1983) and money was recycled in the national economy.

There have been ambitious attempts in recent years outside Germany to give precise, rational meaning to the precautionary idea by the natural sciences (risk and probability analysis), a combination of natural and social sciences, as well as legal and economic theory (Pearce et al 1992).

Most significantly in replying to the economic criticism, however, is the argument that the German precautionary approach looks towards the future and remains committed to industry and the manufacturing sector, even though private firms generally do not like government intervention and tend to be opposed to *Vorsorge* in practice. They fear that *Vorsorge* legitimises government use of national cost benefit calculations rather than those of individual firms.

The German approach sets decision frameworks in a broader spectrum than in the world of 'real life' economics, taking political and social dimensions more explicitly into account. Risks include not only environmental but also political and social costs (as measured by political processes). Benefits include the potential for stimulating and disseminating technical change and hence markets for new products. By adding these dimensions at an early stage, the boundaries of the environmental problem are expanded, incentives for action strengthened and opposition by risk aversion business weakened. This encourages the formation of a broad coalition in favour of stringent abatement action and for technology forcing.

Reflections

While vague, the idea of precaution has played a powerful role in the German environmental policy process by setting ambitious goals and indicating a number of mechanisms through which policy should progress in order to achieve them. This enables official activism when other considerations might have counselled restraint. The duty of precaution endows public authorities with responsibility for the protection of the natural foundations of life and of maintaining the physical world intact for future as well as present generations. It can therefore be used to counter the short-termism endemic in all democratic, consumption oriented societies.

The concept of *Vorsorge* as a duty of 'good' government predicated on the belief that economic development and environmental protection are mutually supportive, helps to explain why the German State may adopt a very proactive stance in environmental matters in order to establish its constitutional authority. *Vorsorge* therefore provides a philosophical principle and tool of persuasion to justify the setting of ambitious environmental targets. There is no legal or institutional requirement to 'prove' damage scientifically or to cost it accurately, before action is legitimate. The promulgation of these targets may therefore become the responsibility of every citizen, industrialist and administrator.

Vorsorge alone gives little guidance as to what instruments are to be adopted, for its aim is primarily to overcome the political and legal opposition of vested interest to public policies. The precautionary principle therefore helped to lay the conceptual and legal basis for a proactive environmental policy which, once spread into Europe, was also directed at ensuring 'burden sharing' in order that German industry would not lose its competitive edge, but rather gain new markets for its environment-friendly technology and products.

Underlying the precautionary principle is a commitment to change which goes considerably beyond doing more research. For the academic world, this implies dangers and opportunities. Basing policy on precaution and knowledge may mean that it is no longer sufficient to describe and understand the world as it is or was. Instead, science is invited to predict and prescribe, engage in persuasion and advocacy. A rational and objective, i.e. scientific, argument in favour of more environmental protection is to be provided on the basis of predictive theory. This is reminiscent of Marxist philosophy and has already created difficulties for scientific institutions giving 'relevant' scientific advice, for example, in the global change debate (Boehmer-Christiansen 1994).

The acceptance of the concept of precaution into public policy also raises questions about different models of environmental policy formation and implementation.

Two policy models are indicated, one pro-active and inviting policy convergence and the other reactive, 'purer' and discouraging convergence. The German case illustrates the former, with the *Vorsorgeprinzip* acting as moral legitimation and legal justification for activism (Boehmer-Christiansen 1992). This in turn helps to overcome a tacit collusion which is possible between conventional economics and the natural sciences in favour of highly complex decision rules. Both disciplines require that causality is fully understood, or probabilities are known. It is well understood that this is rarely the case for major environmental problems (see e.g. O'Riordan 1992). Even removing the onus of providing proof from victim to polluter does not alter this. Policy has difficulties with the 'academic' approach because it remains, in essence, stuck in the diagnostics of the problem. *Vorsorge* and *Stand der Technik* do not overcome, but rather by-pass the problem by justifying technical change with reference to environmental threats (Freeman

1992). While this may produce a tendency to 'overgild' the lily and 'waste' money better spent elsewhere, such waste is difficult to judge in advance and 'better' spending is difficult to ensure. Precaution above all requires a society able and willing to invest in the future, the need for which cannot be 'proven' in advance, but must remain a matter of faith.

To become meaningful and implementable the *Vorsorge* principle cannot be applied in isolation. What really counts for effective environmental policy-making is the capacity of political institutions to motivate 'society' as polluters and consumers, to invest, change attitudes and alter behaviour. Ambitious principles enable and encourage, but do not prescribe solutions. A weak state is unlikely to find the principle to its taste. If the state becomes a strong supporter of Vorsorge, however, regulation will be sought in which the future plays a major role in the rhetoric used to justify policy. The 'future' as a decision criteria can be appealed to by many policy goals, the obligation of acting with *Vorsorge* therefore has the advantage of encouraging policy convergence or linkages which promote the pursuit of non-environmental goals in addition to environmental ones. The danger is that in the absence of such convergence, environmental protection may be neglected.

Bibliography

Bund Deutscher Industrie BDI (Federation of German Industry) 1993. International Environmental Policy - Perspective 2000, 64.

Bundesministeriam für Umwelt, Naturschutz und Reaktorsicherheit BMU (Federal Environment Ministry) 1993. Umwelt, 9, 355.

BMU 1986. Investionshilfen im Umweltschutz. BMU, Bonn.

Bodansky, D. 1991. Scientific Uncertainty and the Precautionary Principle. Environment, 33(7), 5.

Boehmer-Christiansen, S. A. 1994. Uncertain science and power politics: the Framework Convention for Climate Convention. In B. Spector, G. Sjostedt and I.W. Zartman (eds.) Negotiating International Regimes: Lessons learnt from UNCED. IIASA, Austria, forthcoming.

Boehmer-Christiansen, S. A. 1992. Anglo-German contrasts in environmental policy-making and their impacts in the case of acid rain abatement. International Affairs, 4(4), 295-322.

Boehmer-Christiansen, S. A. 1988. Black mist and acid rain: science as a fig leaf of policy. The Political Quaterly, 59(2), 145-60.

Boehmer-Christiansen, S.A. Black mist and acid rain: science as a fig leaf of policy. The Political Quarterly, 59(2), 145-60.

Boehmer-Christiansen, S. A., Merten, D. and Meissner, J. 1993. Ecological restructuring or environment friendly deindustrialisation: the fate of the East German energy sector and society since 1990. Energy Policy 21(4), 355-373.Boehmer-Christiansen, S. A. and Weidner, H. 1992. Catalysts Versus Leanburn: A Comparative Analysis of Environmental Policy in the FRG and GB with Reference to Exhaust Emission Policy for Passenger Cars 1970-1990. WZB Berlin FS II 92-304, Berlin (also Pinder, 1994, forthcoming).

Boehmer-Christiansen, S. A. and Skea, J. F. 1991. Acid Politics. Belhaven, London.

Deutsches Institut für Wirtschaftsforschung (DIW) and RWIW (for Umweltbundesamt) 1993. Umweltschutz und Industriestandort. Erich Schmidt Verlag, UBA Bericht 1/93.

Federal Environment Ministry 1993. Reactor safety and nature protection. Umwelt, 4, 138.

Federal Interior Ministry (BMI) 1984. Dritter Immissionsschutzbericht. Drucksache, Bonn 10/1345, 53.

Freeman, C. 1992. A green techno-economic paradigm for the world economy. In C. Freeman (ed.) Economics of Hope: Essays on Technical Change, Economic Growth and the Environment. Pinter, London 121-142.

Johnson, N. 1983. State and Government in the Federal Repblic of Germany. Pergamon, Oxford.

Koelke, J. 1984. Zum Verhaltnis von Gesetzen, Rechtsverordnungen und VDI Richtlinien, Staub (VDI), 4, (3).

Langguth, G. 1984. The Green Factor in German Politics. Westview Press, Boulder and London (translated from German).

Mayntz, R. 1975. In Mayntz and Scharpf (eds) Policy-making in the Federal German Bureaucracy. Elsevier.Mayntz, R. et al 1978. Vollzugsprobleme der Umweltpolitik. Empirische Untersuchung der Implementation von Gesetzen im Bereich der Luftreinhaltung und des Gewässerschutzes. Materialien zur Umweltforschung, hrsg. vom Rat von Sachverständigen für Umweltfragen, Band 4, Wiesbaden.

von Moltke, K. 1991. Three Reports on German Environmental Policy. Environment, 33(7), 29.

von Moltke, K. 1988. The Vorsorgeprinzip in West German Environmental Policy. Royal Commission on Environmental Pollution, 12th Report, Best Practicable Environmental Option, Appendix 3, HMSO, London, February 1988.

Muller, E. 1986. Die Innenwelt der Umweltpolitik, Westdeutscher Verlag, Opladen.

Narjes, K. H. 1988. Europe-the technical challenge: a view from the European Commission. Science and Public Policy, 15(6), 383-394.

O'Riordan, T. 1992. Shaping environmental science. In E. Lykke (ed.) Achieving Environmental Goals, Belhaven, 181-196.

Pearce, D. W., Turner, R. K. and O'Riordan, T. 1992. Energy and social health: Integrating quantity and quality in energy planning. World Energy Council Journal, December 1992, 76-89.

Salzwedel, J. and Preusker, W. 1982. The Law and Practice Relating to Pollution Control in the FRG. Graham and Trotman.

Vernon, R 1993. Behind the scenes: how policymaking in the European Community, Japan, and the United States affects global negotiations. Environment, 35(5), 12-20, 35-43.

Wey, K. G.1993. Umweltpolitik in Deutschland. Westdeutscher Verlag, Opladen.

Wicke, L. 1986. Die okologischen Millionen, Koesel, Munchen.Wynne, B and Mayer, S. 1993. How science fails the environment' New Scientist, 1876, 32-35

Part II

Implications for Science

Editorial Introduction

Science has never shirked from facing up to uncertainty. It seems to be part of the human condition to accommodate to probability by placing numbers on it and assuming that the numbers provide an aura of certitude. In Chapter 7 David Pearce summarised some of this literature in the context of establishing perceived gains and losses from embarking on uncertain courses of action. Very small probabilities can disappear to zero for convenience or for avoidance, for example belief in being struck by lightning. But the same small probabilities can escalate out of all proportion to their statistical meaning. For example many millions of British people stopped drinking fresh milk for a few days following the Chernobyl radio caesium fallout presumably because they believed that they may have become unhealthily irradiated.

The time-honoured pastime of gambling permits a punter to envisage a rate of return on investment against what is genuinely an unknowable outcome. Comfort comes in the numbers that are set, partly by experience and social conditioning, and partly by the very act of gambling. As bets pile on a particular unknowable outcome, so the odds shorten. This is not because the outcome is any more certain. It is merely a commercial hedging of liability, should the probability prove right. Uncertainty, therefore, is not really a scientific construction. It is a socially and individually mediated artifact that allows us to live with the unease or the thrill of not being sure what is likely to happen from a given set of circumstances.

Uncertainty comes in three fundamental forms, and science seeks to cope with each in a very different manner.

Uncertainty as lack of data

Traditionally the most common form of uncertainty is ignorance, because the evidence is lacking. For the most part this is because the historical record has never been monitored.

So flood heights and frequencies on a river or on a coast can only be framed on the basis of circumstantial evidence and the fading memories of old timers. A plankton bloom in the southern North Sea may be an episodic event tied to ocean currents, sea surface temperature and estuarine discharges, occurring with cyclic regularity, say every 150 years. We cannot know, unless the sediment record shows pulses of organic detritus. But to get such a record costs enormous amounts of money, mostly for precious little payoff.

To overcome these deficiencies, the scientist tries to model the historical record, or to place probabilities on certain combinations of circumstances. This is the so-called Newtonian view of estimating uncertain outcomes, utilising the logic of extrapolation from careful observation and experimentation, coupled to experience and peer reviews. But as Malcolm MacGarvin notes in his contribition, such an approach is couched in assumptions about natural processes, predator-prey relationships and the significance of the presence or absence of indicator species that do not stand up to serious scrutiny when searchingly examined. The very basis of biological monitoring may be flawed because the knowledge frame is built on shifting sands of presumption and selected guesswork. Only by investing in more painstaking monitoring and careful collaborative comparisons of many ecological conditions, can any certainty be created. This is not the stuff of modern science, nor is it attractive to founding agencies, so a necessary ingrediant of improved science in the face of established uncertainty languishes in its societal marginality.

Uncertainty as variability of process

Right now dozens of scientists are scouring the surface of the oceans with expensive telemetric equipment to measure the release of sulphur aerosols from surface plankton, and to discover how much any increase in ultraviolet indication affects the reproductive and other biological functions of various species of plankton and the zooplankton (shrimps etc) that graze upon them at the exposed surface. As Jim Lovelock indicates in Chapter 5, the elimination of cloud-forming plankton under conditions of ocean surface swarming may have a self-reinforcing effect on global temperature increase, at least initially, as the geographical extent of cloudiness becomes confined to nutrient rich estuaries and coastal margins. But this has to be pure speculation.

We know the tolerability of marine plankton to surface temperature, but we are woefully ignorant of the adaptive capabilities of such plankton to slow but steady changes in surface temperature and sea surface conditions. All that peer review can do is integrate guesswork. How the peer review is conducted, for example by networking, or by regular face to face meetings, or by iterative reaction to the views of others in open or closed debates, will more likely influence the collective guesswork to a greater degree than the variations in knowledge, prognoses and institutional bias. Again, such an assertion, while plausible, is impossible to prove.

Similarly the possible effect of greater concentrations of ultraviolet light on oceanic microlife could alter the whole ecological relationships of the high latitude oceans. Such variations could be induced by the removal of ultraviolet absorbing ozone in the outer stratosphere over 50 kms up, caused by the combination of industrial waste gases and sunlight on a system that has never heretofore experienced the hand of humankind. Again, we do not know fully the processes involved, even if we did, we would probably find that the relationships are extremely variable and subject to chaotic fluctuations that are not adequately modellable. So the very basis of Newtonian science is affected by unmodellable natural variability that challenges the most sophisticated computer simulation.

As we have noted, science seeks to overcome these deficiences by authoriative peer review. In effect, this means gathering the judgements of experienced individuals and networks of collaborators to exercise judgement born of knowledge, authority and perspective. There is always the danger of group fallibility in such exercises. The only adequate answer is to ensure that such constellations of opinion have the widest range of views, and are open to examination, so that unusual interpretations get a proper airing. Even today in the realms of more open opinion formation, such exposure and enlightened self criticism are rare.

In her assessment of the management of risks associated with the controlled release of genetically modified organisms, Julie Hill in Chapter 10 explains that the widening of the basis of judgement to include environmental action groups, consumer associations and those with an interest in the ethics of manipulating nature helps to produce a forum that is more truely representative of a cautious public mood.

Uncertainty as indeterminacy

Creates serious difficulties for conventional science. Here ignorance or inspired guesswork are not sufficient attitudes. Indeterminacy means that the systems being studied operate to processes that cannot be encapsulated in traditional scientific terms (Wynne, 1992 provides a useful summary of the arguments). Either they are chaotic, that is they operate in a manner of genuine unpredictability where any forces initiating condition in its guide to final outcome. Or they apply close to a phase change threshold, where the conditions of stability or instability dramatically change, as for example when nutrients accumulate in shallow waters, toxic materials build up in food chains, or human experience is transformed by a wholly relevatory shift in perception. An example of the last was the reapproachment of Israeli Palestinian relations symbolised by a three second handshake between the Israeli Prime Minister and the Leader of the Palestinian Liberation Organisation - men who had fought each other as guerrilla warriers only a generation before.

Indeterminacy creates open-endedness in scientific assessment. Imagine trying to pin down the relationship between the alteration of surface landcover, which changes the pattern of rainfall and temperature in ways just modellable on the uncertainty as variable data principle. Then trying to predict how far all this exacerbates climate change which itself is pushed by greenhouse gas emissions and non-human factors of which only a very few are known. This combination of two layers of uncertainty defy scientific calculation. Yet as Wynne (1992, 119) has observed, such indeterminacies do create models of cause and effect that influence policy and human behaviour. For better or worse, the forthcoming UN Framework Convention on Desertification will reflect these scientific "certainties" while trying to control behaviour on the ground by millions of people whose needs, aspirations and perceptions are a million miles away from the conceptualisation of the alleged links between desertification and climate change.

What, you might ask, has all this to do with precaution? As noted in the introductory chapter precaution is an amalgam of concepts with little cohesion and no internal consistency. In Chapter 8 Robin Attfield develops this point admirably, hinting that precaution may become meaningless in policy terms, ironically because it is too jumbled in rich meanings. These three modes of uncertainty suggest different forms of reapproachment between precaution and science. On the data deficiency theme, much can be done by selective monitoring, more sensitive modelling and greater engagement with informed public opinion. On the data variability issue peer review can be widened, made more reflective and open, and subject to informed policy debate, hopefully beyond party political lines. For the indeterminacy theme, a more radical concept of science-democracy partnership is envisaged.

This raises the issue of civic science, or a negotiated science in which participation becomes a means of brokering knowledge and valuation between scientific processes and public opinion. Precaution opens up the scope for this, because precaution encourages thoughtful and creative dialogue between an activated citizenry and the wider scientific community. For this to occur there needs to be a new relationship between science and the community. Frederick Warner reminds us that risk management is a part social science and a part statistical science. It is the welding of science and creative democracy through such processes as stakeholder mediation and public trust that leads to the evolving notion of risk management as a civic science rooted in open and friendly structures of communication and consensus-seeking.

Intriguingly, this has considerable significance for regulation of risks. The "market testing" of all regulatory bodies in the UK has opened up avenues for greater internal and external accountability. This is connected to the slowly evolving significance of the citizens' charter as a mechanisms to ensure more openness and responsiveness in public service. At present and this is a bit of a muddle, because no one is sure what the charter actually means, and management changes in regulatory agencies have convulsed their operations without yet providing greater effectiveness. But the scope for extending civic science into the precautionary domains of environmental management is considerable. There would be greater opportunity, for example, to examine the merits of a more thoughtful and proactive cost benefit analysis, though this could work to the detriment of precautionary safeguards, as Charles Clover concludes in Chapter 9. But there could be a better dialogue with active citizen groups and the workforce as to the basis on which danger is evaluated, or occupational safety levels are arrived at. Ironically all this prospect is occurring at a time when the government is trying to deregulate the structures of public interest management, when openness is still being officially resisted, and when pressure group cash and memberships are falling. The opportunity is there, but it may not be grasped. This is partly why we conclude in Chapter 6 that precaution should come in slowly, without unnecessary fuss and bother.

In Chapter 6 Jane Hunt shows how uncertainty is mediated via social contexts, some of which shape the scientific research budgets in which science progresses, while others condition the legal and political arrangements that permit precaution to be given its place in the order of things. So liability and onus of proof subtly shift more and more onto the promotor of social change, to show how the net effort will be positive, even if mistakes of judgement are made.

This is why precaution is becoming such a powerful concept in modern environmental management. It is brushing against the revolving doors of a minor revolution in science and an equally important revolution in policymaking and institutional design for coping with uncertainty in all its various forms.

Placed in a constructive and enabling context, precaution can act as an invaluable catalyst in the renogotiation of the appropriate roles for science in an age where uncertainty is recognised for what it is - a sobering indication of human fallibility in its construction of its world.

Reading

Malcolm MacGarvin provides an invaluable insight into the changing conception of science vis a vis assimilative capacity studies. An even more detailed treatment of the factors of the statistical method can be found in Brett Kettle (1993) Statistics, pragmatism and the precautionary principle: exploring the boundaries of the scientific method in a series of papers published by the Institute of Environmental Studies at the University of New South Wales, Sydney, Australia, under the title The Precautionary Principle and edited by Ronnie Harding. Other papers of note in this valuable symposium include Gavin McDonnell (1993) Risk management and the precautionary principle: coping with decisions, and David Farrier and Liz Fisher (1993) Reconstituting decision making processes and structures in the light of the precautionary principle.

For the view of the ecological economist read Robert Costanza and Laura Cowell (1992) The 4P approach to dealing with scientific uncertainty, Environment 34(9) 12-20. This argues for a shift in the onus of proof with more attention being given to liability funds created up front in advance of any activity subject to varying degrees of uncertainty. Brian Wynne (1992) Uncertainty and environmental learning Global Environmental Change 2(2) 111-127 covers in more detail the journal reviewed by Jane Hunt in Chapter 6. For a more accessible version see Brian Wynne and Sue Meyer (1993) How science fails the environment New Scientist 6 June, 33-35.

Chapter 3

Precaution, Science and the Sin of Hubris

By Malcolm MacGarvin

This chapter is mainly about the environmental policies concerning marine issues, particularly pollution, that have adopted by countries around the North East Atlantic, especially around the North Sea; the extent to which these policies depend upon science; the flaws in that science; and what we should do once those flaws are recognised. My excuse for such limited coverage is that the policy developments in this area, with their emphasis on the precautionary principle, are particularly interesting, and there will be many parallels with environmental policies elsewhere in the world.

In the 1960s and 70s environmental policy treated the marine environment as a resource, whose exploitation was limited only by considerations of the effects of one group of people upon another. Thus the effects of pollution on marine species was considered mainly in the context of whether the levels of contamination posed a threat to human consumers. In all such considerations the burden of proof of environmental damage rested on those seeking to protect the environment.

However this 'permissive principle' was shaken by a sequence of unpredicted events (contaminants such as pesticides, PCBs, CFCs and the ozone hole, and nutrients). The precautionary principle, a reaction to problems such as these, first came to international prominence when introduced, during the 1980s, as part of a significant shift in north-west European marine environmental policy. Until then most people had assumed that the North East Atlantic was so vast that it would be little affected by human chemical contamination. However it became apparent that substances were by no means rapidly diluted and dispersed from inshore waters and coastal seas such as the North Sea and the Baltic (e.g. Stebbing, 1992). Moreover, when historical records were examined it became clear that since the 1930s there had been huge and detrimental changes in the species composition of extremely important parts of the ecosystem, such as the Wadden Sea, a vast shallow coastal region of the North Sea stretching along the Dutch, German and Danish coastline (Figure 3.1).

A major stimulus has been provided by three Ministerial North Sea Conferences (1985, 1987, 1990) held by environmental ministers, and one 'Interim Ministerial Meeting' (IMM) of environment and agricultural ministers (1993), with a Fourth Conference due in 1995. The most significant development, the precautionary principle, was given explicit form at the 1987 conference. It was to be applied to avoid potentially damaging impacts of substances, 'even where there is no scientific evidence to prove a casual link between emissions and effects'. The developments at the North Sea Conference were rapidly introduced into the work of the Oslo and Paris Commissions, (OSCOM and PARCOM) which cover the entire North-East Atlantic, and also into the Helsinki Commission (HELCOM), which protects the Baltic. The need for precaution was used to justify decisions made in all these fora to reduce by 50-70 percent or more, or even eliminate, contamination by substances such as synthetic chemicals, heavy metals, and nutrients, and to cease practices such as ocean incineration and dumping.

Yet the precautionary principle is far more than a plea to add an extra margin of safety to old practices (Sperling, 1986). It is based upon the realisation that it is extremely difficult to determine 'safe' levels of contamination; a precautious policy can hardly be centred on the discharge of substances into the environment, followed by attempts to monitor them to see if they have any adverse effects. Nevertheless, in practice the precautious headlines of the Ministerial Declarations have been grafted onto a body of policy still based on the use of the presumed assimilative capacity of the environment, and the setting of reduction targets. The result is a contradictory mess. Policy makers have been slow to set in motion a thorough reappraisal of environmental policy in the light of the recognised need for precaution.

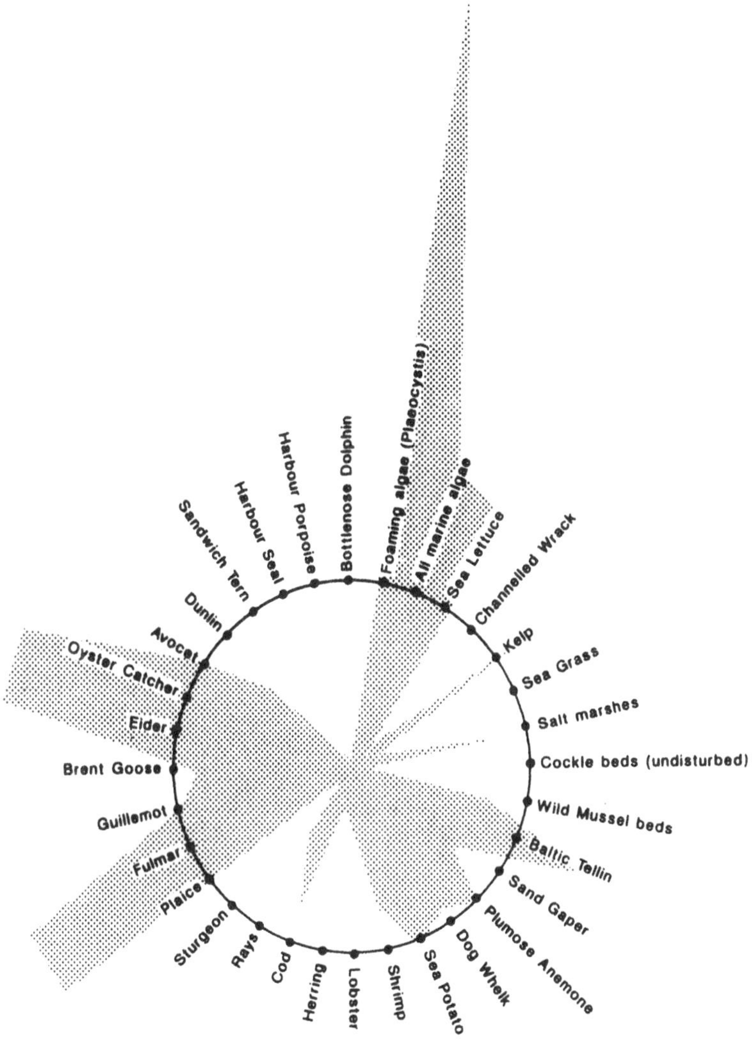
Bottlenose Dolphin
Foaming algae (Plaeocystis)
All marine algae
Sea Lettuce
Channelled Wrack
Kelp
Sea Grass
Salt marshes
Cockle beds (undisturbed)
Wild Mussel beds
Baltic Tellin
Sand Gaper
Plumose Anemone
Dog Whelk
Sea Potato
Shrimp
Lobster
Herring
Cod
Rays
Sturgeon
Plaice
Fulmar
Guillemot
Brent Goose
Eider
Oyster Catcher
Avocet
Dunlin
Sandwich Tern
Harbour Seal
Harbour Porpoise

This is no abstract point. Since the 1990 Ministerial Conference it has become clear that the problems that the North Sea have by no means been largely solved or overexagerated, which appears to be the perception of at least some of the media and politicians. For example, in 1990 the UK Department of the Environment commissioned a major study along the western coastline of the North Sea, from the Shetlands to Kent, to examine the effect of environmental stress, including toxic pollution, on the 'scope for growth' of mussels. The results showed a linear, declining trend in scope for growth from north to south with "consistently lower values south of the Tyne estuary (NE England), reflecting the general increase in human population numbers, industrial activity and associated environmental contamination". Indeed at 8 of 10 sites south of Filey Brig, in Yorkshire, the mussels were classified as highly stressed (Anon. 1992). A little further from the shoreline, Research by Cameron and Berg (1994) between 1984 and 1992 has established that there are worryingly high proportions of fatal malformations in fish egg embryos in the estuaries and inshore waters of the UK and continental Europe - in 1991 46 percent of fish eggs (of all species) from the German Bight (off the Elbe estuary) had these defects, 43 percent off the Rhine, 47 percent off the Thames estuary, 55 percent off the Firth of Forth, and 57 percent of the Tyne. Further offshore the levels were much lower, down to 13 percent. Similar results were obtained in 1992 with a maximum of 60 percent, off the Thames, compared to offshore values down to 6 percent. Moreover there has been no sign of any dramatic decline since survey work started in 1984. Cameron and Berg point the finger of suspicion at pollutants, particularly organochlorines, which are now know to sharply reduce the viability of eggs produced by contaminated fish such as flounder and herring in the Baltic, and whiting in the North Sea, at body concentrations far lower than once thought to be a problem. There are also concerns that the eggs of the species surveyed by Cameron and Berg, which float close to the surface, may come in contact with the 'surface microlayer', a thin film of natural oils, in which fat soluble contaminants, such as organochlorines, are concentrated.

Concern over this contaminated microlayer was highlighted by the Bremerhaven Workshop - a major collaborative effort between leading European marine laboratories (summarised in

Stebbing et al. 1992a, b). This work, based on a transect extending from the German Bight to the Dogger Bank, in the mid-southern North Sea, gave similar results for fish egg embryos as that of Cameron and Berg. They also found that adult dab had elevated levels of defense enzymes that are triggered in response to organochlorines, polyaromatic aromatic hydrocarbons and, interestingly, for organophosphorus and carbamate pesticides - a group that are supposed to break down so rapidly that their impact in marine environment have received relatively little attention.

The workshop confirmed, for the first time in the field, the astonishing result that the concentration of contaminants in the surface microlayer is sufficient to be directly toxic to marine life. Another surprising result was that although all these trends generally declined the further offshore they went, high levels were encountered over the Dogger Bank. This lends support to yet another piece of recent research, summarised by Krönke (1992), which documents remarkable changes in the bottom living fauna of the Dogger Bank between the 1950s and 1980s, including a switch in species from long lived bivalve shellfish towards opportunistic short-lived species, accompanied by a 2.5 to 8 fold increase in biomass. And contrary to expectation, high levels of contamination of the heavy metals lead and cadmium were found in the sediments, benthic species and in dab, greater that those in the German Bight and Danish coastal waters, both acknowledged as being highly polluted. It is believed that the high concentrations of these, and of nutrients (which Krönke argues may be the cause of the faunal changes) probably result from contaminants in water from the UK meeting those from the Rhine, Wesser and Elbe and accumulating in the central southern North Sea. Even remoteness, it seems, is no guarantee of protection.

Two points are clear even from these few examples. First, there are still severe concerns about the health of the North Sea, a decade on from the First North Sea Conference. Secondly research is still turning up unexpected and disturbing results, despite the North Sea being amongst the most intensively studied marine area in the world. While its problems may have diminished in the public eye, and consequently are receiving less political attention, they most certainly have not gone away.

Assimilative capacity, sound science and monitoring

Notwithstanding his commitment to precautionary measures, Mr Yeo, the then UK Minister for the Environment, whilst at the 1993 North Sea Interim Ministerial Meeting, frequently referred to the need for decisions to be based on 'sound science'. By this he meant proof of harm, rather than what his civil service advisors see as the unproven hypotheses that lead many other North Sea countries to demand protection measures.

But assimilative capacity places an enormous burden on science to determine and then monitor for 'safe' levels of contamination. This burden has increased still further now that the objective is not just the protection of human health, but also, in the new (1992) Paris Convention, to conserve and, where possible, restore marine ecosystems per se (Oslo and Paris Commissions, 1992a). Chemical monitoring of the level of contamination of marine sediments, water and biota has its difficulties, but these pale into insignificance compared to the task of biological effects monitoring - surveying the biota to ensure that no significant harmful effects are occurring in the marine ecosystem (often referred to less precisely as 'biological monitoring'). In this chapter I argue that these shortcomings are so severe - indeed insoluble over a time span relevant to current policy makers - that they require us to find alternative means of environmental protection. I also make some observations about the role of science within a precautious policy framework.

But before doing that, to avoid confusion, one has to be quite clear about the distinction between monitoring (and within that biological effects monitoring) from the more general scientific research that sometimes alerts us to environmental problems. Biological effects monitoring is the detection and attribution of adverse changes amongst the biota. Measuring the concentration of a contaminant in a plant or animal is chemical monitoring, not biological effects monitoring. Note also that simply determining that changes are taking place, without knowing their cause, is not biological effects monitoring - although it is an essential step along the way - because monitoring has the aim of ensuring that the assimilative capacity of the environment for various contaminants is not exceeded. The prime attribute of monitoring is that it must be systematic, unambiguous, and part of a control process. Chambers 20th Century Dictionary (Kirkpatrick, 1983) defines it as a means of keeping a variable quantity within prescribed limits. The systematic monitoring received in a cardiovascular unit, or the quality control of an industrial process, are two examples. A change is detected, its cause is known, and the corrective treatment is applied. There is nothing hit or miss here. The situation with monitoring is very different.

The shortcomings of monitoring

Determining the effects of human activities on marine species populations is extremely challenging. As a result the implementation of biological effects monitoring programmes by bodies such as ICES (International Council for the Exploration of the Sea) and PARCOM (Paris Commission) lagged well behind those for the measurement of the levels of contaminants and the determination of 'safe' levels of contamination in marine foodstuffs for human consumption (McIntyre and Pearce, 1980; ICES Advisory Committee on Marine Pollution, 1985; Stebbing, Dethlefsen and Thurberg, 1990; Hoogweg, Ducrotoy and Wettering, 1991; MacGarvin and Johnston, 1993).

Problems at the outset

Even before assessing the impact of the contaminant on an ecosystem there are a number of obstacles that have not been resolved, despite many decades of effort. First there is the cost of trying to systematically determine the effects of thousands of chemicals - at least $10,000 per chemical to test bioconcentration and acute toxicity for a few organisms, and $100,000 to $1,000,000 or more for a more detailed (Nirmalakhandan and Speece, 1988) but still uncertain assessment. Shortcuts have been suggested, such as QSARs (Quantitative Structure Activity Relationships) which attempt to predict the environmental effect of one chemical from its structural similarities with chemicals whose effects are thought to be well known. But such methods are of limited reliability (Matthiessen et al. 1993), and in any case fails to pick up novel and unpredicted effects, a major source of problems over the last four decades. Overall there are huge gaps in our knowledge. For example in one extensive sampling program of industrial chemicals present in the Tees area, no ecotoxicological data could be found for 75 percent of the chemicals isolated (Law et al. 1991) Moreover this does not take into account the possible synergistic effects of many chemicals acting in unison. The concentrations of individual chemicals present in the Tees apparently did not give cause for concern, but when oyster larvae were used to test the water quality, high levels of mortality ensued: indeed in one site in the upper Tees estuary all the larvae died!

This last example illustrates a different approach, to measure the stress induced by contaminants, even where the exact effect of the contaminant, or even the contaminant itself, is unknown. The mussel scope for growth, fish egg embryo surveys cited earlier are also examples of these. Another is the interpretation of physiological and biochemical changes that may be associated with the organism's attempts to detoxify certain contaminants, such as the elevation of mixed function oxidases (MFOs) enzyme activity and metallothionein induction. Yet such techniques need to be treated with great care because of many possible complications; for example organisms can show differing responses at different contaminant concentrations (Köhler and Pluta, 1994), or be stimulated by other stresses, such as reproduction (Stebbing et al. 1992b). Because of such complications the conclusions to be drawn from such studies often remain controversial. In addition, to some extent with the induced defence work, and even more so with that such as scope for growth and fish egg embryos, the work has the serious defect that it indicates that a problem exists, without identifying what it is.

But even were an effect well understood, attempting to monitor concentrations of that chemical in the environment, with the intention of keeping these within the presumed assimilative capacity of the environment, requires a massive sampling programme to reduce the uncertainties introduced by widespread spatial and temporal variation. In reality sampling programmes fall far short of that required. This is true both of the local sampling of, for example, what the UK DoE considers to be the most problematic substances entering the North Sea (the 'Red List', UK DoE 1988) (Agg and Zabel 1990), through to the biggest overall assessment of the state of the North Sea to date, the 1994 North Sea Quality Status Report, undertaken as part of the North Sea Ministerial Conference process. This concluded, with regard to the reductions achieved in the North Sea so far, that 'There have been few serious attempts to assess changes in contamination concentrations over time and there are few good data sets which allow reliable conclusions to be drawn' (North Sea Task Force 1994).

Therefore while the examples cited here can be useful in highlighting the possible effects of human activities, they are more appropriate as a spur to politicians than as part of a fail-safe environmental policy (although, as we shall see later, even this can be a double edged sword). However it is also deficient in yet another major aspect. Physical scientists (Sünderman, 1994) and biologists (Matthews, 1994) alike are now beginning to emphasise that the models and tests of the effects of contaminants in the marine environment are crippled by a lack of information on the ecological interactions that maintain ecosystems. It has sometimes been suggested that it is not necessary to have a detailed understanding of ecosystem dynamics to ensure protection of the marine environment. But this is simply not true, at least within a policy based on assimilative capacity.

Ecology - the Achilles heel of monitoring

The desire to side-step ecology is understandable but inadmissible. Indeed, even the determination of energy and other flows through the food-web does not provide the relevant information to predict ecological effects. We cannot assume that because a species is relatively rare, it is relatively unimportant. To establish the role of a species demands long term detailed observation and the experimental manipulation of populations (Underwood, 1985; Simberloff, 1988). For example a species such as the blue-rayed limpet *Helcion pellucidum* makes up a minute portion of the biomass of European kelp forests. But they bore into the holdfasts of kelp, weakening them so that they are prone to detach from the rock and subsequently die. As a result any factor that influences the abundance of such animals could quite possibly have drastic effects on the community as a whole, even though their biomass might appear insignificant in a study of energy flows consumed by this species. Similarly the increase of nutrients in coastal waters is very likely responsible for the massive increase of *Phaeocystis*, the algae responsible for the masses of foam that disfigure many North Sea beaches (Lancelot et al., 1987; Cadée, 1990). Because species of zooplankton, such as copepods, have feeding preferences for different species of phytoplankton (Davies et al., 1992), and because they in turn are important links in the marine food web, the change in *Phaeocystis* abundance could well have important implications for coastal North Sea ecosystems in general and for fisheries in particular. Yet even a partial untangling of the effects on the food web is a slow process requiring dedicated, painstaking work (Hansen, 1994).

Unfortunately even sheer hard work does not guarantee success. In fact the expectations of theoretical ecology in general and marine ecology in particular have been sharply reduced in the last few years. This leads to the central point of this chapter - that our understanding of ecosystems such as the North Sea is so poor that attempts to determine the effects of contaminants by monitoring are unlikely to succeed for all but the most obvious cases. The uncertainty and soul-searching that has dominated theoretical and 'pure' marine ecology since at least the mid 80s has implications which have been surprisingly slow to trickle through to applied sciences such as monitoring. At least four relevant areas can be identified; the confounding effect of many different human activities, the downward assessment of progress in marine ecology, the reduced expectations of theoretical ecology in general, and the uncertainties introduced by the possibility of chaotic population dynamics. Any one of these has crippling implications for our ability to predict the effect of our actions; taken together they remove the scientific justification for basing pollution policy on the attempt to find 'safe' levels of contamination.

Confounding effects

Modern ecological methods emphasise the importance of rigorous experimental and statistical design that allow different hypotheses to be isolated and tested (Peters, 1991). High natural variability in areas such as the North Sea make it extremely difficult to determine human effects (Gunkel, 1994), and to make matters worse many different human activities take place. But research by different groups almost invariably concentrates on single issues, such as fishing or contamination, without attempting to untangle the interactions. In addition research is confounded because the gathering of basic information during this century has been coupled with unprecedented and increasing human effects. As a result we can have no clear idea of how the natural ecosystem would function, nor do we have true controls with which to compare areas affected by human activities.

Marine ecology reassessed

Toxicologists assume that it is possible to monitor just a few species, using these as indicators for the whole ecosystem. Up until the early 80s the principle could perhaps be partly supported by research on temperate rocky intertidal areas, whose population dynamics were regarded as the best understood of any marine habitat (Underwood and Denley, 1984). This research indicated the existence of just a few 'keystone' species, where changes in their population levels resulted in a cascade of effects throughout the food-web. Alteration of the population levels of most other species, it was thought, had little effect (Dayton, 1984). This concept of keystone species was nested within a wider model of rocky shore community structure that predicted that physical survival would be the most important factor on exposed coasts, predator control would be the most important force in sheltered areas, with competition between species on the same trophic level playing the most important role at sites with intermediate physical exposure (Menge and Sutherland, 1976). It was also expected that research would reveal keystone species in other compartments of the marine ecosystem.

However keystone species need not be particularly common or obvious; instead their discovery requires a detailed programme of population manipulation and exclusion. As a result the number of established cases remains relatively small, albeit with a global distribution (Paine, 1971; Dayton et al., 1974; Menge, 1976; Lubchenco and Menge, 1978). The original work of Paine (1966) in an intertidal area in Washington State remains the most well known. Here the exclusion of the starfish *Pisaster ochraceus* resulted in a dramatic sequence of changes, over the space of two years, from a diverse community to one dominated by the mussel *Mytilus californianus*. But even this work does not mean that a species such as *Pisaster* can be used as a universal indicator - later work showed that it is, in the words of Paine (1980) 'just another species' at another location because of the absence of *M. californianus*.

On soft-bottomed habitats the type of manipulation experiments that are necessary to explore community regulation are far more difficult, and there are very few candidates for keystone species, such as the starfish *Solaster dawsoni* that feeds on sea pens in the subtidal areas of Puget Sound, Washington (Birkeland, 1974). Meanwhile the difficulties of experimental manipulation in open water is an important reason why ecologists such McGowan and Walker (1979) and Dayton (1984) were forced to concede that little progress has been made in resolving the 'paradox of the plankton' (that vast numbers of species apparently find ways of coexisting in this simplest possible of habitats) pointed out over 30 years ago by Hutchingson (1961). And while the current emphasis on physical processes in planktonic ecology gives another dimension to the analysis (e.g. Mann and Lazier, 1991), it is not clear that this guarantees a resolution of the paradox.

Given these difficulties the few species used for biological monitoring are not keystone species. Instead they are selected because they conveniently absorb contaminants (mussels), are quick and easy to test (the oyster bioassay) or need in any case to be monitored for human health (commercial fish species). While the exclusion of keystone species is understandable, it means that monitoring programmes intended to protect marine habitats do not have a firm scientific foundation.

Moreover, the assumption that most non-keystone species play minor roles in ecosystems and, by implication, can be ignored by biological monitoring programmes must be questioned. Species are often innocuous because they are kept rare by predators, parasites or disease, and can increase dramatically when introduced into a new habitat free of such constraints, as a host of terrestrial, freshwater and marine examples testify. It is possible that contaminants (or other human activities) could also adversely affect the dynamics, resulting in outbreaks of species which then disrupt the ecosystem. More complex effects could occur involving a web of species. In either case work based on individual species may give no hint of human involvement.

Apart from the problems associated with the search for keystone species the synoptic model of community structure of rocky habitats, structured along a gradient depending on physical exposure, has also been found wanting. A growing unease that its conclusions were simplistic were given focus by Underwood et al., (1983) and Underwood and Denley (1984). Their work on intertidal barnacles indicated that the number of adults was determined by the number of larvae that survived their plankton phase and settled onto the rocks - which varied hugely from one year to the next. Perhaps the most remarkable feature is that many others before were aware of such huge annual variation in rocky shore recruitment, but had instead simply seen it as a nuisance to be filtered out of the results, rather than the key feature. The result of this and other work (Gaines and Roughgarden, 1985; Lewin, 1986; Roughgarden, 1989) is that the ecology of rocky shores, once considered to be a show-case for marine ecology - indeed all ecology - has gone back to reconsider basic principles (Underwood and Denley, 1984). There are lessons here for monitoring, notably the way in which the momentum built up by a theory kept it alive long after the weight of evidence was against it. It also shows how it has proved impossible to isolate research in one compartment of the ecosystem. Instead, understanding of the rocky shore - once regarded as the easiest to study - is intractably linked to events in the plankton, a graveyard for ecological aspirations.

The reappraisal taking place amongst marine ecologists is just part of a general stock-taking by theoretical ecologists since the subject changed direction in the 1950s to adopt a more rigorous scientific and mathematical approach. The outcome has been a drastic lowering of expectations.

One key area for both pure and applied research during this period has been the search for density dependant mortality. These are those causes of death that must regulate the population of a species if it is to have a characteristic level of abundance. They kill proportionately more of the population if it rises above this level, and relax their pressure when the population falls. Comprehensive data, systematically accounting for and distinguishing between all causes of death over a number of generations sufficient to encompass the range of population densities, is essential. Without it the interactions between density dependent and independent causes of mortality cannot be determined. Nor can accurate predictions be made of future population levels - including those resulting from human perturbations.

Given the amount of effort that has been spent gathering data on marine fish, particularly in the North Sea, some may be forgiven for thinking that here at least we must have good data. Unfortunately the truth is rather different. The size of each generation of marine fish is largely determined between the release of eggs and the recruitment of young adults into the fishing stocks, a period when it is extraordinarily difficult to gather information. As a result population predictions have proved highly inaccurate. Even within the field Wootton (1990) notes 'it takes an act of faith to take the resulting curves seriously', and Rothschild (1986) has drawn attention to the need for a radical reappraisal of fisheries biology methods and goals. Theoretical ecologists from other fields, knowing the difficulties in gathering sufficient information even under the most favourable circumstances, view with incredulity the attempts of fisheries biologists to predict population fluctuations. Peters (1991) speaks for many when he says 'Fisheries management is so accustomed to inaccuracy in its basic models that striking differences between model and observation are scarcely noted . Nevertheless, fisheries biologists fit data to models that are clearly inaccurate and make decisions on that basis'. Few others have commented as directly as Peters, but it is significant that population and theoretical ecologists outside fisheries biology largely ignore their work, as is evident from the lack of citations.

The difficulty of following discrete populations extend to marine species other than fish. The result has been the creation of a rich mass of incomplete and conflicting data, capable of inspiring faith in any number of theories, yet from which it is impossible to draw firm conclusions. However some clues might be gained from terrestrial systems. They, too, have their fair share of confusing evidence. But fortunately some species, particularly amongst insects, lead lifestyles that are amenable to the systematic attribution of the causes of death over many generations that is necessary for an analysis of density dependent mortality (Caughley and Lawton, 1981) - 19 years in the case of a winter moth *Operophtera brumata* population living in an Oxfordshire wood, which formed one of the earliest yet most comprehensive studies (Varley et al., 1973).

But it became clear that even work of this type was still severely limited when it came to predicting future trends. Although the studies could sometimes account for an impressive proportion of deaths, the remaining uncertainties rapidly multiply over a projection of just a few generations, creating a huge degree of error compared to events in real life - as demonstrated by Harcourt's (1971) study of the potato-infesting Colorado potato beetle *Leptinotarsa decemlineata*. The size of this error might be reduced, for instance, by having a better understanding of the factors that made the numbers of natural enemies fluctuate, with the result that they failed to bring the original species back to its mean population size. But this would require a cascade of studies similar to that on the original species, and a vast increase in work that would result in only a slight improvement of the estimates. Problems such as these indicated that all attempts to predict populations would rapidly come up against a barrier that no additional funding or new techniques could overcome.

For theoretical ecologists, unlike applied biologists, this was not too much of a blow. They felt they had what they needed; an understanding in principle of how population regulation worked. Rather than pursue the diminishing returns of further such studies, by the 1970s much of their effort was directed instead towards the deeper understanding of individual aspects of density dependant mortality, such as the searching behaviour of natural enemies or the effects of habitat heterogeneity, using a combination of mathematical models, laboratory and field studies (e.g. Caughley and Lawton, 1981; Hassell, 1981). A variety of species were used, selected for ease of study of the particular character of interest. Many felt that reasonable progress has been made given the immense complexities of the subject.

However the 1980s saw a increasing sense of frustration at the apparent inability to produce a grand unifying theory. The reassessment of rocky shore ecology has been just a small part of this storm. Heated debates occurred, at first over the relative importance of competition or natural enemies in the regulation of populations, and then increasingly over flaws in experimental design, statistical analysis, and the formulation and testing of hypothesis in general (Strong et al., 1984; Roughgarden et al., 1989; Peters, 1991). Underlying this has been a more profound mood change in theoretical ecology, a feeling that the new methods have not delivered the goods expected of them 30 years ago. Major journals now carry editorials asking why ecology, unlike biochemistry or the physical sciences, hasn't solved the problems it set itself (Lawton, 1991). Other influential ecologists such as Roughgarden (1989) and Kareiva (1989) have concluded that the science lacks solid foundations, and that for the time being ecologists should give up any idea of forming grand unifying theories, and concentrate instead on far more narrowly defined studies.

The fact that theoretical ecologists, working in far easier fields than marine ecology, are now asking such searching questions of their methods highlights how unreasonable it is to expect that we can predict the effect of human actions upon marine ecosystems with any accuracy.

Chaos

The possibility of chaotic population fluctuations is yet another unwelcome complication for applied scientists. Assessing the significance of chaotic population fluctuations will be formidable, because it will require new data, carefully gathered, extending over perhaps hundreds of generations. No research programme it seems, however vast, can do anything to speed the gathering of such information.

The uncertainties are highlighted in an analysis by Godfray and Blyth (1990) of the population fluctuations of copepods. The data was gathered by the Continuous Plankton Recorder (CPR) in the seas around the British Isle for over 40 years - one of the most comprehensive data sets available. Yet sophisticated mathematical decoding techniques were unable to determine whether the fluctuations in their numbers during this period were due to random events, or a simple (but unknown) cause that resulted in chaotic fluctuations. The run of data is simply too short for such techniques. The implication is that one might have to gather data for hundreds of years before being able to (possibly) determine whether a factor such as increased nutrient concentrations has an effect on an ecosystem!

The mobility of the CPR introduces uncertainties about whether the same population is being sampled. But data from fixed sites does not necessarily resolve this problem. Other difficulties exist, such as sampling taking at a fixed time of day (missing diurnal migrations or tidal effects) and changes in recording methods. In brief the need to unravel the possible influence of chaotic fluctuations reduces even further the remote hope of predicting the effects of human actions upon marine ecosystems.

Regrettable but inevitable?

Clearly there are many intractable problems associated with biological effects monitoring. It seems inevitable that any debate will reach a point where those arguing for such methods acknowledge the imperfections and weaknesses, but state that we have no choice but to use such methods, because the alternative, of pollution prevention, is impractical. The lack of scientific rigour is conceded, but to continually highlight this appears a council of perfection.

However, from what we already know it is clear that substantial reductions in contaminant inputs are still required. There is a growing policy view that it is imprudent to have any level of synthetic, artificial, compounds in the marine environment. The OSPARCOM 1992 Ministerial Declaration makes the commitment that 'discharges and emissions of substances that are persistent, toxic and liable to bioaccumulate, in particular organohalogen substances, and which could reach the marine environment should be reduced, by the year 2000, to levels that are not harmful to man or nature, with the aim of their elimination.' This commitment was reiterated in the Ministerial Statement of Conclusions of the 1993 Interim Ministerial Meeting, while the 1994 Quality Status Report extends this, by implication, to persistent and toxic compounds in general. (North Sea Task Force 1994, also included as Annex 2 of the Ministerial Statement of Conclusions). So it appears that, here at least, judgement of the appropriate level of synthetic contamination is being removed from the scientific field.

But what of anthropogenic inputs of naturally occurring substances? Well, given that they have their greatest concentrations and effects in rivers, estuaries and coastal zones, where historic burdens are also available for remobilisation (e.g. Dickson, 1987; Eisma and Irion, 1988), it can be expected that the range of debate for no-effect input levels when calculated for the North or Irish Seas *as a whole* will lie between zero and a few percent of natural inputs. Yet the actual levels of metals and nutrients entering these seas are far higher - often 10, 25, 50 percent or more of natural levels (Gerlach, 1988; Salomons, 1988; Boelens 1990).

It therefore seems clear that although one can continue the technical debate about no-effect levels of naturally occurring substances the practical outcome is already apparent; current production practices and product usage will have to change drastically if we are serious about protecting marine ecosystems. It will require a switch to pollution prevention strategies and closed loop production processes that exceed those currently required by national and international programmes.

Clean production

Fortunately new pollution prevention techniques have far greater potential than those outside the field are often aware. These are know collectively as 'clean production' (Baas et al., 1990, Jackson 1993, MacGarvin 1994); a super-set of clean technology that emphasises that pollution prevention involves new operating practices as well as new technology - although in practice the distinction is often blurred. Clean production grew out of the realisation that pollution prevention is the only practical means of implementing the precautionary principle, and that earlier attempts at prevention, such as no- and low-waste technology, were seriously flawed because they concentrated only on pollution caused by waste from manufacturing processes.

Clean production methods can be summarised as those which meet the needs of society - for food, water, energy, transport, goods and services - without damaging the natural world or risking the health of workers or the wider community. They cover all aspects of a product's life cycle - design, raw material extraction, manufacture, use and eventual fate. They aim to avoid the use or manufacture of hazardous products or waste. They are designed to employ only reusable and renewable materials and to conserve energy, water, soil and other raw materials.

Moreover, there are now numerous examples to demonstrate that clean production methods need not be more expensive that conventional process, even when judged at the level of the production process. It is extremely important for all to be aware that the attempt to use assimilative capacity is not the only option. The first question that should always be asked about a contaminant is not what is an acceptable level of pollution, but can there be a safer means of extraction, production and use?

Clean production has been recognised since 1989 by the United Nations Environmental Programme (UNEP Governing Council, 1989), and in UN maritime agreements, such as the London Dumping Convention (ad hoc group of experts on annexes to LDC Convention, 1992), whose provisions have binding force on North Sea states, as elsewhere. Similarly the new Convention for the Protection of the Marine Environment of the North-East Atlantic, agreed in Paris in September 1992, contains many of the elements of clean production (Oslo and Paris Commission, 1992a). This legally binding document commits the countries in this region to the reduction and elimination of *substances* that may cause severe problems in the marine environment, rather than of *pollution* by such substances which, being impossible to define, resulted in endless argument and prevarication. There is a requirement, and a mechanism, for establishing clear goals and timetables for phase-outs and product bans. The accompanying action plan (Oslo and Paris Commission, 1992b) also highlights organohalogens, and requires the elimination of those that can be substituted by other materials. This is true of at least all significant uses, so this appears to mark the beginning of the end of organohalogen production. This, and the many other measures set out, will only be possible by the implementation of techniques associated with clean production. This convention marks a significant point in the metamorphosis of the environmental policy into a consistent, precautionary, framework. And among the many implications it and similar developments have are those for marine monitoring.

What role for science in a precautionary era?

The future of marine monitoring

Clearly, for the reasons already advanced, attempts to establish safe levels for the ecosystem are severely flawed; logic dictates that the precautionary principle surely applies as much to methods that are open to 'reasonable grounds for concern' (Oslo and Paris Commission, 1992a) as it does to the contaminants themselves. But does this mean that the implementation of a precautionary environmental policy would mean that there would be no monitoring at all?

The answer is no. Monitoring should continue, but with a different purpose. Pollution prevention measures are usually phased in, with a series of reduction targets. Until now assessment of whether these targets are met are largely based on dubious, incomplete, incompatible and out-of-date calculations about the levels of inputs believed to enter areas such as the North-East Atlantic by various routes (e.g. Paris Commission, 1991). Instead the assessment should be based on measurements made in the marine environment itself. If they show that reduction measures are falling short of the target, then this will require a intensification of the steps being taken to reduce contamination.

This information will play an important, albeit subsidiary, role in the implementation of clean production methods. There will still be a need for precaution, as considerable degree of error will be present due to inadequacies in analytical (Johnston and MacGarvin, 1989) and statistical methods (Peterman and M'Gongle, 1992). This will require monitors to err on the side of caution when faced with a range of estimates. Nevertheless monitoring will no longer carry the impossible burden of attempting to demonstrate that a particular level is safe The continuing attempt to do so is currently destroying scientific credibility.

Where does science fit in?

So what role is there for science that searches for the effects that our activities have on the environment? This is actually a difficult question to answer. First the easy part. The definition of the precautionary principle in the 1987 and 1990 North Sea Ministerial Declarations, and in the 1992 Paris Convention makes it quite clear how research should not be used, to demand proof of harm before action is contemplated. So, clearly out of order is the UK's attitude, in particular, requiring proof of the substances responsible for, for example the reduction in mussel scope for growth, or of fish egg embryo malformations, and other microlayer effects. Worse still, is the DoE's denial that certain UK 'test case' estuaries, such as the Ythan in Aberdeenshire, have serious eutrophication problems, even though they are aware of the contrary conclusions of the body with the responsible for assessing the Ythan's status, the North-East River Purification Board. Their conclusion, based on the unambiguous criteria laid out in the EU Nitrates Directive, is that the Ythan is quite clearly eutrophic. Such action simply brings the UK into disrepute.

Now a more difficult part. No matter what the formal commitment to the precautionary principle, there is no doubt that it helps to have good evidence, better still clear proof, that a particular substance is causing a particular problem. Environmentalists will want to point to research that shows how bad the situation is; indeed I did the same at the start of this chapter. This may seem reasonable - the precautionary principle then means that both sides have to gather their evidence, but the burden of proof has shifted significantly towards the discharger, rather that those with responsibility to protect the environment.

However there are significant problems with this approach, which should also be apparent from this chapter. We have little idea about where to look for effects on the marine ecosystem, or to demonstrate the cause of a problem when the effects are apparent enough. In short we are in no position systematically to make a risk assessment. Instead we rely on serendipity to bring problems to our attention, hopefully before significant harm is done. However the result has been truly frightening: there is now little that we can do about the levels of immune and reproduction suppressing PCBs, or of ozone depleting CFCs, that are now out of our control, and which will now work their way into the marine environment, or the atmosphere. Instead we are forced to trust in luck. Rather more subtly, if society still demands detailed and convincing evidence of cause of harm before action is taken, just how far have we come, despite reference to precaution? In practice the process will still get bogged down in counter arguments which, given the lack of information, will always be possible.

This is worrying because if one looks back at the major problems that have arisen, these were often not the result of disagreements over the degree of uncertainty. They resulted from ignorance, and it is not necessarily the case that the clean bill of health they were given were a result of scientific incompetence. Technical ignorance will always be with us (Wynne 1992). We cannot assume that our skills are so great that we will always be able to detect and resolve problems caused by contamination before serious consequences arise. The sin of hubris lies behind our current approach - that of "insolence: arrogance such as invites disaster", to quote Chambers 20th Century Dictionary once more.

Instead we have to side-step the problem and look to clean production methods. Three points arise. First, environmental policy needs to give still greater emphasis to existing clean production techniques. The greatest barrier at the moment is lack of awareness and inertia, not the means or economic cost. Second, we need to consider carefully how naturally occurring chemicals are taken from, and returned to, the environment, with an emphasis on closed production loops within the human economy where appropriate. Third, the experience with synthetic chemicals is such that there should be a general presumption against their release out of our control and into the environment, with outright bans for groups of substances where there are doubts, such as organohalogens.

Whether we are capable of making such a change, I must admit I am rather pessimistic. Ironically, at the superficial level that these debates are carried out, it is all too easy to caricature the requirement for action without recourse to further research as irresponsible extremism. And of course there are many other problems beyond those discussed here, even more so considering the world as a whole. Nevertheless, we can take some inspiration - and perhaps even our manufacturing processes - from living organisms. The chemical processes that underpin our modern society, although complex, are nevertheless completely outclassed by those utilised by plants and animals. Their enzymes operate to extraordinary standards compared to the chemical industry. For example the enzyme nitrogenase catalyses a reaction reducing nitrogen gas to ammonia at ambient temperatures and neutral pH (Price and Stevens, 1989). The reaction is 100 percent efficient - no waste products are created. By contrast equivalent industrial processes requires temperatures between 700 and 900 K, pressures between 10 and 900 atmospheres and the presence of iron and other catalysts. Many industrial processes produced yields only measured in a few tens of percent. Enzymes build up extraordinarily complex compounds of remarkable diverse form and function. And all chemical synthesise have to take place in the middle of a living cell, without disturbing its metabolism. Substances are also broken down by other enzymes or by physical processes, back into simple chemicals. Despite the enormously complex materials and chemicals that animals and plants synthesise - including some highly toxic substances - and the billions of years that this has been happening, there are no areas of the Earth that have to be fenced off because of the accumulation of hazardous materials from biological processes. Moreover this has been done without depleting raw materials. Given that living organisms have found ways of sustainable production, then so can we.

References

Ad hoc group of experts on annexes to LDC Convention 1992. Report of the 4th meeting, LDC/SG 15/ 2 Annex. LDC Secretariat, London.

Agg, A.R. and Zabel T.F. 1990. Red List substances: selection and monitoring. Journal of the Institute of Water and Environmental Managers 4: 44-50.

Anon. 1992 Plymouth Marine Laboratory 1991-1992. Annual Report. Plymouth Marine Laboratory, Plymouth, UK.

Baas, L., Hofman, H., Huisingh, D., Huisingh, J. Koppert, P. and Neumann, F. 1990. Protection of the North Sea: Time for Clean Production. Erasmus Centre for Environmental Studies, Erasmus Univ., Rotterdam, 79 pp.

Birkeland, C. 1974. Interaction between a sea pen and seven of its predators. Ecological Monograph 44, 211-232.

Boelens, R (ed.) 1990. Irish Sea Study Group Report. Part 2: Waste Inputs and Pollution. Liverpool University Press. 165 pp.

Cadée, G.C. 1990. Increase of *Phaeocystis* blooms in the westernmost inlet of the Wadden Sea, the Marsdiep, since 1973. In Lancelot, C., Billen, G. and Barth, H. (eds.) Eutrophication and Algal Blooms in North Sea Coastal Zones, the Baltic and Adjoining Areas: Prediction and Assessment of Preventive Actions. Commission of the European Communities, Brussels, 105-112.

Cameron, P. and Berg, J. 1994. Biological monitoring of the North Sea employing fish embroyological data. Helogländer Meeresuntersuchungen 49, 000-000.

Caughley, G. and Lawton, J.H. 1981. Plant-herbivore systems. In May, R.M. (ed.) Theoretical Ecology. Blackwell Scientific Publications, Oxford, 132-166.

Davies, A.G., de Madariaga, I., Bautista, B., Fernández, E., Harbour, D.S., Serret P. and Tranter, P.R.G. 1992. The ecology of a coastal *Phaeocystis* bloom in the North-Western English Channel in 1990. Journal of the Marine Biological Association U.K. 72, 691-708.

Dayton, P.K. 1984. Processes structuring some marine communities: Are they general? In Strong, D.R. Jr., Simberloff, D., Abele, L.G. and Thistle, A.B. (eds.) Ecological Communities:

Conceptual Issues and the Evidence. Princeton University Press, Princeton, 181-197.

Dayton, P.K., Robilliard, G.A., Paine, R.T. and Dayton, L.B. 1974. Biological accommodation in the benthic community at McMurdo Sound, Antarctica. Ecological Monograph, 44, 105-128.

Dickson, R.R. (ed.) 1987. Irish Sea Status Report of the Marine Pollution Monitoring Group: Aquatic Environmental Monitoring Report Number 17. MAFF, Lowestoft, 7-8.

DoE 1988. Inputs of Dangerous Substances to Water: Proposals for a Unified System of Control. UK Department of the Environment, London.

Eisma, D. and Irion, G. 1988. Sediment matter and sediment transport. In Salomons, W., Bayne, B.L., Duursma, E.K. and Förstner, U. (eds.) Pollution of the North Sea: An Assessment. Springer-Verlag, Berlin, 20-35.

Gaines, S. and Roughgarden, J. 1985. Larval settlement rate: a leading determinant of structure in an ecological community of the marine intertidal zone. Proceedings of the National Academy of Sciences USA 82, 3707-11.

Gerlach, S. 1988. Nutrients - an overview. In Newmann, P.J. and Agg, A.R. (eds.) Environmental Protection of the North Sea. Heinemann Professional Publishing, Oxford, 147-175.

Godfray, H.C.J. and Blyth, S.P. 1990. Complex dynamics in multispecies communities. Philosophical Transaction of the Royal Society of London B 330, 221-233.

Gunkel, J. 1994. 100 years Biologische Anstalt Helgoland: A cliff in the sea bathed in tides and currents of history.

Helgoländer Meeresunters.

Hansen, F.C. 1994. Trophic interactions between zooplankton and *Phaeocystis*. Helgoländer Meeresunters. 94.

Harcourt, D.G. 1971. Population dynamics of *Leptinotarsa decemlineata* (Say) in eastern Ontario. III. Major population processes. Canadian Entomologist 103, 1049-61.

Hassell, M.P. 1981. Arthropod Predator-Prey Systems. In May, R.M. (ed.) Theoretical Ecology. Blackwell Scientific Publications, Oxford, 105-131.

Hoogweg, P., Ducrotoy, J. and Wettering, B. 1991. The North Sea Task Force: The First Two Years. Marine Pollution Bulletin 22, 328-330.

Hutchingson, G.E. 1961. The paradox of the plankton. American Naturalist 95, 137-45.

ICES Advisory Committee on Marine Pollution 1985. Biological Effects Studies. In Report of the ICES Advisory Committee on Marine Pollution 1984, 17-21.

Jackson, T. (ed.) 1993. Clean Production Strategies: Developing Preventative Environmental Management in the Industrial Economy. Stockholm Environment Insititute. Lewis, Boca Raton.Kareiva, P. 1989. Renewing the dialogue between theory and experiments in population ecology. In Roughgarden, J., May, R.M. and Levin, S.A. (eds.) Perspectives in Ecological Theory. Princeton University Press, Princeton, 68-88.

Kirkpatrick, E.M. (ed.) 1983. Chambers 20th Century Dictionary. Chambers, Edinburgh.

Köhler, A. and Pluta, H.J. 1994. Responses of central detoxifying and biotransforming enzyme systems during the tumorgenesis in the liver of flat fish in the North Sea. Helgoländer Meeresunters. 94.

Krönke, I. 1992. Macrofauna standing stock of the Dogger Bank: A comparison: III. 1950-54 versus 1985-87. A final summary. Helgoländer Meeresuntersuchingen 46, 137-169.

Lancelot, C., Billen, G., Sournia, A., Weisse, T., Colijn, C., Veldhuis, M.J.W., Davies, A. and Wassman, P. 1987. Phaeocystis blooms and nutrient enrichment in the continental coastal zones of the North Sea. Ambio 16, 38-46.

Law, R.J., Fileman, T.W. and Mattiessen, P. 1991. Phthalate esters and other industrial organic chemicals in the North and Irish Seas. Water Science and Technology 24, 127-134.

Lawton, J.H. 1991. Ecology as she is done, and could be done. Oikos 61, 289-90.

Lewin, R. 1986. Supply-side ecology. Science 234, 25-7.

Lubchenco, J. and Menge, B.A. 1978. Community diversity and persistence in a low rocky intertidal zone. Ecological Monograph 48, 67-94.

MacGarvin, M. and Johnston P. 1993. On precaution, clean production and paradigm shifts. Water Science Technology 27, 469-480.

MacGarvin, M. 1994. The implications of the precautionary principle for biological monitoring. Helgoländer Meeresuntersuchingen 94.

Mann, K.H. and Lazier, J.R.N. 1991. Dynamics of Marine Ecosystems: Biological-Physical Interactions in the Oceans. Blackwell Scientific Publications, Boston, 466 pp.

Matthews, J.B.L. 1994. Pinocchio in the plankton - on the need to breath life into model organisms. Helgoländer Meeresunters 94.

Matthiessen, P., Thain, J.E., Law, R.J. and Fileman, T.W. 1993. Attempts to assess the environmental hazard posed by the complex mixtures of organic chemicals in UK estuaries. Marine Pollution Bulletin 26, 90-95.

McGowan, J.A and Walker, P.W. 1979. Structure in the copepod community of the North Pacific central gyre. Ecological Monograph 49, 195-226.

McIntyre, A.D. and Pearce, J.B. 1980. Foreword. In McIntyre, A.D. and Pearce, J.B. (eds.) Biological Effects of Marine Pollution and the Problems of Monitoring. Rapp. P.-v. Réun. Cons. int. Explor. Mer. 179, 5.

Menge, B.A. and Sutherland, J.P. 1976. Species diversity gradients: Synthesis of the roles of predation, competition, and temporal heterogeneity. American Naturalist 110, 351-369.

Menge, B.A. 1976. Organisation of the New England rocky intertidal community: role of predation, competition and environmental heterogeneity. Ecological Monograph 46, 355-393.

Nirmalakhandan, N. and Speece, R.E. 1988. Structure-activity relationships. Environmental Science and Technology 22, 606-15.North Sea Task Force 1994. Quality Status Report of the North Sea, Chapter 3. North Sea Task Force, London.

Oslo and Paris Commission 1992a. Convention for the Protection of the Marine Environment of the North-East Atlantic. Paris Commission Secretariat, London. 50 pp.

Oslo and Paris Commission 1992b. Action plan of the Oslo and Paris Commissions, 1992. Oslo and Paris Commission Secretariat, London. 8 pp.

Paine, R.T. 1966. Food web complexity and species diversity. American Naturalist 100, 65-75.

Paine, R.T. 1971. A short term experimental investigation of resource partitioning in a New Zealand rocky tidal habitat. Ecology 52, 1096-1106.

Paine, R.T. 1980. Food webs: linkage, interaction strength and community infrastructure. Journal of Animal Ecology 49, 667-685.

Paris Commission 1991. Report on Land-based Inputs of Contaminants to the Waters of the Paris Convention 1989 (PARCOM 13/6/3-E). Paris Commission, London.

Peterman, R.M. and M'Gonigle, M. 1992. Statistical power analysis and the precautionary principle. Marine Pollution Bulletin 24, 231-234.

Peters, R.H. 1991. A Critique for Ecology. Cambridge University Press. Cambridge, 366 pp.

Price, N.C. and Stevens, L. 1989. Fundamentals of Enzymology. Second Edition. Oxford Scientific Publications, Oxford.

Rothschild, B.J. 1986. Dynamics of Marine Fish Populations. Harvard University Press, Cambridge, Mass., 277 pp.Roughgarden, J. 1989. The structure and assembly of communities. In Roughgarden, J., May, R.M. and Levin, S.A. (eds.) Perspectives in Ecological Theory. Princeton University Press, Princeton, New Jersey, 203-26.

Roughgarden, J. 1989. The structure and assembly of communities. In Roughgarden, J., May, R.M. and Levin, S.A. (eds.) Perspectives in Ecological Theory. Princeton University Press, Princeton, 203-226.

Roughgarden, J., May, R.M. and Levin, S.A. (Eds.) 1989. Perspectives in Ecological Theory. Princeton University Press, Princeton.

Salomons, W. 1988. Heavy metal chemicals - an overview. In Newmann, P.J. and Agg, A.R. (eds.) Environmental Protection of the North Sea. Heinemann Professional Publishing, Oxford, 245-255.

Simberloff, D. 1988. The contribution of population and community biology to conservation science. Annual Review of Ecology and Systems 19, 473-511.

Sperling, K.R. 1986. Protection of the North Sea: balance and prospects. Marine Pollution Bulletin 17, 241-246.

Stebbing, A.R.D., Dethlefsen, V. and Thurberg, F. 1990. Report on the ICES/IOC North Sea seagoing workshop. In North Sea Pollution: Technical Strategies for Improvement. IAWPRC/ EWPCA/NVA Amsterdam, 41-45.

Stebbing, A.R.D., Dethlevsen, V. and Carr, M. 1992a. [check with author]

Stebbing, A.R.D., Dethlevsen, V., Addison, R.F., Carr, M., Chapman, P.M., Cofino, W. P., Heip, C., Karbe, L., Moore, M.N. and Vethaak, A.D. 1992b. Overall summary and some conclusions from the Bremerhaven workshop. Marine Ecology Progress Series 91, 323-329.

Strong, D.R., Simberloff, D., Abele, L.G. and Thistle, A.B. (eds.) 1984. Ecological Communities: Conceptual Issues and the Evidence. Princeton University Press, Princeton, 613 pp.

Sünderman, J. 1994. The ecosystem of the German Bight - The PRISMA concept. Helgoländer Meeresunters 94.

Underwood, A, Denley, E. and Moran, M. 1983. Experimental analysis of the structure and dynamics of mid-shore rocky intertidal communities in New South Wales. Oecologia 56, 202-19.

Underwood, A.J. and Denley, E.J. 1984. Paradigms, explanations and generalisations in models for the structure of intertidal communities on rocky shores. In Strong, D.R. Jr., Simberloff, D., Abele, L.G. and Thistle, A.B. (eds.) Ecological Communities: Conceptual Issues and the Evidence. Princeton University Press, Princeton, 151-180.

Underwood, A.J. 1985. Physical factors and biological interactions: The necessity and nature of ecological experiments. In Moore, P.G. and Seed, R. (eds.) The ecology of rocky coasts. Hodder and Stoughton, London, 372-390.

UNEP Governing Council 1989. Decision 15/27 Precautionary approach to marine pollution, including waste dumping at sea. UNEP, New York.

Varley, G.C., Gradwell, G.R. and Hassell, M.P. 1973. Insect Population Ecology. Blackwell Scientific Publications, Oxford, 212 pp.

Wootton, R.J. 1990. Ecology of Teleost Fishes. Chapman and

Hall, London, 404 pp.

Wynne, B. 1992. Uncertainty and environmental learning: reconceiving science and policy in the preventative paradigm. Global Environmental Change 2, 111-127.

Chapter 4

What if? Versus if it ain't broke, don't fix it

By Frederick Warner

Society has always struggled to find the correct mix of risk taking and risk avoiding behaviour. In simplistic terms risk taking carries great advantages that have to be set against obvious and less obvious dangers. And to advance, or to succeed, an element of risk taking seems necessary. Of course excessive or wanton risk taking breeds trouble and ultimate calamity, so risk aversion is the salutary sheet anchor against foolhardiness or excessive and ill-considered zeal.

The classic engineering approach to risk is to define it in terms of a probability that a particular adverse event occurs during a stated period of time, or that the event results from a particular or identifiable challenge (e.g. stress fracture, heavy rainfall, seismic tremor). On this basis a system of risk assessment is constructed with the object of setting out levels for comparison. A typical example would be deaths per million exposed people per year, or per billion kilometers travelled. Any modern design procedure requires the insertion of historical statistics into logic or fault trees as part of a process that is proactive in eliminating risks. In this way conventional risk assessment can claim to be part of the precautionary principle or anticipation.

The regulator seeks to make sense of all this by defining yardsticks for both tolerable and intolerable risks. Figure 4.1 illustrates one approach. The frame is the frequency of fatalities set against the probability of occurrence, the so-called F-N curve. The intolerable zone is set by both commercial and engineering considerations initially, though it will also be influenced by social judgements about the quality of life, the avoidability of death and the degree to which blame should be attributed to poor management or lack of adequate surveillance over the amount of exposure permitted. These last points tend to apply particularly to socially stigmatised facilities such as nuclear power stations, radioactive waste disposal projects and incinerators. To a different extent they also apply to genetically modified organisms as outlined by Julie Hill in Chapter 10. In all these cases, the social construction of risk is more cautious, largely because individuals perceive that they have inadequate control over any dangers that may be associated with such phenomena, and feel that they or their children cannot escape the consequences. So the line between tolerability and intolerability is affected by the social relationships between risk creation and risk acceptance as mediated by such measures as trust, communication, and, of course, precaution. The more the risk adverse elements creep in the more the principles of precaution apply.

Figure 4.1 Fatality-frequency curves for different categories of risk. In the upper right arena the risk would be intolerable, so would not be permitted, if society had the means to control it. In poor countries even this level of regulation is not always available. Precaution applies in the ALARP region where proportionality provides a guide.

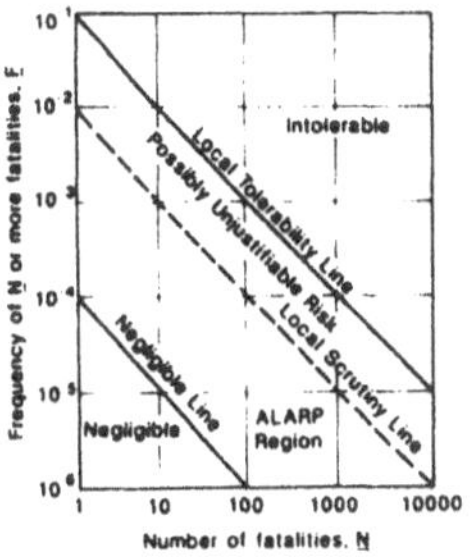

To get round this, the British risk regulator avoids any absolute standard of risk. This emphasis calls upon the risk creator to prepare and justify the safety case. The regulator, when in doubt, will apply two principles, both rooted in the principle of precaution. One is the notion of <u>as low as reasonably practicable</u> (ALARP) when setting safety limits. ALARP applies to an interesting combination of factors including the best technology, very careful indication of quality control in manufacturing, strict rules and procedures over maintenance and operator training, and regular tests of post emergency procedures. In short, ALARP presumes that the worst may happen, and insists that the operator is fully prepared both in anticipation of danger, and in anticipation of failure. The other principle is that of modifying the application of best available techniques by the caveat of not entailing excessive costs. This matter is given fuller treatment in Chapter 7.

The second principle is that of proportionality as outlined in the introductory chapters and reinforced by Nigel Haigh in Chapter 13. Again proportionality, or a variant of cost benefit analysis, is not a single minded notion applied similarly in all circumstances. It is constructed to ensure the public that value for money is being achieved by the application of sound safety procedures. For outcomes carrying very low risk the costs of safeguard may exceed benefits by a factor of up to 10000 to 1 (as in the case of certain nuclear safety procedures). Normally the rule of thumb is 1000 to 1 for genuinely problematic uncertainty and 10 to 1 for typical uncertainty. Here, it will be noted, the normal rules of cost benefit analysis, namely that at the margin costs and benefits should equate, do not apply. Precaution places a premium on avoidable action, largely because, in effect, society inflicts the benefit of playing safe when considerable uncertainty exists, or is perceived to exist.

This approach also applies to commercial risk in the engineering industry. The normal requirement is that safety should be assured to a level of 1 in 100,000 to 1,000,000 per year. This does not however form the basis of any insurance cover. The insurance industry sets its premium on the assumption that there is no profit to be made by going below a probability of one in a thousand. The industry caught a cold when underwriting BP shares at 0.018 percent. In this sense the insurance industry is also applying the precautionary mode, as is now reflected in more hazard conscious setting of premiums throughout the world.

Precaution and risk aversion

Much of risk prevention is uncontested. Anticipationism has a reputable scientific background in prophylaxis, inoculations, dietary prescription and epidemiological studies of active or passive smoking. Largely as a consequence the chance of surviving to middle age, which was only 50 percent a century ago is now 97 percent. Yet 14 percent of deaths in males and 17 percent in females both aged between 35 and 69 are due directly to tobacco-related illness (Cox et al., 1992, 82-83). Evidence itself is not a cause for taking precaution. This serves to remind us that precaution is a cultural phenomenon that manifests itself in varying circumstances and political settings. It is not a strictly comparable notion.

Risk management in the area of epidemiology and food hygiene depends a lot upon statistical inference. Luckily the improvement of statistical techniques makes it much easier to separate cause from consequence, and to improve the necessity of probability arrays. But as was mentioned in the introduction, any statistical analysis is at the mercy of the assumptions made about the pattern of events and the logical meanings attached to them. Data themselves are subject to interpretations for measurement and the biasses of the institutions that collect and disseminate them. As Barlow et al. (1992, 64) conclude in their assessment of epidemiology studies and legal proof:

> Given the inevitable imprecision of some of the measure ments on which toxicologists rely, the complexity of the systems under consideration and the possibility of differ ences of interpretation of data, informed expert judgement after consideration of all the evidence is likely to continue to provide a better basis for risk reduction and management than a mechanistic scoring or a decision tree, desirable though these may be on legalistic grounds. This strengthens the need for public interest participation in taking decisions on issues relating to risk.

Precaution and distortion

Regulatory authorities have to straddle the marshy terrain between expert opinion, public anxiety and political expediency. Regulation is rarely left to the specialist, even when the kind of public interest participation is also involved as advocated by Barlow and his colleagues in the above quote. In Chapter 12 Dan Bodansky signals how much of US environmental law is pushed on the outer tides of precaution, where the economical justification for the additional margins of safety become the battlegrounds between various vested pressure groups whose resolution of dispute does not always constitute the "public interest". In the European context the decision by the European Community to limit nitrates in drinking water to 50 mg per litre, and the control of sheepmeat sales on very low concentrations of radiocaesium post Chernobyl have no foundation in scientific thinking. Precaution is evidently placing science in new and unaccustomed positions in the order of things. Currently there is a public furore over pesticide residues in drinking water, with the official water price regulator seeking to raise the acceptable lower limit in order to avoid very costly replacement work on removal measures. Again this move, handled largely to protect the customer from excessive water bills, is being challenged just because a given set of figures raised upwards in terms of safety margins, becomes a focal target for the precautionary debate.

Part of the difficulty here is that scientists or courts of law are still in the process of defining yardsticks for the quality of life under conditions of illness imposed by exposure or injury. As yet society is not particularly good at indicating the payoff between avoiding death and avoiding injury. This is partly because there is no single dimensional numerical indicator for morbidity. Attempts to calculate a measure of quality-adjusted life years, i.e. some idea of the loss of wellbeing associated with disease or disability, have so far not been readily convertible into cost benefit analysis.

Intellectually or even morally these problems are paradoxical, absurd or even metaphysical. Time and resources are spent in the application of the precautionary principle in inverse proportion to the magnitude of the problem in terms of death, injury or financial loss. The pursuit of the hypothetical takes more and more resources with insistence on proof by society as against the methods of scientific and engineering analysis of risk based on statistics whose history and reliability are known. These statistics also face the nature of risk as part of just living - limited but approaching the level of 1 in 100 per year. The quality of danger is an essential part of existence for many people who feel better off for surviving exposure in face of hazards that constitute that risk. To eliminate risk is not in human nature: precaution carried too far, even with the qualification of proportionality, must become counterproductive. For the pragmatic approach of common law, based on its tests of reasonableness and fairness, as well as the considered judgements of expert but widely representative commissions of enquiry, still carries insufficient weight. The application of the subsidiarity principle in the new European Union should allow for greater national flexibility in the interpretation of precaution, but this is less likely for transboundary problems as outlined in the introductory chapter.

Risk management is passing though a transition through which greater weight is being given to the aversive anxieties of particular interests than the scientific evidence and historical record justify. This transition is institutional in that it is not only generating a more participatory framework for setting safety standards. It is also creating new arrangements for the determination of appropriate margins of safety. These matters are given a fuller airing by Julie Hill in Chapter 10. With risk management culture evolving, so precaution takes greater hold. This may not always be a bad or a good trend, because there are too many variables to make any simplistic judgement. But precisely because it is surely not all good that this shift in perspective is taking place and a more open cost-benefit framework is required, as David Pearce argues in Chapter 7, then society needs continually to reexamine how far precaution should be taken. This task is addressed in the final chapter of the volume.

References

Barlow, S. et al. 1992. Toxicity, toxicology and nutrition. In Royal Society Study Group, Risk: Analysis, Perception and Management. Royal Society London, 35-65.

Cox, D. et al. 1992. Estimation of risk from observation on humans. In Royal Society Study Group (op. cit.) 67-87.

Chapter 5

Taking Care

By James E. Lovelock

Let's assume that the Earth self regulates; that on our planet organisms, rocks, air and ocean all act in unison to keep the climate and chemistry comfortable. I am not asking you to suspend science and believe in some mysterious Earth mother with teleological powers. All I ask is that you imagine a planet sized ecosystem, Gaia, something that emerged when organisms and their material environment evolved together. Why do it anyway? Simply because the need for the precautionary principle is more clearly seen in a view of the whole Earth than in the subdivided parts of it.

Conventional wisdom sees the facts of the Earth all explicable, but separately, according to the languages and customs of the different Earth and Life sciences. I do not doubt the importance for science itself of this specialist approach in the understanding of fine detail, but we do need also a top down view of the whole Earth. A full understanding of the links between climate, atmospheric chemistry, and the metabolism of regional ecosystems, is unlikely to come from the specialist sciences alone. Conferences that include scientists from different disciplines rarely work. Think of a geophysicist listening to an account of how chordates are naturally selected according to the frequency of their species, or of a biologist trying to become enthraled by mesospheric aeronomy. The real world is not subdivided. If you look at the Earth from above you will see that climate, atmosphere and surface are noticeably coupled. The clouds over the 70% of the surface that is ocean cover the same areas of ocean that are sites of dense algal growth. Over the tropical forests you will see their moist climate coupled to the growth of trees. Over the land masses, if you could look for as long as a million years, you would see the organisms on the rocks and in the soil participate in weathering away the mountains. Mountain levelling is the only long term sink for carbon dioxide, and the rate of its removal from the air depends on how vigorously the plants grow. Growth in turn depends upon the local temperature.

I will now try to show how the Earth self regulates, how Gaia works by closing the loops that link growth, surface and atmospheric chemistry. Then try to use this knowledge to see more clearly the consequences of what we are now doing.

Planetary homeostasis

Professional aeronomists who model the atmosphere according to conventional science do not include the organisms. Many of their models do not even include the oceans and the clouds. If they think about living organisms at all, they assume them merely to adapt to changes in climate or chemistry. They see them as bystanders not as active participants. Purely geophysical models can predict positive feedbacks and surprises, but climate and atmospheric chemistry models are usually rational. For example, they suggest that as greenhouse gases accumulate in the air there will be a proportionate global warming. Disagreement among the forecasters is mostly over the rate of change and the final state reached.

Gaia theory, the expression of the top down view, predicts resistance to change when all is well, but sudden or catastrophic change with too much stress. Feed back systems are only stable dynamically. They need a goal, energy, and feed back in the right sense. If the power fails, or the feed back turns positive, they become unstable and either vacillate or drift spontaneously to their natural equilibrium. The Earth is undoubtedly in deep disequilibrium, yet it has a more or less stable climate and chemistry. If this stability comes from dynamic self control, then failure could be catastrophic; like an airplane whose engines fail while taking off. Few seem aware of the extent to which the climate and atmospheric chemistry of the Earth are in disequilibrium. The expected state, if only geophysics and geochemistry mattered, would be that of a planet interpolated between Mars and Venus. Without life, Earth would now have an atmosphere dominated by carbon dioxide and with a mean temperature at least 20°C hotter. Like Mars and Venus there would be no ocean. An Earth that evolved without life is far from the comfortable moist planet we know. Cataclysmic would be the fall to this ground state, were life eliminated.

We know the Earth has recently passed an unstable or critical point, one that marked the abrupt change from glacial to interglacial. The evidence from the analysis of polar ice cores points to a climate and atmosphere that was stable during the ice age when it was cold, but unstable when in the warmth of an interglacial, like now. The present warm spell is not excepted, and well before humans began to change the Earth, the climate was unstable and it still is. By unstable I mean climate control is in positive feedback. Regulators like the natural abundance of carbon dioxide, and the albedo of clouds, both respond to temperature change in a way that destabilizes climate. A change of climate to greater heat, or greater cold, magnifies itself.

You might well ask what justifies a theory of the Earth that sees it as self regulating when it clearly is not. You might go on to say: surely this is evidence that Gaia does not exist and proves that the climate is arbitrarily determined by geophysical forces alone. Far from it. Periods of unstable, even chaotic behaviour, are characteristic of working control systems and of living organisms. The dead are more stable than the living, being so much closer to the final state of equilibrium. Remember the last time you had a fever. At the onset you would have felt cold and shivered and your skin would have been dry and hot. In a fever we, wonderfully self regulated though we are, go into positive feed back. Shivering, increased metabolism and a dry skin are all things that should warm us when cold, yet perversely turn on in a fever. Think of the interglacial warm spells as brief fevers troubling an otherwise well regulated Earth. We still need to ask: why with increasing heat does the carbon dioxide greenhouse grow thicker and why do the cooling clouds disappear? The answer may come from a better understanding of the ideal temperature for plant growth. Laboratory experiments show that land plants and marine algae grow best when the temperature is about 22°C, well above the

Earth's mean temperature of 15°C. Further heating should therefore lead to more growth and consequently a negative feedback on temperature. The reason it does not is because the ideal temperature for Gaia is not the same as that for plant growth, but lower. Algal ecosystems of the oceans grow best when the sea surface temperature is about 12°C. Not necessarily because the ocean organisms are different in their temperature response to land plants, but because for geophysical reasons the ocean surface layers tend to form a stable inversion, the thermocline, when the heat flux increases. In practice, the thermocline forms when the surface layers exceed about 12°C. When this happens the cooler, nutrient rich, waters below the thermocline cannot mix with the surface water and the organisms are starved.

Orbiting satellites take measurements of surface temperature, algal growth, and cloud cover. Their view from above sees dense growth only in ocean regions where the surface temperature is near or below 12°C, they also see that these regions are cloud covered. The tropical, and warm temperate, ocean appears as beautiful clear blue water, but marine organisms living in polar waters would compare them with a desert. Algae can grow well in warmer waters when there is an ample supply of nutrients, but such favoured regions tend to be small in area and close to the estuaries of large rivers.

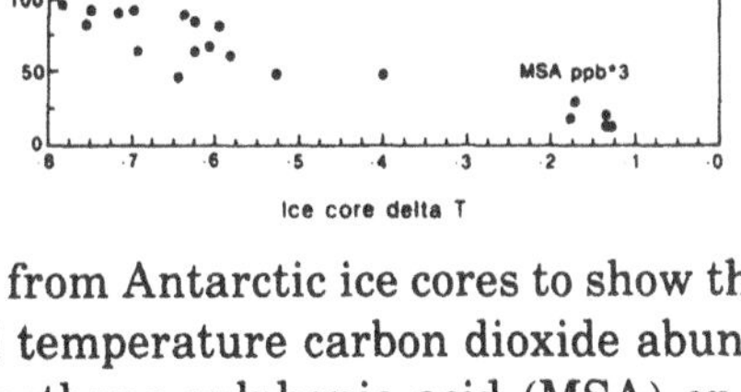

Historical date from Antarctic ice cores to show the relationship between global temperature carbon dioxide abundance and the deposition of methane sulphonic acid (MSA) on the polar ice. Note how carbon dioxide rises and MSA falls with increasing temperature, suggesting the climate is in positive feedback with the greenhouse effect and with cloud albedo.

In the last cold period pack ice extended, in the Atlantic in winter, as far south as the Canaries, latitude 30°N. At the same time there was five times more algal sulphur deposited on the polar ice than now. We can guess from this increased rain of sulphur compounds that algal growth was proportionately greater, as was cooling by clouds. During the 100,000 year long cold spell, carbon dioxide pumping and the albedo increase of cloudiness, acted to regulate and keep the goal of cool conditions. In this view the present interglacial is like a fever, a pathological state distinguished by positive feedback.

Is there similar evidence to link a decline of plant growth, and of the carbon dioxide sink, with increasing land surface temperature? The land regions between 30°N and 30°S latitudes are notable for the prevalence of desert and arid regions, although this is less obvious than the sparse growth of algae in tropical waters. Even where growth is dense, as in the humid forests, we know that forest ecosystems are themselves able to regulate water supply and keep local temperatures low. Certainly the clearance of tropical forest is often irreversible. On the land surface, as in the ocean, geophysics, not biology, sets the limiting temperature for growth. When the temperature is high the rate of evaporation of rain water exceeds the rate of fall and the soil dries out. In hot regions, lack of water tends to limit plant growth more than heat alone. Lack of water therefore slows the removal of carbon dioxide from the air. The sink of carbon dioxide by rock weathering is slow with a response time greater than 10^5 yr. This is fast enough to account for the low carbon dioxide of the last glacial period, but too slow to explain the sudden rise of carbon dioxide into the interglacial. The positive feedback on carbon dioxide with rising temperature must have another cause. Among several possible explanations, a likely candidate is the decrease in area of ocean available to those algae that remove carbon dioxide. The pump down of carbon dioxide by ocean algal growth has a much shorter response time than weathering, approximately 100 yr. The failure of algal carbon dioxide pumping would add a pulse of carbon dioxide to the atmosphere, one that would take thousands of years to remove. Similar to the time it will take to remove the surge of carbon dioxide from burning fossil fuel.

The need for foresight might be more immediately comprehensible if we could place a value on Gaian services. If I am right about the role of the algal ecosystems, and that of the land plants that control rock weathering, their value is as great as that of life itself. This is so far beyond price that understanding comes easier from thinking about the value of one of the smaller ecosystems, the forests of the humid tropics. We are destroying these forests at a ruthless pace. We know it is wrong but argue for keeping the tropical forests on the feeble grounds that they are the home of rare species of plants and animals, even of plants containing drugs that could cure cancer. They may do. They may even be slightly useful in removing carbon dioxide from the air. But they do much more than this. By evaporating vast volumes of water vapour, and by making gases and particles that are the nuclei of cloud droplets, the forests serve to keep their region cool and moist. They do it by wearing a sunshade of white reflecting clouds and by bringing the rain that sustains them. It is easy to calculate the value of the tropical forests from the energy required to provide the same air-conditioning and irrigating service. A service far more valuable than the use of the forest land for farming. It is worth about £10000 per acre or for the global tropical forests worth about £300 trillion a year. Yet every year we burn away an area of forest equal to that of Britain and often replace it with crude cattle farms. Unlike farms here in the temperate regions the land of such farms rapidly become scrub or desert. When this happens the farmers fell more trees, and the burning away the skin of the Earth goes on. Beyond a certain point the process becomes irreversible, when only 20 to 30 per cent of a tropical forest ecosystem remains, it can no longer sustain its climate and it collapses. At the present rate of clearance, it will not be long before the forests no longer have the critical mass they need to exist as self sustaining ecosystems. When they vanish, the billion poor of those regions will be left with little to support them and in a harsher climate. This is a threat comparable in scale to a global nuclear war. The human suffering, the refugees, the guilt and the political consequences of such an event have all been described by Sir Crispin Tickell. It will happen at a time when we in the first world are battling with the surprises and disasters of the greenhouse effect, intensified by the extra heating from the forest clearance. We could be unable to help.

Even if we reform immediately we shall still see the Earth change and we, its first social intelligent species, are privileged to be both the cause and the spectators. The change in climate imminent is as large as between the last ice age and now.

To comprehend the magnitude of the change ahead glance back to the depth of the last ice age, some tens of thousands of years ago. Then the glaciers reached as far south as latitude 35° in North America and to the Alps in Europe. The sea was more than 100 metres lower than now, and therefore an area of land as large as Africa was above water and where plants grew. The tropics were like the warm temperate regions are now. In all it was a pleasant world to live on and there was more land. What will happen, as a result of our presence so far, will be a change as great as that from the last ice age until about 100 years ago.

To understand what has already begun and will develop in the next century, imagine the start of a heat age. Temperatures and sea level will climb, by fits and starts, until eventually the world will be torrid, ice free, and all but unrecognisable. Eventually is a long time ahead, it might never happen to that extent; what we have to prepare for now are the incidents of a changing climate, just about to begin. These are likely to be surprises, things that even the most detailed of big science models do not predict. Think of the ozone hole, this was a real surprise. The most expensive computer modelling and monitoring of the Earth's ozone layer failed to see or predict it. It was seen by observers looking at the sky with simple instruments. Surprise may comes as climatic extremes, like ferocious storms, or as unexpected atmospheric events. Nature is nonlinear and unpredictable and never more so than in a period of change.

This is an occasion when we cannot look to Gaia for help. If the present warm period is a planetary fever, we should expect that the Earth left to itself would be relaxing into its normal comfortable ice age. Such comfort may be unattainable because we have been busy removing its skin for farm land, taking away the trees that are the means for recovery. We also are adding vast blanket of greenhouse gases to the already feverish patient. Gaia is more likely to shudder, then move over to a new stable state, fit for a different and more amenable biota. It could be much hotter, but whatever it is, no longer the comfortable world we know. These predictions are not fictional doom scenarios, but uncomfortably close to certainty. We have already changed the atmosphere to an extent unprecedented in recent geological history. We seem to be driving ourselves heedlessly down a slope into a sea that is rising to drown us.

We must, in our own interest, recognize that our planet is at least as important as we are. If we continue to pollute and destroy for narrow self interest, we could bring about the end of the Pleistocene and the dawn of a new hot Earth. The future depends on decisions made now on the supplies of food and energy. We must moderate our passion for human rights and begin to recognise the rest of life on Earth. Individual risk, such as of cancer from exposure to nuclear radiation, or to products of the chemical industry, are to be prevented, but they are no longer the most urgent concern. First in our thoughts should be the need to avoid perturbing Gaia and exacerbating its present natural instability. Above all we do not want to trigger the jump to a new but unwanted stable climate.

Among the things we must not do is cling to the illusion that we could be stewards of the spaceship Earth. Stewardship implies that contemporary science can fully explain the Earth, and that people are willing and able to work together to keep the Earth a fit and comfortable place for life.

These assumptions are naive, like expecting the passengers of a plane, whose pilot had died, to land it safely with no more help than the pilot's manual. Does anyone believe we, intelligent carnivores prone to tribal genocide, could, by some act of common will, change our natures and become wise and gentle gardeners, stewards, taking care of all of the natural life of our planet?

It takes a lot of hubris even to think of ourselves as stewards of the Earth. Originally a steward was the keeper of the sty where the pigs lived; this was too lowly for most humans and gentility raised the styward so that he became a bureaucrat, in charge of men not only pigs. Do we want to be the bureaucrats of the Earth? Do we want to be made accountable for its health? I would sooner expect a goat to succeed as a gardener as expect humans to become stewards of the Earth. There can be no worse fate for people than to conscript them in such a hopeless task; to make them responsible for the smooth running of the climate. To make them responsible for the chemistry of the oceans, the air, and the soil. Something, that until we began to dismantle it, Gaia gave free.

I have written as an independent scientist, and it may seem that by stressing the need to take care of the Earth I am indifferent to human needs. Nothing is further from my mind, I want my grandchildren to inherit a world that has a future for them. To make sure that this happens we first need to recognise that human rights are not enough and to survive we must also take care of the Earth. There is no tenure for anyone on this planet, not even a species.

Chapter 6

The Social Construction of Precaution

By Jane Hunt

The adoption of the precautionary principle in a range of environmental policy arenas reflects growing attention to the identification and management of scientific uncertainty. Implicit in most interpretations of the precautionary principle is the recognition that scientific knowledge cannot adequately predict the potential environmental consequences of human activities. On this basis, it is argued, we should act more cautiously, particularly where potential hazards have already been identified, such as the discharge of toxic chemicals into the environment. Scientific uncertainty and its management is now a major consideration for environmental policy.

Discourses about uncertainty, however, expose the awkward nature of the term. It is used to denote different aspects of knowledge and to imply different responses; it is also used as the generic catch-all signifying all cases where scientific knowledge is disputed, or where scientists themselves consider available evidence to be inconclusive. Confusion therefore arises as to the precise meaning of 'uncertainty'.

Wynne (1992) has characterised uncertainty in four ways: as risk, uncertainty, ignorance and indeterminacy. Risk is considered as knowing the boundaries of the system under consideration and being able to quantify the factors involved. Uncertainty represents knowledge of the parameters of a system, but not of the quantitative significance of the factors involved, i.e. uncertainty is contained within a framework of understanding. Ignorance is that which is not known; however, in order for ignorance to be identifiable, new knowledge must be discoverable as possible. Indeterminacy is a more complex concept, involving recognition of the essentially open-ended and conditional nature of all knowledge and its embeddedness in social contexts. In part, indeterminacy is a product of the unforeseeable and thus unpredictable actions of individuals or groups whose behaviour is influenced by the events that are so uncertain. An example might be the removal of land cover as a result of climate drying - an act that would add locally to climate change. It also incorporates the recognition that scientific knowledge is essentially a sociocultural process and is thus subject to change in social attitudes and understanding: scientific interpretations produced metaphorical representations of natural processes but not direct contact with those processes, so is always mediated by the forms of our understanding.

In the conventional classification, risk and uncertainty are perceived as amenable to resolution by the production of 'more science' to fill the gaps. Risk, uncertainty and ignorance can be conceived as a linear scale from more to less knowledge. However, Wynne argues that indeterminacy, particularly that of a social kind (which is then incorporated in knowledge production) is implicated in risk, uncertainty and ignorance and is a feature of all forms of scientific and technical knowledge.

The risk framework has been used extensively in environmental management, for example in assessing radiological hazards. It provides a useful policy tool by quantifying risks and allowing these to be weighed against perceived benefits, and by providing numbers which enable the setting of regulatory standards. However, as the arena has become more controversial, the underlying assumptions involved in risk appraisal have been challenged. This opens it up to reconsideration and reanalysis through the highlighting of previously ignored uncertainties and ignorance. From ecological pathways and bioaccumulation mechanisms to effects of low-level radiation on human health, the assessment of radiological hazard has moved from risk mode to that of uncertainty. Whilst for proponents of risk assessment, and particularly for the institutional groupings involved in its production, radiological risk analysis remains valid, its credibility has been largely undermined in the public mind by the critique used by anti-nuclear groups. This is complicated by the insights within the public understanding of science that institutional trust is a key factor in maintaining scientific and technical authority: the nuclear industry has been its own worst enemy in this respect, tending to take a condescending and non-negotiable stance, so is increasingly perceived as untrustworthy. In contested arenas, then, previously certain scientific knowledge can become uncertain as social groupings focus on rhetorics of scientific argument; additionally, whether knowledge is determined to be certain, amenable to risk analysis, or uncertain, differs from one social context to another. This will be evident in the discussion of biotechnology.

Uncertainty as such has been highlighted in the North Sea Ministerial Conferences, and has been a mainstream factor in justifying precautionary approaches. Whilst, broadly speaking, the parameters of the North Sea ecosystem are considered to be understood and the main factors identified (e.g. circulation patterns and the transport of pollutants are considered to be important, although this is qualified by new research which may provide different understandings or create new questions), understanding of the detail of the mechanisms and, in particular, the causal relationships involved, are acknowledged as incomplete and uncertain. The relationship between fish disease and pollution, and of the effects of nutrient inputs, fall into the category of uncertain knowledge. Uncertain knowledge perhaps provides the clearest illustration of the limitations of existing scientific practice: the detailed knowledge of fish population dynamics and natural disease occurrence are missing from the current understanding of the fish disease and pollution relationship, and are hard to come by. Understanding of the effects of nutrient inputs are equally restricted by the lack of detailed knowledge. Both cases suffer from the lack of long term data sets. Even if data were to be collected over, say, the next 20 years, the questions for which the data are originally gathered may well change by the time the data are fully collected. But the fundamental problem is that scientific practice is largely structured around controlled experiments in the laboratory. It is not possible to control real world environmental conditions in the same way; in any case, these conditions change and only broad generalisations can be proffered for the effect of changing conditions.

The discourse of ignorance, whilst not as widespread as those of risk and uncertainty, is nonetheless also acknowledged. The consequences of loss of biodiversity, or of climatic change, are sited in at least some quarters as belonging to the realm of ignorance. In addition, there is a partial recognition, born of the experience of the last 20 years, that environmental management is operated in the realm of:

> 'what men do! what men may do! what men daily do, not knowing what they do! (Much Ado about Nothing IV.i.(19)).

As environmental pigeons have come home to roost, there is increasingly a recognition that potentially disastrous consequences, which we cannot predict, attend our actions. However, the policy response to ignorance is in the realm of 'if we don't know it, we can't act', rather than adopting more flexible, smaller scale policies with the ability to respond more rapidly to changing circumstances.

The story so far presented is one of scientific knowledge which is necessarily provisional and socially located, which can be read as a failure of science to provide legitimacy to policy. However, there are abundant counter-examples, where science is taken as certain, uncertainties amenable to resolution, and knowledge as complete. The consequences of cigarette smoking and of lead pollution are now largely accepted, having moved from uncertainty to risk. The shift to 'certainty' or anyway, adequate proof, cannot be attributed to the power of the scientific 'proof' alone but must also be encouraged by cultural factors. Uncertainty in scientific knowledge appears to be a product of social conflict, rather than of the science itself. It is the location of the knowledge claim, not so much the science itself, which determines the uncertainty of the claim. On the same lines, responses to scientific uncertainty vary across contexts: government scientists argue that enough is known about the input of toxic chemicals to the marine environment to be able to argue for (limited and controlled) discharges, and this is accepted within at least some parts of government, although highly contested outside it. The point here is that scientific certainty and uncertainty vary from one social and political context to another.

Further, it is not always the case that government agencies project certainty which environmental groups then criticise by highlighting uncertainties: in the acid rain case, it was the CEGB who argued during the early 1980s that knowledge was insufficient to take (expensive) remedial action, whilst environmental NGOs argued that knowledge was sufficient to premise action. Uncertainty, then, is part of a rhetoric of science, an argumentative strategy which can be employed for a variety of purposes. It is the opposite side of the coin to the equally negotiated term 'adequate proof'.

The various contending definitions and understandings of the precautionary principle which have been proposed by different authors, in different contexts, can be reduced to two basic types in relation to their treatment of uncertainty. The lesser version accepts that environmental discharges may cause harm which science cannot 'prove' in time, but it still in effect recognises only uncertainties in the sense of 'facts beyond science's current eyesight'. Thus this version pushes the burden of proof out a bit, into the anticipation of possible harm, or expected proof of harm. The more radical version of the principle has been read as demanding the impossible - proof of safety before discharge is allowed. However the substantial version has nothing to do with this; it implicitly recognises and takes seriously the indeterminacy of scientific knowledge (e.g. why is it built around this or that end-point? how does it recognise multiple interacting possible causes?) and thus opens the normally closed-off connection between the intrinsically open question, how much harm might this discharge do?, and the social question, how much do we need this process which causes that discharge?

The determination and management of uncertainty and the responses to it are themselves representative of the range of positions held in the environmental debate. Greenpeace (and other environmental NGOs, e.g. see Campbell, 1985) have utilised a strategy of challenging the scientific authority which legitimates policy by bringing to the fore uncertainties in scientific knowledge claims. For example, in the case of the building of a deep underground repository for radioactive waste at Sellafield, they have consistently pointed out the range of uncertainties and ignorances regarding e.g. water movement through rock, geological movement, as well as the social indeterminacies of such a long term project. They argue for a highly precautionary strategy in response to such uncertainty, linking this to the argument for the necessity of developing cleaner technologies with less demand on environmental knowledge.

Central government, and particularly industry, are less willing to adopt such a wide application of the precautionary principle, arguing that the costs involved in taking action under conditions of uncertain knowledge mean that the first response should be to increase the knowledge base, so that unnecessary and expensive remedies are avoided. In the Sellafield case this means more research, on the assumption that current uncertainties can be resolved. Precaution can thus be seen as an expression of environmental value phrased in the rhetoric of science. The innovative element of the precautionary principle if pursued in the fuller sense is that it signifies the scale of the problematic, potentially opening up a much larger array of questions about what is at stake and ultimately, about what sort of society we want (and about how much choice we have in creating it).

What becomes apparent is that whilst contention exists over the correct management of the environment (or perhaps about human relationships with the environment), scientific uncertainties will continue to be used in the argumentative strategies of the participants. The significance of science here is its legitimatory capacity, operating through its claim to be able to provide a rational and accepted basis for decision making. What the expanding discourse of uncertainty illustrates is that this legitimatory function is threatened. If scientific uncertainty is taken as representing dissent, then consensual science requires agreement over a wider range of values than that of the purely scientific. Science does not provide the answers to this wider range of questions. It has been amply demonstrated that when environmental disputes are sited as scientific, then scientific dispute, and the production of uncertainty, follow (e.g. Jasanoff, 1990). It is important to note that this is characteristic of 'normal' science: scientific closure, or facts (i.e. our understanding of the natural world), are produced through a process of negotiation between social actors, not through being dictated in any absolute sense by nature (e.g. see Collins, 1985; Latour, 1987). This is not to say that science has nothing to offer to environmental management, but that if social disputes are cited as scientific, then scientific uncertainty may well be the result, rather than resolution.

One response to this problem has been to suggest that scientific advice must be produced in isolation from the policy process (e.g. Floistad, 1990). This is essentially unworkable: if scientists, thus isolated, were to achieve consensus, the conflicts would emerge immediately the knowledge had to be interpreted into application. It is the institutional forms of scientific advisory groups and the ways these institutional forms both define the problem and translate the science, to which attention should be more critically addressed.

Another proposed solution is that scientific advice be subjected to some form of external review and validation process. In the US, this task has traditionally been undertaken by the law courts, but the adversarial nature of this system tends to produce further examination of scientific claims, rather than resolution (Jasanoff, 1990). Some form of 'office of assessment' which codifies scientific review processes is unlikely to be able to encompass the widening array of issues involved. To be effective such an office would require a highly radical, flexible and open-ended method of operation, which was both inclusionary and able to negotiate widely, and had the power to influence decision making, as well as being able to respond to ever changing scientific knowledge, then it would be likely to reproduce the current problems.

A third solution comes under the label the democratisation of science. This tallies with other calls for a 'greening' of science (e.g. Johnston and Simmonds, 1991), or for new scientific forms which are seen, at least in some quarters, as necessary. In part, this is taken as meaning a wider basis for the composition of advisory groups, and public access to their deliberations. Current exclusions from, for example, the North Sea Task Force (whose remit is to produce a Quality Status Report of the North Sea) mean that the process is neither open and amenable to public scrutiny, nor inclusive of the range of positions held. Where environmental organisations are included in the process, their contribution may be subject to the interpretations of government officials and chairpersons who ultimately decide what advice should be given. In addition, the often confrontational and divisive relationship which exists between, for example, MAFF and Greenpeace, is likely to be exacerbated rather than resolved by current institutional formats. The NGOs then resort to public critique (and hence re-examination of uncertainty) rather than being given negotiating space. This public dispute, and hence loss of authority and legitimacy (Mazur, 1973), often exacerbates conflict.

Three priorities would thus seem to be called for. The first is widened participation in groups producing scientific advice. The second is that participants should have equal status; no participant should have institutionalised power over others (there are of course associated considerations here, such as the access to funding or research capability of particular groups). The third is that the procedures and debates within groups should be open and publicly accessible. Ideally, this might have similarities to the public inquiry system, where full transcripts and documentation are available. Freedom of information is a basic requirement of conflict resolution and legitimation, unless public trust in decision making bodies is sufficient to grant such bodies authority. In many cases, for example that of regulation of the nuclear or chemical industries, is patently not the case at present. Such a liberation of advisory groups would enable production of scientific knowledge which, whilst it might acknowledge its inherent uncertainties, might manage them to produce consensus rather than to utilise them in conflict. The legitimatory function of Science could be re-established through trust in the decision-making bodies which manage it.

More radically, the nature and role of science per se could be addressed. I have argued that science is not the producer of hard, objective facts about the natural world in the positivistic sense, but a socially mediated process, with an important legitimating function. Nature of course has a voice in scientific knowledge, but it is not a voice uninfluenced by social and cultural positions. As science has increasingly been used as the location for environmental problem-solving this results in the critical exploration of scientific certainty. If the status of scientific knowledge shifts from being the objective, final arbiter to a more conditional and consensus seeking knowledge form, which allows other forms of knowledge equal standing (and there is some evidence that this is occurring), then its legitimatory function may be reaffirmed through a more realistic, and less rhetorical, appreciation of what science can and cannot do with respect to environmental management.

References

Campbell, B. 1985. Uncertainty as symbolic action in disputes among experts. Social Studies of Science 15, 429-453.

Collins, H. 1985. Changing Order: Replication and Induction in Scientific Practice. Sage, London.

Floistad, B. 1990. What makes scientific advice appear legitimate? International Challenges 10(2), 12-16.

Jasanoff, S. 1990. The Fifth Branch: Science Advisors as Policy Makers. Harvard University Press, Cambridge, MA.

Johnston, P. and Simmonds, M. 1991. Green light for precautionary science. New Scientist 3.8.91.

Latour, B. 1987. Science in Action: How to Follow Scientists and Engineers through Society. Harvard University Press, Cambridge, MA.

Mazur, A. 1973. Disputes between experts. Minerva XI(2), 243-262.

Wynne, B. 1992. Uncertainty and Environmental Learning: Reconceiving science and policy in the preventative paradigm. Global Environmental Change. June, 111-127.

Part III

Implications for Management

Editorial Introduction

The application of the precautionary principle presents many a dilemma for the analyst and decision maker. One obvious reason is that precaution has as yet no clearly defined set of rules against which to test current practice. It is both amorphous and shifting in its significance for environmental problem solving. Another reason is that precaution is deliberately being wrenched out of its slow evolution by interests who wish to exploit it for their own ends. The British government berates the loss of "good science" as a basis for determining environmental standards. It is dubiously using the principle of subsidiarity, ie. freedom of action by sovereign states to reach their own conclusions as to how to proceeed in a framework of collective responsibility, to give it room for maneouvre over the standards applying to drinking water and bathing beaches. According to a Department of Environment memorandum quoted in The Guardian (14 December 1993, 3) "sound scientific knowledge should provide the basis for precautionary action" and because of scarce resources nothing more should be spent to protect human health until a figure can be scientifically confirmed. On another level environmental groups such as Greenpeace and Friends of the Earth exploit the uncertainties inherent in such simplistic conceptualisations of the scientific method and argue vehemently for a more proactive and polluter pays approach by forcing would-be discharges to swallow their own waste.

For the economist precaution presents a problem in that precaution is not absolutist, so it is difficult to define what level of safety or cleanliness is actually preferred. This tends to make cost benefit analysis a more fluid exercise, with possibilities of negative relationships, i.e. costs exceeding benefits, under circumstances of genuine uncertainty or where phase changes at thresholds may occur. Under these circumstances, usually not the domain of science alone in prediction or justification, the usual economic yardsticks do not readily apply and other decision criteria have to be included. David Pearce shows how various approaches to risk aversion can be incorporated in expected utility analysis, though the assumptions have to be made very explicit. He also suggests that a more rigorous use of economic valuation on the merits of playing safe should encourage both estimates of possible damage and repair costs assuming probabilistic outcomes and that this rigour is sorely required. As yet the application of precaution is not creating the best conditions for extended cost benefit analysis, but the time is approaching when such studies will become more uniformly sought. This is very much the mood of Sir Frederick Warner's remarks in Chapter 4.

For a philosophical viewpoint safety margins, giving the earth a little space, and allowing a little spare assimilative capacity to future generations all provide an ethical foundation to the application of the precautionary principle. Presented carefully, precaution should clarify ethical stances on such matters as the right to test for natural processes and species whose presence and functioning are vital for the survival of life on earth. Similarly, again if treated openly and with care, precaution should clarify how we determine fairness fo future generations, and why we should put weight on the scope for burden sharing between those who should give, and those who have some justification to take. Robin Attfield explores many aspects of these issues, and includes that precaution contains a number of layers and ethical considerations that give it a distinctive quality in environmental decision making.

Sadly these are troublesome concepts for the media who generally distance themselves from convoluted arguments not capable of being simplified into summary paragraphs, memorable phrases, or sound bites. As Charles Clover argues, the media and precaution are frequently at cross purposes, since the media thrives on crisis rather than too much "wolf-calling", on novelty rather than established dispute, and on social conceptions of reality in which uncertainty plays a less constructive role. Yet ironically constructive use of the media to clarify uncertainty, to explicate choices, to open up the debate on how various courses of action could be justified or related to the rights of people and nature - all of this is media material, though not in the format and timescales of commercially driven news gathering and opinion formation.

Where uncertainty is truly great, and where ethical issues of great movement are involved, institutional arrangements are being created which address the science and ethics of precaution quite explicitly. Julie Hill sets the scene for the creation of the Advisory Committee on the Release to the Environment of Genetically Modified Organisms (ACRE). This influential body incorporates a wide cross-section of opinion, where that "non scientific" views are given due weight, and a fair degree of opinion and trust operates in the Committee's deliberations. This is partly because hypothesis testing is not available in many cases, and prediction is more a case of imposing clear safeguards then guessing likely consequences. Monitoring of any release is much more intense than monitoring of any other environmental change, and the liability rules on release agents are tighter. These are the institutional frameworks for precaution in the modern age. Though the process is still scaling down, the procedures reveal just how much is being learnt about the management of precaution in an area of focussed public and scientific interest.

By way of contrast Janice Morphet and Tony Hams regard the onset of precaution as a valuable reason for reasserting the proactive, managerial and civic guidance roles of local government in the UK, namely that has been missing from a large part of the 1980s. Irrespective of precaution local government is passing through a more constructive transition whereby its role in shaping the health, education and environment of its citizens is being reassessed. Admittedly the policies of the ruling Conservative government, by its own admission, is to bring local authorities to head on the major issues of spending, public services as opposed to private sector provision, and education in the cause of cost effectiveness and consumer choice. As with the advent of the sustainable development mandat arising out of the UN Conference on Environment and Development, and the more prominent role for local authorities as a key player in local sustainable development strategies, the scope is there for a reassessment of the working practices of local government and facilitators of civic mindedness in the face of climate change, biodiversity loss, waste minimisation, education for global citizenship and the emergence of a frugal society living without its earthly means. Involved thoughout all this is the more radical concept of precaution, namely its role as a creator of global responsibility at the level of the communal household. This is bound to be a tortuous path to travel, but at least a promising start has been made.

Chapter 7

The Precautionary Principle and Economic Analysis

By David Pearce

The economic paradigm

Until recently, economists have had little truck with the precautionary principle, or, at least, not with the precautionary principle as it has been interpreted by some environmentalists. The precautionary principle (PP) implies:

a) an emphasis on prevention rather than cure, and

b) an emphasis on taking strong preventive action in a context of uncertainty. (For a detailed discussion of alterna tive definitions of the PP see Ramchandani and Pearce 1991).

Note that one may prefer prevention to cure even where one if certain about the damage. For example, it could be cheaper to prevent damage than to suffer the consequences and then clean up the damage.

Because of the second characteristic, the PP implies a high degree of risk aversion on the part of the decision maker. Economists have traditionally developed their rules in the context of risk neutrality and risk aversion. Risk neutrality produces what is known as the expected value concept (EV). Risk aversion produces the expected utility concept (EU).

Under EV one takes a set of uncertain outcomes - say they

have the magnitudes -10, +10 and +20 - and attaches a probability to each, say, 0.1, 0.5 and 0.4. Then the EV is:

$$0.1(-10) + 0.5(10) + 0.4(20) = -1 + 5 + 8 = +12$$

If these are benefits, then the +12 would be compared to the cost, say 8. Then since 12 › 8, the decision is to proceed with this policy despite its uncertain benefits.

The EV approach is clearly unsatisfactory since it implies that a unit of loss is valued equally with a unit of gain. In the example, the -10 has been valued in the same way as the +10 - the only factor applied to it is the probability of its occurrence. This is the assumption of risk neutrality. But most people are very averse to losses, so we might expect the -10 to get a bigger weight than the +10 in the example. Also, an extra unit of gain might not be as important at high levels of gain as at low levels of gain, so the risk aversion procedure should take that into account. This is done by using not expected value but expected utility (EU). With EU we weight losses more heavily than gains and additional gains less if there are already significant gains compared to a situation in which gains are low. For example we might adjust the example above by saying that the -10 would be a disaster and is therefore weighted by a factor of 10, the +10 by a factor of 1 and the +20 by a factor of 1.5, i.e. the +20 is not twice as important as the +10. This converts the values into 'utilities' and the computation becomes:

$$[0.1 \times (-10) \times 10] + [0.5 \times (+10) \times 1] + [0.4 \times (+20) \times 1.5]$$

$$= -10 + 5 + 12 = +7$$

which has significantly reduced the value of the outcome and, compared to the hypothetical cost of 8, means that the project is now not worth undertaking.

It seems fair to say that most economic analyses of policies and projects where there is uncertainty are analyzed using the EV or EU rule. Strictly it should be the latter, but there are obvious problems of finding the weights to convert values to utilities. (In the economist's jargon, this is a problem of specifying the 'utility function').

The expected utility approach seems able to handle the problem of disastrous outcomes. In our example, the minus 10 can be thought of as a potential 'disaster'. In the expected utility approach, then, we would attach a large utility value (or 'disutility' value if it is a loss) to the outcomes we most like or dislike.

Some attempts have been made to estimate 'disaster aversion' measures. How, then, do the public perceive disastrous events? Many of the points that follow are covered in the report of the Royal Society Study Group on Risk (1992) as discussed in more detail by Warner in the preceeding chapter.

Everyone is familiar with news items about road accidents in which multiple vehicles are involved and the deaths are several or many. This is the phenomenon of the 'group accident'. It partly explains why aeroplane crashes, boat sinkings, gas explosions, nuclear accidents and natural disasters such as hurricanes and tornados are news. Yet the deaths from such events rarely exceed 25 people and the events themselves are not very common. Compare that to the more than 5000 people who die every year in road accidents in the UK. What it suggests is that individuals perceive group accidents differently to accidents in which one person dies. Put another way, if 10 people die in one accident this is seen as being somehow far more serious than if a single person dies in each of 10 accidents. There is what is known as disaster aversion. Allowing for disaster aversion in assessing environmental risks is perfectly legitimate if the requirement is that individuals' preferences should count. Moreover, disaster aversion is consistent with the economic theory of risk aversion. Table 7.1 shows some suggested rules taken from contexts in which safety investments have to be decided upon. But we shall discover that other aspects of human behaviour toward risk are not consistent with the received theory of risk aversion.

Summarising the economic approach to uncertainty, then, we have:

(a) expected value approach:

compare costs with expected value of benefits where the expected value of benefits is equal to:

$p_1.B_1 + p_2.B_2 + p_3.B_3$ etc, or $p_i.B_i$.

where p is probability and B is benefit measured in non-utility terms.

We can now see that the expected value approach is acceptable if we have reason to suppose that society is risk neutral, i.e. if it is indifferent between two outcomes with the same expected value, even though the variance about those expected values is different. But as soon as risk aversion is relevant, the expected value approach is not appropriate. Then the expected utility approach appears more applicable.

(b)Expected utility approach:

compare costs with the expected utility of the benefits, i.e. with

$p_1.U_1 + p_2.U_2 + p_3.U_3$ etc, or $p_i.U_i$

In this case the value of the 'U's should enable the decision-maker to capture society's aversion to particular risks.

Table 7.1

Disaster Aversion

The table below shows some possible rules for deciding on the 'value' of a disaster. Suppose we know that the 'value of a statistical life' (V) is $2 million, i.e society is willing to pay up to £2 million to save a single life in road accidents, health programmes etc. Assume that the accident in question has a 1 in a million chance of happening (f = frequency of the event) and that it might involve 100, 500 or 1000 people dying (N = 100, 500, 1000). Then the 'value of the accident' depends on how people view the group accident event. It has been suggested, and some regulatory agencies use this rule, that an accident involving 100 people is regarded as being the equivalent of 100x100 deaths in individual accidents (the 'square rule'). Others suggest that it is equal to 300 times the number of actual deaths, and so on. Which rule is chosen matters a great deal. In the table it can be seen that one would spend only $4000 to avert a one in a million chance of 1000 people dying in a single accident if no aversion factor is present, but $4 million if the square rule is used.

f = 1/1,000,000		
N = 100	N = 500	N = 1000
fN = 0.0001	fN = 0.0005	fN = 0.001
fN^2 = 0.01	fN^2 = 0.25	fN^2 = 1.0
300fN = 0.03	300fN = 0.15	300fN = 0.3
vfN = £400	vfN = £2000	vfN = $4000
vfN^2 = £40,000	vfN^2 = £1,000,000	vfN^2 = $4,000,000
v300fN = £120,000	v300fN = £600,000	v300fN = $1,200,000

In practice we know that people very often obey neither the expected value rule nor the expected utility rule. They simply do not behave according to the predictions of expected value or expected utility. Prospect theory suggests that attitudes to uncertainty are very complex.

Prospect theory

The expected utility model is attractive, but extensive research suggests that it does not describe how people actually behave. Recall that if individual preferences count, then actual behaviour must be studied to see what people actually care about and why they behave as they do. This can be contrasted with the view that ignores how people actually behave and builds up an approach based on how they ought to be behave if they are to be judged 'rational' or 'consistent'. It is not always easy to keep this distinction in mind. After all, the very purpose of analysing decisions is to make them better. Better decisions could be ones that always obey the axiom that what people want is best. But we know that societies have always abrogated some individual sovereignty to the state in order to override individual preferences.

In practice, psychologists and economists have uncovered many kinds of behaviour which are inconsistent with expected utility theory. Just a few are listed below:

i) people seem regularly to confuse probability with plausi bility. The more they think it could happen ('it seems reasonable') the higher the probability they attach to it occurring. This conjunction fallacy is especially important if the event in question is described in some detail - e.g. the effects of a nuclear accident, islands disappearing under rising sea levels etc. This often happens in association with events that are easy to imagine (explosions, flooding) while events that are hard to imagine tend to attract low subjective probabilities (the issue of availability);

ii) people often suffer from the 'it can't happen to me syndrome'. Because it hasn't yet happened, people think it won't happen. This is the fallacy of optimism;

iii) experiments show that people do not correctly perceive low probabilities. Many seem to ignore them altogether, and much depends on how the risk is described. In many other cases, people exaggerate the low probabilities, believing some accidents to be more likely than, say, the risk of fatality in a road accident. This is the under or over-weighting of low probabilities issue;

iv) people seem 'anchored' to wherever they are at the point in time they are asked to make a decision. This is their 'reference' point, and people value risks with reference to that point rather than in abstract in the way the expected utility approach assumes. They also value losses from the standpoint of the reference point more highly than equivalent gains (the phenomenon of 'loss aversion'), whereas economics has traditionally taught that there will be little difference in these values. This helps explain the difference between willingness to accept and willingness to pay in economic valuation. Asked what they are willing to accept (WTA) to tolerate a nuisance and what they are willing to pay (WTP) to avoid it, the former generally exceeds the latter by a substantial margin. Yet, for small changes in risk, economics tells us that the two magnitudes should not differ much (Pearce 1993). People also tend to make the risk problem simpler than it really is, as if they cannot cope with a more complex issue. These features of decision-making, together with the distortion of low probability perception, define prospect theory. Prospect theory seeks to explain how individuals behave with respect to risk in light of the apparent failure of expected utility theory to explain that behaviour;

v) prospect theory also suggests that people put the various contexts for valuing risk into separate mental boxes, or 'mental accounts'. They then have little difficulty in weighing up costs and benefits within each account, but find it difficult to make comparisons across mental accounts. If this is true then it goes some to explaining how people can seemingly entertain contradictory notions at the same time. For example, benefits might be in one 'account' and costs in another. This does not invalidate cost-benefit thinking since the idea of cost-benefit is to prescribe actions. But it raises again the awkward problem of when individuals' actions can be regarded as 'rational' and when they cannot;

vi) much also depends on the context of risk. A risk of being injured or catching a disease is regarded as being very different if it is involuntarily borne as opposed to being voluntary. So, the risk of dying from lung cancer through smoking (a voluntary process, at least initially) is often seen as being less than the risk of cancer through exposure to nuclear radiation (involuntary), even though the former probability is substantially greater than the latter. The context issue can be complicated. Risks in the future are usually thought to be less important than risks now (the phenomenon of 'discounting'), but recent research suggests that people often tend to value future risks more highly than present risks, and future benefits more highly than present benefits. This is because they sometimes like to 'leave the best to the last' (in the case of benefits), or dread being vulnerable when they older and perhaps less capable of looking after themselves (in the case of risks).

All in all, the issue of how people actually behave in the presence of uncertainty and risk turns out to be complex. It seems fairly clear that neither expected value nor expected utility are adequate to explain that behaviour, even if expected utility can accommodate many issues, such as disaster aversion. Other theories of risk-taking - such as prospect theory - have been developed to account for the inadequacies of expected utility. They tend to suggest that the context of the risk is important, and that we cannot advocate a single rule to deal with all risk and uncertainty contexts. The phenomenon of loss aversion is important for the environmental context because it is often the case that we are dealing with environmental losses rather than gains. Loss aversion means that those losses may be valued very highly by society. The issue of risk context means that we cannot analyse low probability, high damage events in the same way as we value 'every day' risk. Somehow we have to account for perceptions of low probability events.

Theories of uncertainty suggest all kinds of ways in which people can be encouraged to deal with risk. As just one example, in some countries it is fairly usual to compensate people if a project perceived as risky is located in their vicinity. This might be a nuclear power station or even a waste landfill site. Compensation may work as a means of getting a more 'rational' appraisal of risk not just because bearing the risk is itself compensated, but because the compensation creates a new context of sharing in risk compared to the uncompensated case in which the owner of the landfill site, or the nuclear power station is seen to be 'imposing' the facility. Other approaches include trying to build a bridge of trust between the neighbouring community and a risk-generating facility, in the form of a community liaison panel, or educational facility, or risk communication programme.

Risk and risk perception

Table 7.2 assembles some risk data for the USA. The data is objective in the sense that the deaths per million are either based on actual past data, or on expert assessment of future risks. But the public often perceives risk in very different ways to experts. This disparity between public and expert risk assessment is absolutely fundamental to the problem of coping with risk and uncertainty. The economist's cost-benefit way of thinking involves us in a process of recording individuals' preferences for or against some change. Economists tend not to ask where the preferences come from, or whether they are 'good or bad' (subject to the law, that is). This is because cost-benefit approaches try to be 'democratic' by using individuals' preferences rather than some expert's view.

When it comes to assessing risks, however, there is a problem. Suppose the expert assessment of risk is that some dreaded event, say a core meltdown in a nuclear power station, can only happen with a probability of 1 in a million reactor-years (10^{-6}). That is, the chance of an accident of this kind would only occur once in 1 million years of producing electricity from one nuclear reactor, or, once in 1000 years if there are 1000 nuclear reactors. This is an extremely small probability. And it is one that tends to be used when designing modern reactors in the developed world. Most people would agree that such a risk is so small it is not worth worrying about. Yet the fear of a nuclear accident is so great that in the United States no nuclear power station of any significance has been commissioned for the last twenty years. Clearly, there seems to be a marked disparity between what the public worry about and what the experts think is important. And this disparity has major implications for many projects and policies, e.g. the development of certain energy sources and the siting of allegedly hazardous facilities. Indeed, it generates the 'NIMBY' syndrome ('not in my back yard') whereby people oppose the siting of such things as waste disposal sites, incinerators, and power stations in their area. They do this despite the expert evidence that the risks to health from such facilities are very small.

Table 7.3 shows the contrast between expert and public opinion. The expert information is for the USA but the public's opinion can be gleaned from surveys in the USA and the UK. It can be seen that what concerns the public is fairly similar in the two countries, and most of the exceptions are readily explained. For example, the US has debated the risks from exposure to radon (naturally occurring radioactivity) in domestic dwellings for quite some time and it has been a regular feature of media programmes. This concern is somewhat more recent in the UK and hence did not figure prominently in the 1989 public opinion polls used here. There have been similar investigations into indoor air pollution generally in the USA but, to date, very little has been said about this in the UK. Perhaps of more interest are the items that the US experts implied did not matter very much, but which the public thinks do matter. These are very much in a general category of 'accidents' - nuclear, industrial, oil spills, underground storage tanks in the USA and problems with the nuclear fuel cycle. The only exception is bathing water which has been a specific problem in the UK because of a Directive from the European Community on the matter. The issue of 'group accidents' was analyzed above.

Table 7.2

Risks of Death in the USA: Selected Environmental Hazards and their Cost of Reduction

	Deaths per 1 million people exposed:	*Cost to Avoid 1 death: ($ mill)*
Trihalomethane in Drinking Water	420	0.2
Radionuclides in Uranium Mines	6300	3.4
Benzene Fugitive Emissions	1470	3.4
Benzene Occupational Exposure	39600	8.9
Asbestos Occupational Exposure	3015	8.3
Arsenic/Copper Exposure	63000	23.0
Acrylonitrile Occupational Exposure	42300	51.5
Coke Ovens Occupational Exposure	7200	63.5
Hazardous Waste Land Disposal	2	4190.2
Municipal Solid Waste Landfill Standard	1	19107.0
Hazardous Waste: Wood Preservatives	<1	5,700,000

The risks shown relate to numbers of mortalities for the relevant exposed population. All the hazards shown are the subject of environmental legislation in the USA, so, for example, the risk that is affected by the piece of legislation is the numerical value shown here. Notice that expressing the risks as 'per million' makes some of them look large. The largest risk, for arsenic/copper exposure, is 0.063 when expressed as a fraction, or 63 in 1000 or just over 6 in a 100. The manner in which risk is expressed often influences the extent to which people react to the risk.

The legislation costs money. The right hand column shows what happens when this cost is divided by the numbers of lives that the legislation is expected to save. In this way, cost and 'effectiveness' (lives saved) can be compared.

Source: The Council on Environmental Quality, Environmental Quality: 21st Annual Report 1990, US Government Printing Office, Washington DC.

Table 7.3

Comparing Perceptions of Risk: Experts vs the Public

US Environment Protection Agency Scientific Advisory Board Unranked Priorities:	*USA Public Opinion Poll March 1990* *% Saying 'Very serious':*	*UK Public Opinion Poll May 1989* *% Saying 'Very worried':*
Ecological Risks		
Climate change	48	44
Ozone layer	60	56
Habitat change	42	45
Biodiversity loss	na	45
Health Risks		
Criteria pollutants*	56	34-40
Toxic air pollutants**	50	33
Radon	17	na
Indoor air pollution	22	na
Drinking water	46	41
Pesticides	52	46
Issues Regarded by the Public as Important but not by the Experts		
Oil spills	60	53
Hazardous waste sites	66	na
Industrial water pollution	63	na
Nuclear accidents	60	na
Industrial pollution accidents	58	64
Radioactive waste	58	58
Leaking underground storage tanks	54	na
Contaminated bathing water	na	59

Sources: UK Department of the Environment; 'Counting on Science at EPA', Science, Vol.240, August 10, 1990; D.W.Pearce et al, The Development of Environmental Indicators, Report to UK Department of the Environment, April 1991.

If individuals are very averse to environmental risk, it suggests a sound basis for the precautionary principle. Indeed, the insights from risk experiments and prospect theory go a long way to explaining the attraction of the precautionary principle, particularly where there are low probabilities and potentially high damages, where the risk is involuntary, and where the risk is of loss rather than gain.

The precautionary principle may take several forms. In its strictest interpretation it suggests that no action should be taken if there is any likelihood at all, however small, that significant environmental damages could occur. This likelihood may be independent on the scientific evidence. That is, unless there is certainty that there are no detrimental effects, actions should not be taken which, for example, release harmful pollutants into the environment.

Construed in this way, the precautionary principle can be thought of as one approach to the 'zero-infinity' problem in which the probability of damage is small or unknown, but the consequences are potentially very large. As such, the precautionary principle can be held to apply to both risk and uncertainty contexts.

A second interpretation requires that there be a presumption in favour of not harming the environment unless the opportunity costs of that action are, in some sense, very high. Put another way, no significant deterioration of the environment should occur unless the benefits associated with that deterioration heavily outweigh the costs of the deterioration. Effectively, this safe minimum standards approach says that the benefit-cost ratio of any project or programme which incidentally damages the environment should be high. While this formulation is somewhat vague, it can be contrasted with the typical cost-benefit rule to the effect that the benefit cost ratio should be greater than unity.

The precautionary principle is embodied in some national environmental legislation, is espoused generally in European Community environmental legislation as discussed by Haigh in Chapter 13, and in some international agreements, see the contribution by James Cameron in Chapter 15. Clearly, adoption of the precautionary principle can be expensive. If the benefits forgone are substantial and new information reveals that the measure turns out not to have been warranted, then there will be a high net cost to precaution. On the other hand, if new information reveals that precaution was justified, nothing is lost. This suggests that some balancing of costs and benefits still must play a role even in contexts where the precautionary principle is thought to apply.

If we interpret the PP as implying something like safe minimum standards, then the question arises as to the need for economic valuation of environmental costs and benefits. As is well known, such procedures are controversial and some people may feel happier with decision rules which avoid valuation. But there is no escape from valuation, not least because whatever rule we adopt it will imply an economic value. If we adopt the safe minimum standard rate, for example, it effectively says that the avoidance of environmental damage is worth the sacrifice of the economic benefits from the environmentally damaging activity. We still have to have some idea of the cut-off point: when is the forgone cost so large that it justifies environmental damage?

One way of looking at this has been examined by Ramchandani and Pearce (1992). They sought to examine the relative costs of applying various "rules" to the costs and benefits of pollution control. The four conditions were:

i) strict precaution when only discharges proven or likely not to harm ecosystems or diminish environmental quality were permitted.

ii) precaution coupled to best available technology for dis charges likely to result in environmental damage.

iii) application of the critical load principle, with some safety margin, to accommodate assimilative capacity insofar as it is known, and

iv) the use of a proportionality clause, best available tech niques not entailing excessive costs, within the broad rubric of precaution.

Figure 7.1 shows how each of these positions compare on a highly simplified pair of cost and benefit curves. Arguably the cost of meeting the very strict precautionary standard may be so high in relation to any measurable gains as to divert resources from other more needed returns. Even the critical load approach, if fully complied with, imposes costs at a point where no measurable environmental gains can be increased.

This is a useful analytical device, but it depends enormously on the evidence of assimilability, critical load, ecological health and resilience that, as pointed out by MacGarvin and others, are not readily to hand. So valuation of precautionary action is problematic, but still a goal worth pursuing even if only by the heuristic means already mentioned.

A more sophisticated argument for ignoring valuation arises in the context of biodiversity conservation (Perrings and Pearce 1993). The loss of the world's biological and cultural diversity is probably the gravest of all the environmental threats to humankind. It is perhaps necessary to explain why. There is much talk today about sustainable development and how to achieve it. Both the economic approach to sustainable development and the ecological approach have common themes. The economist speaks of ensuring that future generations have the same kinds of choices that we have today. Limiting choice is to limit human wellbeing. Providing the basis for choice means provided technical capability for choice, and that means ensuring that the next generation has no less 'capital' than we have today. But that capital includes 'Nature's capital' - the stock of all environmental assets, including biogeochemical cycles, biological diversity etc. So, for the economist, sustainable

Figure 7.1 The cost-benefit analyses of different levels of precaution. Strict or strong precaution assumes a damage function so steep that the product or process should be banned or stopped from being released. BATNEEC applies the principle of proportionality, where the damage functions

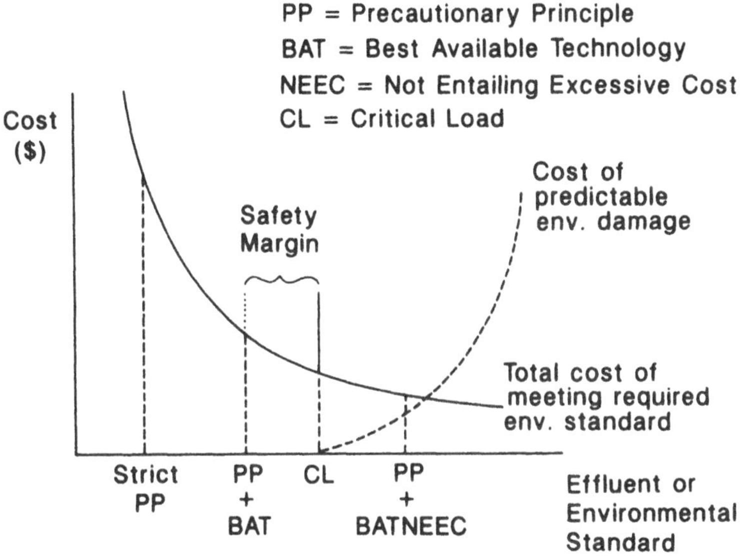

development is about ensuring that the next generation is no worse off than this one by leaving bequests of all kinds of capital. This is the 'constant capital' rule. It is familiar to any businessman - no business is sustainable if it lives off its capital.

The ecologist speaks of the resilience of ecological systems - the ability of those systems to withstand stress and shocks. While it is a disputed proposition in ecology, there is some evidence to suggest that resilience increases with system complexity, and complexity can be measured by biological diversity. In that way, the more diversity there is, the more resilience there is and hence the more sustainable the system is.

The link between these economic and ecological definitions is that biological diversity conservation is common to both of them. And we should extend that to cultural diversity as well - the range of cultures and indigenous knowledge systems that occupy the world.

How does this relate to economic valuation and the precautionary principle? The connection is that ecological systems may not be 'smooth and continuous' like the economist tends to assume economic systems are. There may be discontinuities such that it is possible to 'nibble away' at a system without any evident effect until one trips over a threshold and the system itself collapses. If that is true we can interpret the precautionary principle as implying that we should avoid the thresholds. The only relevance for economic valuation would lie in determining where to settle in the system prior to the threshold. But the threshold itself would be determined by 'physical' concerns - ecological information, for example. If we think we are in the region of a threshold, valuation could be irrelevant: we need to know where the threshold is and take precautions to avoid going beyond it.

Such an approach is persuasive but problematic. In the first place, life science seems ill-equipped to tell us where the thresholds are. We cannot therefore say when valuation is relevant and when it is not. We may be so far to the left of any threshold that valuation remains important.

We may be past the thresholds, in which case we should be witnessing system collapses all round us - and perhaps we are with global warming, loss of coral reefs, the spread of environmentally transmitted diseases and so on.

Here there are implications for the advocacy of market based economic instruments for controlling environmental problems. If such problems are regarded as close to thresholds, and hence may have the characteristics of irreversibility, then economic instruments will be inefficient ways of keeping just below the thresholds. It may be better to adopt traditional standard setting. But this is debateable: there is a strong case for a combination of both approaches. This is an area when the economics of precaution need further investigation.

Integrating risk and uncertainty in decision-making

The previous analysis suggests that there are no simple or comprehensive rules for integrating risk and uncertainty into decision-making. But addressing the problem of risk and uncertainty should be an integral part of programme and project design and management. Certain steps in the procedure can be set out:

(a) potential sources of risk and uncertainty need to be identified at the outset, including the physical attributes and mechanisms of environmental systems likely to be affected. Systems simulation models are often a useful means of understanding the relevant natural processes;

(b) the quality of information needs to be assessed. For some effects very little will be known or predictable. For others, information may be available for upper and lower bounds. In still other cases it may be possible to fit a probability distribution to the pattern of effects. If possible, identifica tion of thresholds is critical;

(c) risk information can be portrayed in probability distribu tions and can be 'reduced' to single numbers as expected values (if risk neutrality seems appropriate) or expected utility (if risk aversion seems appropriate). But the use of expected utility as a model is open to question. If cost-benefit analysis is meant to obey the value judgement that individu als' preferences count, then the observation that people often fail to obey the axioms of expected utility is problematic. If, on the other hand, cost benefit analysis is supposed to reflect some representative 'rational' decision-making, it may be legitimate to adopt the expected utility model. In such cases, economic valuation remains of paramount importance;

(d) Where probabilities are small but impacts are very large (the 'zero infinity' dilemma) recourse may be had to the precautionary principle or safe minimum standards, but some reference to the opportunity costs of adopting these principles is required. In such cases the focus of economic valuation shifts from estimating environmental damages to estimating the economic value of the activity giving rise to environmental damage. Contrary to popular opinion this is often just as complex as estimating the economic value of environmental damages;

(e)uncertainty information can be portrayed in payoff matrices, but the matrices themselves do not enable a choice to be made. This requires some choice rule based in turn on the outlook and disposition of the decision-maker;

(f) the issue of delaying a decision needs to be investigated. This will be especially true where the issue is one of pollution prevention or remediation. The costs and benefits of delaying the action need to be compared with the costs and benefits of acting now.

The precautionary principle sets an important new discipline on economic analysis of environmental protection, especially where science suggests phase changes are possible, or where long term uncertainties encourage a strategy of hedging against possibly serious damage costs. This inevitably puts pressure on the appropriate role of cost-benefit analysis, for it is possible that a commitment where costs exceed likely benefits, but not possible damage costs would be acceptable under precautionary cost-benefit rules. This is not unusual in the risk arena: it may become more commonplace for certain aspects of global change.

References

Pearce, D.W. 1993. Economic Valuation and the Natural World, Earthscan, London.

Ramchandani R., and Pearce, D.W. October 1991. Alternative Approaches to Setting Effluent Quality Standards: Precautionary, Critical Load and Cost-Benefit Approaches, Water Research Centre, Report LR 93, Medmenham.

Perrings C., and Pearce, D.W. 1993. Biodiversity Conservation and Economic Development, Centre for Social and Economic Research on the Global Environment, University College London, Working Paper.

Royal Society Study Group 1993. Risk: Analysis, Perception and Management. Royal Society, London.

Chapter 8

The Precautionary Principle and Moral Values

By Robin Attfield

Before certain moral issues raised by the precautionary principle are discussed, it is necessary to tackle some key questions about the principle itself, such as the first five given here:

(i) What is here taken to be the precautionary principle?

(ii) Is it consistent?

(iii)Is it a basic or a derivative one, an absolute or a qualified one?

(iv) What is its scope?

(v) Which values are implicit in it?

The discussion of these questions then introduces further ethical issues:

(vi) How do the implicit values related to recognised moral values?

(vii) What are the implications for compensation, conditionality and sustainability?

What is here taken to be the precautionary principle?

I shall take the precautionary principle to consist in the four assumptions outlined in the editors' introductory chapter, plus some of the further claims subsequently made in that chapter. The four assumptions are: "(1) prudent action in advance of scientific certainty, (2) shifting the burden of proof into the would be developer to show no unreasonable harm, (3) ensuring that environmental wellbeing is given legitimate status, and (4) developing best practice techniques in the pursuit of management excellence."

The further claims, reconstructed from the ensuing text, are these: (5) precautionary action in advance of conclusive scientific evidence is justified at least where either environmental change is globally pervasive, or where irreversible change would be intolerable to human beings, or where vulnerable ecosystems have reached the critical point where further interference would subvert them, as in the principle of critical load. Further, (6) an equivalence of burden or responsibility falls upon all countries with powers of action in a given environmental zone, in the matters of conserving the relevant resource, a responsibility owed, at least in part, to the other partners. Besides, (7) while the BAT of BATNEEC holds (best available techniques of environmental management), the NEEC (not entailing excessive costs) will frequently be superseded through the critical load approach (see claim 5), through cost-effectiveness analysis (implicit in assumption 4), and through precaution itself (assumption 1). While the principle may include other claims, I am inclined to think that the remaining claims mentioned in the introductory essay are implicit in one or more of the seven tenets already indentified.

Is it consistent?

It could be denied that these tenets add up to a principle at all. Thus they, or at least the four assumptions, are not couched in universal terms, and for that reason fail to tell us on which kinds of occasions specific classes of agents are obliged to act or forbear, or how far-reaching their interventions are to be. Disobliging people who paid lip-service to these tenets could readily wriggle out of them in practice, since they all need constructive interpretation before clear cut applications can be identified. So as not to be disobliging, I will henceforth assume suitable constructive interpretations, and they that these tenets each and all make a practical difference.

This allows questions of their consistency to be raised. While assumption (1) calls for prudent action in advance of scientific knowledge, the principle of critical load, which is relevant to claim (5), could only be applied when considerable scientific knowledge was already available. The same probably applies to assumption (3), if crucial aspects of environmental wellbeing are to be identified. There is at least some tension here; but assumption (3) does not require scientific certainty, and claim (5) does not specify conditions necessary for precaution to be justified. Indeed the perennial need to make decisions in face of scientific uncertainty makes precaution normally a pre-eminently sane policy. There is probably more tension when several broad-brush tenets with inspecific boundary conditions i.e. (1) to (7)) are conjoined, and in the absence of rules to priorities them. Indeed perhaps we have something more like a manifesto than a principle. Let us again, however, assume that tensions are minimised by constructive, harmonising interpretations, and move on.

Is it a basic or a derivative principle, an absolute or a qualified one?

Since principles are either derivative or basic, and either absolute or qualified, it is worth asking to which kinds that of precaution belongs. Part of the answer seems to be given by Cameron and Abouchar (1991); precaution applies "to social change generally, and to fundamental principles of justice and welfare", including certain rights, of which the grounding is thus couched: "so that the weak and vulnerable do not get suffocated in the stampede to save the world". If I interpret this aright, there are principles (concerning justice, welfare and rights) more fundamental than precaution, which to some degree underpin it, and which in any case must not be overlooked.

Another part of the answer emerges in the particular claim there is that "risky strategies of precaution" themselves require careful appraisal; the more general point is that none of the elements of the principle is absolute, and that "precaution is not an unfettered principle". Thus the principle has a built-in hypothetical or conditional aspect, presumably answering, amongst other matters, to the importance of rights and of justice. For example, interventions (trade regulations, perhaps) apparently demanded by the principle might need to be rejected because they struck at the long-term needs of the poor of the third world, if we may assume, that either human rights or justice require these needs to be satisfied.

What is its scope?

Does the principle apply to all agents and all action? If clearly forbids many omissions, and mandates many acts of investment. But it must also surely mandates many omissions (e.g. not to initiate development), and correspondingly forbids many actions. This being so, we need to know just which actions and omissions are mandated or forbidden by precaution; otherwise both action and inaction will be mandated in advance of knowledge, and on all occasions.

What are to be forestalled seem to be processes which could lead (as in claim 5) to unreasonable environmental harm, in circumstances of pervasive threats, irreversible change or of critical phases of vulnerable environments. The scope of the principle is thus limited to the kinds of agencies and of actions which can significantly affect such situations; mostly corporate agencies and their policies, except that, as Derek Parfit (1984) points out, the trivial acts of millions (e.g. in using petrol) can have a significant environmental impact when aggregated. Thus they would seem to fall under the principle too.

Which values are implicit in it?

Some of the implicit values are unimpeachable. Thus prudence is immensely preferable in matters of externalities to repenting at leisure, and it is often developers who pose the greatest threats. Yet sometimes threats come not from developers but from conservers of the status quo, as possibly with those who keep Chernobyl-style power-stations in operation. Holders of the principle would thus be ill-advised to assign priority to preserving the actual over all actions which would change it.

Other implicit values call for interpretation, including environmental wellbeing and environmental harm. Clearly a great deal here turns on whether the welfare of nonhuman creatures is valued solely for the sake of human interest or not. The problem seems to be circumvented by stressing the wellbeing of ecosystems, in which many spcies including our own are independent. But there is more to the welfare of nonhuman creates than the intactness of ecosystems. Not even when O'Riordan (1992, 13) writes of the commitment in the German 1970s policy of precaution to "a bioethic, the protection of the intrinsic rights of natural systems to be allowed to operate with a minimum of molestation" do the problems disappear; for even those able to credit that natural systems have intrinsic rights are not committed thereby to the wellbeing of individual nonhuman creatures, as long as such creates are held to be replaceable is such a way as to preserve the systems in which they play a part.

Thus the maintenance of ecosystems is compatible with policies of maximum sustainable yield, which limit the harvest from forests or fishstocks to a level compatible with the replenishment of the populations of the relevant species. In this way ecosystems are preserved, and there is also, spread out over the course of time, the maximum possible benefit to humans from the system. Nonetheless if the species harvested consist of such intelligent creatures as whales or dolphins, plausibly they should not be harvested at all. Maybe harvesting them would be ruled out by the phrase about "the minimum of molestation". But what we are not to molest is natural systems, not nonhuman creatures. Further clarification of the principle would be necessary before it became clear, particularly to parties with interests at stake, that e.g. whaling per se is forbidden by the principle. At particular times, of course, it may be forbidden on precautionary grounds concerning the survival of whale-species being at risk; but grounds such as these will not always prove sufficient.

Nonhuman interests, then, can make a difference to actions and policies; so it is important to know whether appeals to environmental wellbeing recognise them as having intrinsic value or not. Much the same applies to the principle of critical load, which could be focussed simply on the human interest in the preservation of ecosystems. This matter is not further or clarified by talk of the intrinsic rights of natural systems (which rights? how claimed? how grounded?), indispensable as natural systems usually are. Nor can anyone afford to assume that, just because a holistic approach to the study of systems is desirable, a holistic theory of value which locates intrinsic value in systems is the best theory available. Systems, plausibly, are of value not intrinsically but on account of the value of the individuals which they support.

The values implicit in adherence to "best available techniques" depend, of course, on the diverse goals and the constraints of those techniques. Whether they enhance moral values or not must therefore remain an open question for present purposes.

The concern of precaution to avoid irreversible change intolerable to human beings embodies an admirable concern for future human generations, which is equally admirably nondiscriminatory across spatial and temporal boundaries. Its most obvious defence concerns the loss which would otherwise be involved for every generation after the irreversible change took place. Thus it reveals the same concern for human interests spread out over time as the parallel concern to prevent excessive globally pervasive change shows for human interests spread out across space. Perhaps understandably, all this concern is limited to human beings, maybe because only they are potential voters. As it happens, a related concern for nonhuman interests of the future would serve to supplement the grounds for precaution against irreversible species extinctions, and thus for this part of the precautionary principle.

Further values are implicit in the requirement of burden-sharing. Here equivalence of burden is advocated, presumably not an equal burden but one proportionate to GNP. (The difference would be important in areas shared by developed and Third World countries, such as the Mediterranean and the Carribean.) Some supplementary principle may eventually be needed for the responsibilities of countries where one or more other countries refuse to play their part. This problem, however, has been addressed by O'Riordan (1992, 28) who writes favourably of "rights of international agencies to place pressure on non-complying states or agencies through some kind of consensus over environmental security and cooperation". A further supplementary principle is likely to be needed to cover cases where countries are too weak or vulnerable to practice precaution. Here there is a strong case, partly based on self-interest, for international aid, and for burden-sharing among those countries able to supply it.

Yet further values again are embodied in the commitments to cost-effectivness and to preparedness to override the NEEC of BATNEEC, effectively on environmental grounds. This latter commitment makes the package more consistent. Against a background of uncertainty of returns from investment, however, cost-effectiveness could commend inaction where the rest of the principle of precaution commends intervention; presumably it is to be given a subordinate role. This would in any case be sensible, for to give it a pre-eminent role commits people to the abolition of all practices where the ratio of outputs to inputs is less than maximal; and the implications of this stance are ludicrously pervasive. It is worth adding that what count as the "excessive costs" of NEEC cannot be determined independently of a determination of when precaution is on balance necessary; for where precaution is necessary, the costs of precaution cannot be excessive, however much conventional economics may represent them as such.

How do the implicit values relate to recognised moral values?

As previously mentioned, O'Riordan (1992, 28) relates precatuion to social change in general and thus "to fundamental principles of justice and welfare", mentioning a few lines later the need to protect rights, the weak and the vulnerable. To what extent does the precautionary principle uphold such values?

In at least one respect it upholds them well, as it could make the crucial difference to preserving natural systems, without which many of the weak, the vulnerable and the holders of rights would not survive, let alone have their welfare provided for or receive justice.

In other respects it is less clear whether it upholds them well. For it needs to be asked who are the weak, the vulnerable, and the bearers of rights? I have written elsewhere (Attfield, 1987) about the scope of moral concern, or, more technically, moral considerability, and maintained that it includes not only all living human beings, whether near or far. Moral considerability, I suggest, also belongs to all their successors whose existence and wellbeing can be affected by current action, and the members of other living species, present and future, too. While the concept of rights is plausibly inapplicable to people and other creatures who are, as far as current knowledge is concerned, mere possibilities, the concepts of wellbeing and of interests are highly applicable wherever the impacts of current actions and policies could extend. The principle of precaution stands up better than many against this background, as it takes seriously the difference which can be made to the people and the other creatures of many areas for centuries to come. Yet certain interests may still be neglected.

As already mentioned, these could include individual nonhuman animals, about which perhaps enough has been said in the present context. Certain human interests too, however, could be neglected, if responsibilities for environmental management are to be shared on a regional basis; for this could have the result that the environment of developed regions will be much better protected than that of Third World regions. For, while common interests may ensure that steps are taken by Western countries to minimise pollution in Eastern Europe and the Mediterranean, there is a serious risk that too little will be done in more distant sub-Saharan Africa, in Asia, and in Latin America, given the indebtedness and relative powerlessness of most countries there, if responsibility is left to the countries most directly affected by environmental problems.

Just after the passage on environmental cooperation, O'Riordan mentions favourably "rights of sharing and exchanging information, understanding, and intellectual property rights" in a context of benefitting the weak and the vulnerable. If I am right in detecting a reference to the Biodiversity Convention of the Rio 1992 UNCED Conference, then provision is envisaged here for worldwide scientific and technological cooperation. Nevertheless even this is less than the Brundtland Report (Brundtland, 1987) recommend. That report advocated an international fund for the preservation of species and biodiversity in general, and tropical forests in particular, whereby developed countries would subsidise preservation and the lost economic opportunities which it would often involve for debtor countries. It is to be doubted whether the Commission for Sustainable Development, set up at Rio, or even the Global Environment Facility given a financial boost at Rio, will prove capable of implementing this. Sadly, the need is even more urgent, now that several more years of deforestation have passed since the Report was issued. Besides, if natural systems are to survive, what is needed may extend beyond preservation to restoration, involving the setting-aside of corridors linking uncultivated areas, something which would require further international funding. It is unclear whether the scope and content of the precautionary principle extend to such measures, and whether in this regard it can encompass the moral values that such actions call for.

As Brundtland also further urged, environmental deterioration is only likely to be contained if the poverty which often causes it, and which plausibly is also responsible for high rates of population growth, is tackled. Tackling it would involve appropriate economic and social development in the countries concerned, which (except in the cases of the Newly Industrialising Countries of the Pacific rim) would need to be fostered through much more generous loan-terms from donor countries and international agencies like the World Bank and the IMF. It may seem strange for an essay, which begins with a recognition that developers are responsible for much environmental harm and that they should be expected to show the harmlessness of proposed developments, to conclude with advocacy of development, however appropriate, in the Third World. But plausibly that is necessary if avoidable environmental deterioration is to be avoided (see Dower, 1992 for a persuasive argument). It is also, the path of global justice; but that basis is not so much implicit in the precautionary principle, as one of its grounds. Fortunately, as the principle is neither fundamental nor overriding, there is nothing wrong with supplementing it.

Implications for compensation, conditionality and sustainability

One issue which needs to be addressed is the question of who should pay for precaution. If opportunities are foregone (as with decisions made in favour of "ecological buffers"), e.g. by refraining from cutting down a forest, should the affected human parties be compensated?

But this is much the same issue as arises when we impose limits to development for the sake of future people, even though the rationale does not then consist in our current ignorance, but in our understanding of likely harms to such people.

The question about compensation needs to be clarified, for the potential beneficiaries might be rich or poor, secure or vulnerable. Imagine first that the only losers are powerful companies, well placed to diversify their interests. While they suffer lost opportunities, this scarcely entitles them to compensation, either from a national government or from international agencies, if we bear in mind alternative ways of deploying the resources in question, such as the relief of poverty or the conservation of species.

There is also the possibility that the foregone opportunities will affect poor farmers, plus maybe a national government itself desperately in need of foreign exchange to repay international debt. (This is the kind of case very effectively pressed at Rio by the Malaysian delegation.) Such farmers will be nowhere near as well off as other beneficiaries of the ban elsewhere, and the government may stand to forego its only way of solving its financial problems. Here there is an extremely strong case in equity for both international compensation to the government and for national compensation to the relevant farmers. This should plausibly be paid by the better-off beneficiaries in the West and the Far East, in the form of inter-governmental compensation funded from taxes.

Thus the case for compensation arises out of on a range of factors, of which precaution is only one, and its strength varies with different distributions of costs and benefits. But in some cases its strength will be overwhelming.

Should such compensation nevertheless be made conditional on the adoption of policies by the recipient government of sustainable development? The case is strong, but the ethics of conditionality is a complex subject; here it will suffice to commend Dale Jamieson's (1994) recent discussion of its ambivalence.

The ethical issues become yet more complex because the very nations liable to make sustainability a condition of aid or compensation often owe their comparative prosperity to non-sustainable practices in the past. Consistency requires as a minimum that those demanding sustainability of others should currently practice it themselves; sometimes it will also demand additional payments to compensate for past damage to global or regional ecosystems and for past resource depletion, wherever current prosperity is partly due to these practices. I have discussed principles relating to such reparations elsewhere.

If, as I have suggested, the principle of precaution calls both for precautionary measures in the West and, when extended, support (albeit selective support) for development in most of the Third World, some kind of integrated plan is required. Such a plan might draw on the ideas of the second report of the club of Rome, Mankind at a Turning Point (Mesarovich and Pestel, 1975) which commended fostering growth in, for example, India, in conjunction with a voluntary holding-back from growth in the West. (But it would be unlikely to include plans for dams which would involve flooding existing forests and moving tens of thousands of people.) It might also draw on the ideas of the Brundtland report for minimising resource-consumption, and for making growth in the Third World sustainable.

It would in any case involve all the agencies and more proposed by Cameron and Abouchar (1992). Where O'Riordan (1992) summarises their proposals as 'The Extension of Precaution', what has just been described amounts to what might be called an "Extension of the Extension". Yet nothing less is involved in taking seriously the Principle of Precaution, its moral presuppositions and their implications.

References

Attfield, R. 1979. Unto the third and fourth generation. Second order, An African Journal of Philosophy, 8(12), 55-70.

Attfield, R. 1987. A Theory of Value and Obligation. Croom Helm, London.

Brundtland, H.G. (Edair) Our Common Future. Oxford University Press, Oxford.

Cameron, J. and Abouchar, J. 1991. The precautionary principle: a fundamental principle of law and policy for the protection of the global environment. Boston College International and Comparative Law Review, 14(1), 1-27.

Dower, N. 1992. Sustainability and the right to development. In. R. Attfield and B. Wilkins (eds.) International Justice and the Third World. Routledge, London, 93-116.

Jamieson, D. 1994. Global environmental justice. In. R. Attfield and and R, Belsey (eds.) Philosophy and the Natural Environment. Cambridge University Press (in press).

Mesarovic, M.D. and Pestel, E. 1975. Mankind at the Turning Point. Hutchinson, London.

O'Riordan, T. 1992. The precaution principle in environmental management. CSERGE Working Paper GEC 92-03. University of East Anglia, Norwich.

Parfit, D. 1984. Reasons and Persons. Oxford University Press, Oxford.

Redclift, M. 1993. Sustainable development: needs, values, rights. Environmental Values 2(1), 6.

Chapter 9

How the Media respond to Precaution

By Charles Clover

Editorial Introduction

Twenty years ago the American political scientist Anthony Downs applied his "issue attention cycle" to the environmental movement. The result looked like Figure 9.1. This depicts the changing public engagement with environmental problems as they wax and wane in reality and through media coverage. To begin with, and here is the true precautionary mode, only a few knowledgeable insiders know much. They may tip off a journalist or two, or even tempt a television producer. But unless the story is "hard" it is unlikely to capture attention. The ozone hole was not news as a theoretical prediction: only when the satellite pictures revealed the purple aura of depletion. Similarly famine in Ethiopia is not "news" until a fine television journalist engulfed the public conscience with horrendous first time pictures.

The Downs cycle continues through the initial flush of media excitement as stories chase each other and images coalesce to give a disturbing collage of fundamental malaise. Oil spills, nuclear accidents, ploughing of ancient woodlands burning tropical forests, bleached coral, and leaching toxic waste. Media coverage under these conditions tends to be frenetic. Generally speaking journalists are not environmental scientists, so they tend to lack both knowledge and a sense of perspective. This is not the case if they are trained into the job, have good academic and specialist contacts, and spend some time understanding the political culture of environmental problem identification and solution-seeking.

The point of crisis in the Downs cycle is where the

enthusiasm for environment crusading bumps against the harsh realities of falling profits, recession to public fatigue. This is the crunch period, when the underlying crisis is lost in the whelter of recrimination and criticism of the over zealous enthusiam of the dedicated minority. One can imagine that during this crucial phase of reconsideration, the politics of the precautionary principle gain attention mostly because of the skewed cost benefit analysis interest in even more stringent margins of safety, or the sacrifice of lucrative job creation on the alter of biodiversity protection.

The world of the media demands excitement, a sense of rapid movement, clean at issues of high symbolism, and rapid turnaround from breaking story to hard copy. None of these demands suit media treatment of precautionary principle, which as the editors point out in the final chapter, is designed to "seep through the pores" of social change to change the very outlook on anticipatory action and taking care over environmental intervention. The world is greyer, qualifications have to appear. Uncertainty of whatever kind is a nuisance for the journalist hoping to catch the attention of leisure-orientated young who form the battleground for increasing market share. The jostling over "poaching" stores between various established specialists in the business, gender and agricultural columns is also a point of considerable friction. In any case so much depends on the nature of contact with the editors and line managers who ultimately control both timing (if it is a broadcast) and copy placing (if it is newsprint). These are not supportive settings for promoting the cause of the precautionary principle in considered media coverage.

This is, of course, a potentially serious situation. From a pragmatic perspective, the fact that environmental coverage has spilled over into the business and finance pages is to be welcomed - at least in principle. At least there is a foot in the door in domains that until now have largely ignored the environmental dimension, even though arguably they have contributed more than their fair share to its manifestation.

But on another level, the demise of the specialist environmental journalists with hard won knowledge of the basic sciences, politics, legalities and ethics, and with equally painstakingly acquired contacts is a matter deeply to be regretted. The German sociologist-philosopher Habermas characterised modern society as being torn between humanitarian values of fairness and justice and instrumental values of efficiency and wealth creation (see Nohrstedt, 1993, 93). He feared that the organs of media and government would distort communication in such a way as to allow the latter to dominate the former. To a large degree he appears to be right. The media remain obsessed either with economic survival, and the crisis of recession and economic demise for society, the public sphere generally and the degree of latitutde for coming beyond the immediate needs of the household. The precautionary principle, as outlined by the editors in the introductory chapter, covers the humanitarian and ecological qualities of collective existence - giving space to the weak or to the resilient and ensuring a sense of fairness for future human and nonhuman populations.

These are not the qualities that sell news stories or dominate nightly news bulletins. Sadly, if precaution is likely to get coverage, it is when it tackles the efficiency and wealth creating syndromes. Any requirement to cut a profit margin in the name of reducing greenhouse emissions places the spotlight on the uncertainties inherent in the argument. Media coverage tends to be channelled to protecting a variant of business as usual: despite its serious efforts, it is not so good at uncovering the heart of social conscience, particularly where what the editors call "ecological space" and "historical environmental debt repayment" are concerned. We await a more creative dialogue between the advocates of the precautionary principle and the editors of the media who control the message channels.

Newspapers

Newspapers do not deal in abstract concepts like the precautionary principle. Nor does the news on radio or the television. We report events, deaths, crimes, disasters, strikes, deals, court cases, love affairs, scandals, what policy-makers say and do and even what makes people laugh. We explain everything in simple English, in case the reader or listener is hearing about the subject for the first time. So we have no use for phrases of "principles" which require a paragraph's explanation. We do also publish views. But the existence of the views in the newspaper or bulletin is dependent on news values. Views are partly a way of explaining what has happened, partly of provoking further discussion. Comment only follows disaster, atrocity, Cabinet or Summit, triumph or shame. By the time the media get involved, something has gone wrong.

That, I believe, is as it should be. So if you want the reader or watcher of news to understand the precautionary principle, wait for a chemical disaster, a tanker on the rocks, or five dry summers in a row. That is not to say that we in the news media have no part to play in bringing about a more widespread belief in the precautionary principle, or, to put it another way, the avoidance of unacceptable risk. We help to bring about its incorporation into policy by writing about its opposite: disaster. Or, ideally, if we are lucky and well informed, potential disaster. A few well-corroborated scare stories - chemical leaks, rare climatic events, or well-reported court cases against cowboy companies - can be very useful in attracting public attention towards potentially unacceptable risks.

That accounts for the rational side of the job. But we all know there is often something close to the irrational about what grabs public attention. News has fashions. The waves of hype are hard to resist - "The worst tanker disaster to hit Britain's shore" someone inserted in my copy about the Braer disaster. The hype, fanned by the over-zealous enthusiams of the dedicated minority, generally bears along the seeds of the reaction. The media helped create a new understanding of the risks of pollution in the North Sea by banging on, often quite erroneously, about the effects that sewage disposal at sea was having in 1987. (We have had less of an effect on the true disgrace of the North Sea ecosystem, overfishing.) We helped to push government towards precautionary measures on the climate by seizing on dying seals, rainforests, and a froth of disparate environmental ills. Eventually the up-tempo 1980s, turned into the recession-bound 1990s and the mood changed. The public got bored. It was right to do so. The public is always right in our business.

The public does get bored with issues, particularly insoluble ones like Balkan wars and global warming. It is a separate question, not an easy one to answer, whether the down-turn of media interest in environment in Britain was caused by the recession or the arrival of a Prime Minister who gave an ear to those more anxious to stress the costs of environmental measures, of avoiding seemingly-remote risks. Mr. Major's has not been a Government which has had much of a priority for the environment. So the media have rightly concentrated its reporting on what it did see as the Government's agenda.

There is also the down-market pressure which hits all privately-owned media in a time of recession. Editors know that as the winds of war, drought or recession swirl outside, the public, particularly those struggling to survive financially, wants to hear of nothing but trivia, human interest and how the other half lives. These are the moments in which it takes skill to get a story into the news about risks which will affect the public some time in the future, or which threaten something of other-than-economic importance such as landscape or wildlife. But it can be done. To succeed, that story has to be robust, in news or sensation terms, and to explain exactly what it means to each individual. We have a number of often-irritating trigger words - anglers, farmers, motorists, walkers, animal-lovers, nature-lovers - which serve to tell our news editors that we are talking about a significant constituency of interest. The bigger the constituency, the bigger the prominence for the story.

My simple submission on what the media can do about ensuring the principle of precaution is taken seriously in public life is to employ someone on every newsdesk to do a job like mine. The only form of precaution that the media should be concerned with is employing someone whose role is to look sceptically at science, instead of reporting everything scientists say with glee; someone with a broad brief to poach other people's subjects, to make connections between industries, to steal stories from the business correspondent and to recognise disasters real and potential, home and foreign. In short to be an environment correspondent. I am totally opposed to this person being "trained". The best position to be in is not that of the true specialist but that of an educated layman who, as a reporter, *represents* the environmental constituency, which understands these kinds of risks, to the outside world. Wide experience as a reporter is useful. A science subject would help. The only essential is the ability to translate the understanding of the true specialists into layman's English.

We have just been through a testing time for correspondents of this kind - and I like to think that the cynics among the media editors, who thought the environmental boom was a passing fashion, lost out. The environmental media corps grew dramatically in the 1980s. By 1988 everyone, even the Sun, had one. By 1992, there was a reckoning going on. Editors, to a man, scaled down or abolished their environment coverage. Last year the Observer and Daily Telegraph scaled down from two correspondents to one (the Observer losing, in the process, the doyen of environment correspondents, Geoffrey Lean, to the Independent on Sunday). The Guardian maintained a staff of two, and a weekly environment page, but this has moved towards the back of the book. The FT alone maintained the quality of its coverage and the size of its staffing, with the inventive role of "Resources Editor", David Lascelles, in addition to "Environment Correspondent", Bronwen Maddox. But the Press Association made its environment correspondent a science and health correspondent. The Mail never re-appointed an environment correspondent after Sean Ryan. The Express's James Davies took on industry and health as well as environment. The Times lost the excellent Mike McCarthy by underestimating his worth, tried to do without an environment correspondent at all, then found themselves appointing a less-experienced journalist to do the same job within six weeks.

A year on, I think the environment constituency has now won back its place at the media feast, just by the number of events of public interest that need covering every day. Whether it has yet won enough tickets at the feast is another question. Most broadsheet newspapers and some of the broadcast media know that news is a rollercoaster ride. Sometimes your specialist correspondent's stories will not be used at all, sometime they will be on the front page. Their willingness to employ a correspondent who consistently gets little into the news is limited. Rightly. But I am reassured at the coverage still being given in some of the better papers to environmental issues - and therefore to the kind of risks that environmentalists worry about - as we come out of recession. And I am even more reassured by the number of colleagues from the European and American media that I run into at conferences from time to time.

I believe there is a continuing need for what we environment correspondents do. But I am entirely happy that there are still others in the British media do not see it that way. That gives us a competitive edge. There is plenty to write about every day for anyone who understands the principle that the polluter should pay (but usually doesn't); or the precautionary principle should be observed (but usually isn't) because these failures, these instances of neglect or political hypocrisy, are also potential news stories, waiting to be pounded upon when something goes wrong. And the knowledge in the minds of politicians or captains of industry that someone is there reading the wires for precisely these things on newsdesks around the world is a big help in changing the course of political, or industrial debate, ensuring that some thought is involved, at least, before the short-term decision is taken.

I am not sure what makes me think so - perhaps it is, peversely, the growing sense that the Government isn't necessarily handling the sustainability debate too well - but I am now more confident that the British media has recognised that environmental risks are worth covering day-in, day-out than I was two years ago. We have come through. And that is as it should be.

References

Downs, A. 1972. Up and down with ecology: the issue attention cycle. Public Interest 28, 38-50.

Nohrstedt, S.A. 1993. Communicative action in the risk society: public relations strategies, the media and nuclear powers. In. A. Hansen (ed) The Mass Media and Environmental Issues. Leicester University Press, Leicester, 81-104.

Chapter 10

The Precautionary Principle and Release of Genetically Modified Organisms (GMOS) to the Environment

By Julie Hill

Editorial Introduction

The release of genetically modified organisms generates both excitement and apprehension. There is always a tension between a desire to innovate and a fear of creating an uncontrollable outcome with devastating faultlines in the "natural" part of evolution. For this reason the biotechnology industry is subject to unusual scrutiny. It is also very mindful of its awesome responsibilities to creation. This is why there is a heated debate between the industry, regulators and active citizen groups over how far regulation should be based on proactive process-based standards, as opposed to the more familiar, reactive, product-based criteria (Tait and Levidow, 1992; Levidow and Tait, 1992). Because of both genetic complexity and uncertainty of outcome, the precautionary approach is preferred, simply because cause and effect are so difficult to isolate. Indeed, the more such organisms are created and released, the more complicated cause and effect linkages become. Thus there is a presumption that an environmental hazard is possible rather than that proof should always first be required. This puts the onus on the producer to show that no known analogue of an experimental genetic creation has caused demonstable harm.

This in turn poses a problem for the regulatory process itself. How open should it be? What additional safeguards should be imposed? How widely representative should be the review today? How far should it incoporate non-scientific but informed opinion, yet avoid either bureaucratic inertia or undue public anxiety? These are not easy questions to answer because genetically modified organisms apply to such a range of processes, products and circumstances of use. In general countries are taking a cautious line, largely because this particular technological innovation coincided with the emergence of a risk averse culture. Ten years earlier and a more reactive approach would surely have been put in place, as is the case for pharmaceuticals and pesticides. Ten years later and the technology would probably have developed in an even more hostile regulatory environment as society begins to shun natural manipulation for its own sake. The so-called "need" justification of such products would have provided more troublesome regulatory hurdle than it creates at present.

Tait and Levidow (1992, 227) point out that a strong precautionary approach also has considerable implications for the structure and inherent competitiveness of the industry. The small, fleet-of-foot, firm cannot provide the cash for the time and legal backup necessary to ensure a successful product. The industry tends to be dominated by big players in chemical conglomerates with the capacity to withstand litigation and protracted out of court compensatory settlements. Ironically the risk averse culture is also generating the demand for environmentally "friendly" processes and products that save energy and tread lightly on ecosystems. Here is where biotechnology can score success. Hence the unresolved business between innovation and rejection, progress and regress, cooperative competition and industrial hegemony.

Consequently, by default more than by design, the state financially supports the compensatory element of any unforseeable adversity consequent on a GMO release. By backing its regulatory regime, and by accepting that the good faith of regulatory compliance has estimated the state is a basis for financial liability. Society prefers to back the innovative, progressive elements in economic evolution, even at the expense of certain risk. At least for the present, precaution can be regarded as a double edged sword for the biotechnology industry. The more tough the regulatory requirement, and the more representative the review committee procedures, the greater the social acceptance of support following reasonable compliance.

This may turn out to be a heavy price to pay, for the regulatory barriers will be very demanding. Perhaps more attention should be given to the range of regulatory structures and criteria for review than even now exists in all its administrative complexity.

The UK Government's 1993 Strategy for Sustainable Development states that 'The UK adopted a precautionary approach to modern biotechnology because the lack of experience meant that it was not possible to predict the risks to humans and the environment' (HM Government, 1994, 33). On some of the most commonly accepted interpretations of the precautionary principle this is not a valid claim.

What are GMOs?

Genetic modification is a sub-set of a group of technologies which harness biological processes and which are often generically referred to as 'biotechnology'. Genetically modified organisms (GMOs) are any plants, animals or micro-organisms that have had their internal genetic structure altered artificially in order to change their outward characteristics. Most applications of the technology are in the fields of pharmaceuticals and agriculture. For instance, sheep can be given human genes so that they can manufacture valuable substances such as human blood clotting agents in their milk. Potatoes can be given genes from bean plants that help confer a natural insect resistance. Toxins from scorpions can be inserted into viruses that attack caterpillars to make the virus a more effective pesticide. Tomatoes can have their own genes rearranged in order to delay the process of decomposition.

Any experiments or products involving genetic modified organisms which are outside contained facilities such as laboratories or factories are termed 'releases' to the environment. This covers everything from a few plants being put into a field as part of an experiment to tomatoes being sold in the supermarket. Releases have been taking place in the UK since 1986, with around 75 to date. World-wide, the number of releases is estimated to be about 1400 (OECD, 1993).

Why could they be a risk to the environment?

The major concern about releases of GMOs is that they might cause similar problems to some non-modified organisms. There are many examples of plants, animals and micro-organisms introduced into new environments, whether deliberately or accidentally, which have found a competitive advantage, and have become established to the point of being pests. Such 'invasions' of 'exotics' include well-documented examples such as Japanese Knotwood, introduced into the UK as a garden plant and now a major pest in parts of Wales; and Dutch Elm Disease, a fungus introduced accidentally. Very few introductions, probably less than 1 in 100, pose any risk of becoming pests, and often it should have been possible to predict that they would be competitive in advance - for instance if they have high reproduction rates. However, the concern is that in some cases it is very difficult to pinpoint what combination of environmental conditions turns an introduction into a pest, especially as the process can take place over decades. The same uncertainties apply to genetically modified organisms, which, because they carry new genes or have had their own genes rearranged, are effectively 'exotics'.

There is particular concern about the genetic modification of viruses, since the way in which they function as well as their relationship to the wider environment are not, in general, well understood. Lastly, even less well understood or articulated, is the concern that genetic modification, particularly of micro-organisms, might in some way interfere with basic ecological processes such as cycling of nutrients and weather patterns. This is the uncertainty of indeterminacy outlined by the editors in their introduction to this section. This fear of the possibly catastrophic unknown, together with an instinctive dislike of tampering with nature, helps to reinforce a precautionary reaction.

GMOs are also considered to have qualities not shared by chemical hazards. They are living organisms, and thus potentially capable of replicating in the environment. A GMO that becomes a serious pest might be difficult to eradicate: it cannot simply be discontinued in the same way as most chemical discharges. Risk aversion is at its most potent when cause and effect are novel, out of phase with accepted norms of scientific assurance, and potentially uncontrollable.

Where does the precautionary principle come in?

According to the UK Government (1994, 33), 'The UK adopted a precautionary approach to modern biotechnology because the lack of experience meant that it was not possible to predict the risks to humans and the environment'. The main component of this so-called 'precautionary approach' is a regulatory regime that requires anyone proposing to do contained work with GMOs, or release them to the environment to apply for permission to do so. The existence of this regulatory regime in the UK has been driven primarily by two EC Directives agreed in 1990. One was the Directive on the Deliberate Release into the Environment of Genetically Modified Organisms (9644/89). The other was the Directive on the Contained Use of Genetically Modified Organisms. The Royal Commission on Environmental Pollution (1989) strongly recommended precautionary controls. This influential body may well have stimulated UK regulations even without the EC requirements.

The main reason that the regulatory regime is considered precautionary is that it has been put in place in advance of any observed harm from the release of GMOs. The lack of observed harm is not surprising given the relatively small number of releases that have taken place worldwide, and the fact that any problems could take many years to show up. The development of a regulatory regime was widely welcomed by environmentalists and concerned scientists as an attempt to minimise the possible negative effects of a new technology from the very start, rather than waiting until serious problems had been demonstrated.

So how precautionary is the regulatory regime in its operation?

The basis of the system is that all releases in the UK must have a formal consent from the 'competent authority'. In effect this is the Department of the Environment. Anyone proposing to make a release must produce a risk assessment, based on consideration of the characteristics of the organisms being modified, the characteristics of the organism donating the genetic material being used to achieve the modification; the characteristics of the modified result; and the characteristics of the environment into which it is being released. Regulators, taking into account the advice of an advisory body, must decide whether they agree with the conclusions of the risk assessment, and whether they want to put any conditions on the release such conditions, for instance, might include changes to the procedure or instructions for monitoring the results.

However, there are considerable problems in undertaking risk assessments. Firstly, as discussed above, there is limited knowledge about the nature of the hazards involved, since none have been observed as a result of releasing GMOs. There is considerable argument about the validity of the analogy to 'exotics', since these involve introduction of a whole new organism. Many genetic modifications, by contrast, involve only a few genes and result in changes to outward characteristics that are considered by those doing the work as very small and very specific. Many of the subjects of genetic modification, for instance crop plants, are not themselves exotic to the environments into which they are introduced, and anyway require considerable attention and care to survive at all. It is thus argued that they would have to undergo very radical modifications to have a substantially different relationship with the environment to the one they have already.

On the other hand, it is argued that given the complexity of the environment and ecological processes, and our lack of knowledge of they function, GMOs may pose long-term hazards which have not been observed even in non-modified organisms, indeed, have not yet been imagined. It is not just the individual GMOs being introduced that have to be considered, but the extent to which they may be able to pass on their new genes to closely related organisms, and what kinds of unpredicted and unpredictable genetic combinations might result.

If the nature of the hazard is hard to determine, it is even harder to determine the magnitude of the consequence of a hazard being realised. This uncertainty is also related to the complexity of the environment. To some strands of scientific thought, the environment is a robust system capable of absorbing considerable change and perturbation before anything that we might consider 'damage' occurs. To others, ecological processes are delicately balanced and easily disrupted, and any unintended changes are to be avoided. This argument was introduced by the editors in the opening chapter of this volume.

A complication to considering the magnitude of consequences is the lack of any accepted measure of 'damage' in this context. Section 106 of the Environmental Protection Act 1990, which contains the primary legislation for the regulatory regime, effectively defines 'harm' to the environment as any unanticipated change. However, without clear guidelines this would probably be hard to argue in court. The environment is constantly changing, both through its own processes of evolution and through man's activities. In the tradition of British law, the assumption is that some common sense view of what any reasonable person would constitute as damage would emerge as a criterion. Guidance to regulations already makes some assumptions, for instance by asserting that loss of a species would be considered serious damage.

Lastly, determining the probability of realisation of a hazard is effectively impossible. There are so many different variables in terms of the environmental factors that could make a difference that putting numbers to any one of them is a meaningless exercise. The risk assessment system as currently applied seeks only to classify releases into high and low risk based on what is known about characteristics of recipient, donor and a best guess about the characteristics of the resulting GMO. There is, as yet, no scale of specific outcomes following release.

The majority of releases that have come before the regulatory system in the UK so far have been alloed to go ahead, not on the basis that it is certain that they won't cause harm, but harm seem highly unlikely given the specific modifications made. However, it is generally acknowledged that the grounds on which releases are judged safe cannot be assumed to hold in the longer term. This is why the regulations contain provisions for strict surveillance and regulatory reporting.

The regulatory regime is a response to scientific uncertainty in that it seeks to scrutinise proposals for release and to consider their possible implications before they are allowed to take place. However, given the difficulties outlined above, the regulatory system cannot be regarded as rigorously preventative. The judgements made as a result of the risk assessment process cannot be that definitive. If the precautionary principle were to be interpreted as seeking to prevent damage in any absolute sense, application of the precautionary principle would not allow releases to go ahead at our present stage of knowledge.

In their opening chapter, the editors indicate that the precautionary principle may be interpreted as a mechanism for ensuring 'margins of tolerance' or 'ecological space'. Since we have only a limited idea of the nature of the hazard, we can have no realistic knowledge of what the margins of tolerance might be. Some commentators have come forward with the notion of 'genetic pollution', implying that any genes spread in the environment that would not have arrived there naturally should be considered undesirable. This implies no 'margin of tolerance' for GMOs and hence no releases under a precautionary approach. This is the strong precaution principle outlined in the introduction.

There are elements of the regulatory regime that could, on a generous interpretation, be considered to be contributing to a precautionary approach. Those carrying out releases are under a duty to report anything that changes the assumptions made in the risk assessment, whether it is new scientific data or changes to the experimental design, or direct observations on the behaviour of the releases GMOs. They are also required to use the principle of Best Practicable Means Not Entailing Excessive Cost to keep organisms 'under control' and prevent damage to the environment. David Pearce in Chapter 7 considers the application of BATNEEC and the goal of strict prevention to be incompatible: in all probability entailing costs considered excessive.

There are also provisions in consents for monitoring the results of releases, and feeding this information back to the regulatory system. However, monitoring is not geared to identifying long-term effects - it is unusual for monitoring requirements to extend beyond three years. It has been suggested that the time for a descendent of a GMO to show 'weedy' characteristics could be at least 50 years. Many of the discussions about the need for further monitoring founder on the question of what exactly to monitor. This reflects the problem of not knowing clearly what the hazards might be.

In the face of these unknowables, those undertaking risk assessments (i.e. those proposing to make a release) and those whose job it is to verify them (the Department of the Environment advised by ACRE, the Advisory Committee on Release to the Environment) are forced to work on a certain level of generalisation. Under 'fast track' procedures introduced in 1994, proposals are classified as 'low hazard' if the organism being manipulated is judged not to 'possess inherent characteristics that pose a risk of damage to the UK environment' (Department of the Environment, 1994). The present list of genetically modified organisms so classified consists of crop plants that have low prospects of survival in the environment because of frost-sensitivity. In addition the trait being engineered into them is not one that could be expected to alter the ecological competitiveness of the plant or cause any problems if passed to related plants. Such traits include herbicide resistance and certain genetic markers. Proposals may also be classified as 'low risk', meaning that there may be a hazard but of modest significance. Here particular measures are taken as part of the experiment to prevent spread, for instance taking flowers off a plant before pollen has had a chance to form in order to minimise the passing on of genes.

The Department of the Environment felt able to introduce the fast-track procedure because of what it describes as 'the light of experience'. However, it must be understood that this refers to ACRE's experience of considering release proposals and finding itself giving the same kind of advice to certain types of releases. This practice suggests that 'generic advice' could be given through a guidance note, and the secretariat could make judgements on similar future proposals without referring back to ACRE. 'Experience' in this context does not mean experience of the effects on the environment of release of GMOs. In this sense, the 'fast track' procedures do not represent any alteration to the assumptions and methodology of risk assessments, so in this respect they are not any more or less precautionary. However, it could be argued that by-passing ACRE scrutiny and the effort to get proposals through the system more quickly could result in important details being overlooked.

The move to fast-track procedures has been one of the most political issues that ACRE has had to deal with. The Committee is largely composed of scientific experts in relevant fields, including ecology, microbiology and genetics, plus a member with a pressure group background (myself) and a farmer. While most members of the committee recognised from the inception of the system in 1990 that in the long term it would be possible to clear certain proposals more quickly, the introduction of 'fast track' procedures has been speeded up by considerable pressure from the biotechnology industry to reform what they see as an unduly bureaucratic system. Some sections of the industry reject the idea that a precautionary, or pro-active approach to the technology is necessary.

Many commentators agree that the release of GMOs does have the potential, albeit with low probability, of causing irreversible environmental damage, and some have argued for the precautionary approach to translate into a moratorium on releases. There are two major difficulties with this position. One is that a moratorium implies a temporary stop while new knowledge is gained. However, given the practical difficulties of understanding the vast complex of ecological interactions that make up the environment, it is difficult to see what kinds of new knowledge would be both within our reach yet also lead to greater confidence about releases. The second is that the issue of proportionality is inevitably raised. The price of a moratorium may be the loss of applications of genetic technology that actually improve the environment. The possibilities of crops manipulated to need less pesticides and fertilisers, and micro-organisms modified to clean-up pollutants, are often raised. To the extent that the precautionary principle involves a cost-benefit calculation, its application could arguably involve a judgement that a complete stop on release of GMOs is not 'cost-effective'.

References

Department of the Environment 1994. Fast Track Procedures for Certain GMO Releases. DoE, London.

Levidow, L. and Tait, J. 1992. Release of genetically modified organisms: precautionary legilsation. Project Appraisal, 7(2), 93-105.

OECD 1993. Field Review of Transgenic Plants 1986-1992: An Analysis. Organisation for Economic Cooperation and Development, Paris.

O'Riordan, T. 1993. Interpreting the Precautionary Principle, CSERGE Working Paper PA 93-03, University of East Anglia, Norwich.

Royal Commission on Environmental Pollution 1989. The Release of Genetically Modified Organisms to the Environment. 13th Report. HMSO, London.

Tait, J. and Levidow, L. 1992. Proactive and reactive approaches to risk regulation: the case of biotechnology. Futures, 219-231.

Chapter 11

The Precautionary Principle in Local Government

By Janice Morphet and Tony Hams

Introduction

As yet in the UK, there is little explicit discussion on the role and use of the precautionary principle in local government. However, this belies both historic approaches and a recent surge of new initiatives which together make local authorities important instruments of the delivery of the precautionary principle.

Local authorities were set up in their current form over a century ago as an arm of the state primarily concerned with environmental regulation. Early local authorities were concerned with housing, health and sanitation matters as their primary responsibilities in response to rapid urban change. There was a recognition that both the public and the business community wanted at least a preventive if not a precautionary approach to be adopted.

Some of these pressures for precaution also arose in the voluntary sector but were subsequently taken over by local authorities. One good example of the precautionary principle in operation is characterised by the open space movement founded by Ocatvia Hill. She campaigned against to the potential loss of Hampstead Heath to additional housing development. Once the precautionary principle had been applied to the provision of open space, local authorities were seen as guardians of these community decisions.

Local authorities have become one of the main agents of the

Government in the application of environmental regulations. The Environment Protection Act 1990 Section 7, for example places local authorities under an obligation to render harmless releases from works when authorising processes. However, unlike other European countries, e.g. Denmark, local authorities are not the only agencies to have this role. Furthermore, the role of local authorities have been reduced over the last decade as their regulatory functions have been devolved to privatised utilities and other Government agencies.

However, local authorities in the future are likely to have a more central role in both monitoring environmental standards and coordinating the community's role in achieving environmental quality. This will be primarily through the mechanisms of environmental auditing and the development of Local Agenda 21 which are discussed later in this chapter. Unless there is both information and community commitment to sustainable development, then it will be difficult to apply the precautionary principle. Sustainable development requires the acceptance of shared responsibility and ownership from all sectors of the community.

Local authorities as regulators

Regulation is one way of ensuring that the precautionary principle is applied in practice. Existing and future environmental regulations are the teeth of the precautionary principle and without them its application can be no more than a hope. The adoption and implementation of regulations implies that the community has agreed the extent to which the principle should be applied.

Regulations ensure anticipatory intervention and are based on economically effective principles which reflect the true costs of actions. In the short term, these costs may appear higher than current costs, but when the long term or life cycle of a development or product is taken into account, then the precautionary principle may save money. In the Netherlands, for example, there is a national commitment to manufacture products to higher standards so that they do not have to be replaced so frequently.

There are examples where this type of approach is beginning to emerge in the UK. The Department of Transport is considering assessing road construction tenders on the basis of both initial cost and subsequent maintenance. So although a particular method of road building may initially be more expensive, if it requires less maintenance it will be cheaper in the long run. A further example is in the provision of landscaped areas. Grass is the cheapest medium to use, but extremely expensive to maintain - it may need to be cut fifteen times per year! Slower growing shrubs may have a higher initial cost but require far less annual maintenance and can provide better ecological corridors on roadside verges, for example. Such areas can also have a better visual impact.

However, it is in the exercise of its planning functions where local authorities are perceived to have the greatest regulatory role. Since the mid 1970s, this regulatory role has been questioned, not least in respect of its perceived restrictions on economic development. However, during the 1980s, the development boom put pressure on many sites which had become informal open spaces over the years. The response from the public to these pressures was great. Many people found that the planning system, which had been primarily readjusted to 'getting things done', provided no real protection against unwanted development. This weakness in the system was caused both by the local planning authorities failure to produce development plans and the perceived increase in the use of the appeal mechanism.

As a result of this concern, the pendulum has swung back. The planning system is perhaps now stronger than it has ever been before. In 1991, the Planning and Compensation Act, in Section 54a, established a requirement for up to date plans for all local authority areas. It also confirmed that the plan, once adopted, would be the primary consideration against which any planning application would be judged, whether by the local planning authority or the Secretary of State on appeal.

Such an approach should allow better protection for a variety of sites in the future. The strength of the reformed system is that it is proactive and it will provide a coverage throughout the whole the country. The new system will also enable local authorities to identify sites of special nature interest or protect green field sites where these are not identified for development. Section 54a provides a greater potential for the implementation of the precautionary principle than ever before.

The planning framework is also changing in response to post Rio requirements to introduce sustainability concepts the plan making process and the European Union's Fifth Environmental Action Plan, 'Towards Sustainability (1992). The recent full review of the DoE's Planning Policy Guidelines (PPGs), which are critical in the preparation and interpretation of planning policy, has moved consistently in this direction.

The application of capacity planning principles is more common in land use planning systems in other European countries e.g. Denmark but they are already beginning to seep into the U.K. process. As yet, the potential capacity of an area in respect of water provision or drainage or refuse disposal would not be regarded by the Department of the Environment to be valid reasons for refusing a planning application, although this may change in the future. However, there are other areas such as the natural environment and perhaps the capacity of the existing road network which are now being increasingly examined by local authorities in their preparation of plans and consideration of planning applications. It is also clear from the DoE's Guide to Environmental Appraisal of Development Plans (1993) that State of the Environment Reports will be increasingly used to define environmental baselines and capacities.

The local authority therefore has the role of identifying local capacity and applying the precautionary principle. It will also have the regulatory teeth to apply it. The planning system also has a direct role in regulating hazardous substances and in the application of the EU's Directive on environmental assessment, which is currently under review.

BOX 11.1 PPGs: ENVIRONMENTAL CONTENT

PPG 1 General Principles and Policies..the planning system, and the preparation of the development plan in particular can contribute to the Governments objective for sustainable development [para 3]

PPG 4 Industrial and Commercial development and small firms the principles of man made development require the responsible use of natural and man made resources[para 2]

PPG 6 Town Centres and Retail Development promotes town centres rather than out of town retailing in order to minimise the need to travel [para 2, paras 11ff]

PPG 12 Development Plans and Regional Planning Guidance growth and development must be sustainable - Government will develop policies which are sustainable,attention must be given to future generations to ensure that irreversible harm is not done - development plans have an essential role to play in achieving the Government's sustainable strategy[paras 1.8,,6.8]

PPG 13 Transport commitment to CO_2 reduction, public transport, environmental assessment and integrated approaches to planning and transport to be supported; inter and intra urban road pricing to be pursued

PPG 20 Coastal Planning [para 1.1]

PPG 21 Tourism tourism strategies must be fully consistent with the Government's commitment to achieve sustainable development[paras 1.2 and 1.7]

PPG 22 Renewable Energy supported in order to reduce harmful emissions and be more environmentally acceptable [para 5, para 8]

Source: PPGs DoE/HMSO and Index of National Planning Policies CPRE 1993

The practical approaches of local government towards implementing sustainable strategies have been maturing rapidly. Initially many local authorities adopted the Friends of the Earth Model Environmental Charter which endorsed a basic commitment to the environment on the part of the locality. This approach has been supplemented in a variety of ways. Many local authorities have developed environment strategies or Action Plans in an attempt to draw together their commitments.

In terms of the application of the precautionary principle in local government, one of the key initiatives has been the introduction of State of the Environment audits by many local authorities. Until recently, local authorities primarily took an interest in that part of the local authorities environment over which they had some control. However, with the widespread use of State of the Environment reports, local authorities are beginning to amass an increasing amount of information on the local physical environment which aids both long term monitoring and the development of a capacity planning approach.

BOX 11.2 Undertaking an SoE involves ten key stages:

1. establishing a linked internal and external mechanism for dialogue, consultation an partnership based on the round table format;

2. agreeing [via the coordinating mechanism] the environmental components which are to be assessed as part of the SoE;

3. agreeing the sustainability indicators which are to be used and measured;

4. collecting the data and organising it into a management database;

5. using the information in the database to measure the sustainability indicators;

6. presenting the results and issues these give rise to;

7. publishing and publicising the SoE;

8. defining sustainability targets from the indicator/issue analysis;

9. incorporating the targets into environmental policy

10. monitoring the performance of the targets and policy, the effectiveness of the coordinating mechanism and reviewing/updating all three

from Morphet et al. 1994

Once the state of the local environment has been audited, and the local community has developed both a commitment and targets for action, the next concern is to ensure that the process of change is monitored. This can be undertaken in a number of ways. The first is to reaudit the state of the environment at regular intervals. This process can also be allied with a range of targets for improvement. It is also possible to undertake specific consumption audits of energy and waste, again against set targets. Finally, in the longer term, it will be possible to monitor change against a group of sustainable indicators which will incorporate the environmental,social and economic dimensions of community progress towards sustainability. The work to develop these indicators is underway in the UK and is also programmed as part of the EC's Fifth Environmental Action Programme.

All these initiatives, in conjunction with many others, including the use of the environmental management and audit scheme for local authorities, purchasing strategies, environmental awareness training for staff and the development of green accounting techniques, will not, in themselves result in a precautionary approach. Local authorities have also made a commitment to sustainable development through a Declaration issued in 1993 as part of the process of preparing for the UK's National Sustainability Strategy.

However, the real test in any locality will come when the environment and the economy are seen to be in conflict. Is a better environment tomorrow worth more than jobs today? In reality, there does not need to be a conflict between the two. Any company setting up which does not operate good energy management policies or clean technology is unlikely to survive for long in the face of higher standards being demanded by main suppliers. The environment is seen to be an area of comparative advantage whilst the problems left by many industrial processes in urban and rural areas demonstrate daily the wisdom of the precautionary principle. The precautionary principle can save money and jobs in the longer term. As the EC implements its 'environment' first policy in the field of structural funds and through the Committee of the Regions, localities have come to appreciate the benefits such a clean approach can bring.

BOX 11.3 WHAT ARE SUSTAINABLE INDICATORS?

Sustainable indicators will provide a means of assessing the progress towards more sustainable development. Together they will address a range of generic issues including:

* environment and economy
* environment and health
* environmental rights, equity and quality of life
* impact of lifestyles and consumption patterns
* environment and culture

These indicators should:

* provide a representative picture of conditions, pressures and society's responses;
* be simple, easy to interpret and able to show trends over time
* be responsive to changes
* provide a basis for international comparisons
* have a target or threshold against which to compare present state and future change and so that users can assess the significance of the values associated with it.
* be well founded in technical and scientific terms
* be readily available
* be capable of updating

[after LGMB study/IDLG]

Over the last five years local authorities have been seeking to develop their local environmental role. This has been in response to local public opinion and to a view that local authorities are the only locally based agencies which can provide initial community leadership. Agenda 21, which was agreed in Rio in 1992, has an emphasis on participation by all levels of government. This implies an extensive and active contribution by local government.

This approach has been endorsed in Chapter 28 of Agenda 21 and is commonly known as Local Agenda 21 [LA21]. Over two thirds of the statements in Agenda 21, which have been adopted by 178 national governments worldwide, including the British Government, cannot be delivered without the commitment and cooperation of local government. Local Agenda 21 has the backing of the Local Authority Associations and the British initiative was launched in 1992 under the management of a steering group. The national steering group directs future programmes and monitors progress. This group has appointed a project officer who is located at the Local Government Management Board [LGMB]. The programme of work set by the national steering group incorporates a number of key issues including

* sustainable indicators development project

* declaration on sustainable development

* support for international activities through participation in Partnerships for Change and Global Forum

* economic development/environment project

* round tables on specific issues

* development of training packages

* developing the eco-management and audit scheme

* publication of regular update [available from LGMB]

* promoting cooperation with GreenNet

Local authorities are encouraged to develop a LA21 for their community, in effect to define a sustainable strategy at the local level. There are a number of ways of pursuing this task, whilst much of the work which may already have been undertaken within a local authority can be brought within the ambit of LA21. In some local authorities work on LA21 is supported by to a special green team of officers or through the appointment of an environmental coordinator. Elsewhere it is undertaken by mainstream staff.

The implementation of LA21 relies heavily on partnerships involving local authorities, businesses, voluntary and community sectors. This importantly also includes individuals. It is considered that local authorities are well placed to facilitate these partnerships although there is still some way to go in defining the best approach to sustainable development at the local level. One way of doing this through Local Agenda 21 is to establish local consultative processes which can:

* seek consensus on the meaning of sustainable development at the local level

* to establish partnership frameworks to work towards sustainability

* to share and disseminate the information and expertise developed both within the UK and the international local government community

One way of progressing this is to establish a LA21 Forum or Round Table of local interest groups or stakeholders which conform to the groups identified in Agenda 21. The forum may then decide to sub-divide itself into Special Working Groups (SWGs) each to deal with a particular set of problems or the involvement of particular groups. These groups and the forum can have an important role in defining the sustainable strategy at the local level. They can achieve this through dialogue, exchange of information and the commitments of members to good environmental practice.

One of the key elements of this approach is that the local authority acts as a catalyst in forming the environmental forum, acting as an 'enabler'. Once the forum has been formed and begins to operate efficiently, the Council can gradually relinquish its position as leader of the forum to become an equal, participating member. The forum can develop the practices of local sustainability which are then communicated to others outside the forum to adopt where applicable. The Council can also document achievements made by the forum on sustainable development.

The whole approach of LA21 is to explicitly apply the principles of sustainable development at the local level by all stakeholders. The understanding and application of the precautionary principle at the local level must be one of the key tasks to be achieved in the process. Indeed as LA21 gets underway in the U.K. and beyond, the level of understanding of the principle and the best means of application should be advanced rapidly.

Local companies, schools and community groups all have a role to play. There are already some examples of the way in which this is working. In some local authorities there are many small working parties dealing with different issues on behalf of the whole community. Elsewhere, local groups are undertaking detailed surveys of the open or wild spaces and assessing what is required in order to help them function better.

There are also new ways of working with households and

individuals. Based on a Dutch model, ecofeedback schemes are being developed in order to encourage whole communities to monitor their environmental performance, using the principle of changing individual behaviour.

In any community based approach the role of the educational institutions and the media are critical. Local Universities and colleges are often major employers and consumers. They can provide a source of expertise and of community leadership. The press and local radio can also reach many who would not necessarily attend a public meeting or read a local authority leaflet. Both can be important in opinion forming and providing support to community initiatives such as LA21.

BOX 11.4 USING INFORMATION TO CHANGE BEHAVIOUR: ECOFEEDBACK

Several cities in the Netherlands have experimented with eco-feedback, which requires householders to regularly record their energy consumption, compare it to locally and nationally published norm data, which allows the individual householder to judge whether he or she is below or above a national easily achievable savings target. Reports so far suggest that the approach indeed helps to reduce the amount of energy consumed.

Similar experiments are scheduled to start in several cities in the UK, with the introduction of household monitoring schemes from the minimisation of energy, waste, water and transport fields. For energy, communities will be trained in the use of monitoring their consumption against locally adjusted weather tables published in the press. Children will also be trained in these processes at school.

The feed-back mechanism in waste minimisation will be the amount of tonnage reduction achieved by the individual householder which is monitored weekly on bathroom scales; in the transport field the number of trips reduced or length shortened and/or fuel consumption can be monitored. For water, community inflows and outflows can be measured and publicised week on week.

There is also potential to develop this into a community scheme. One U.K. local authority is currently seeking to involve the retailers, pub, petrol filling station, church, medical practice and small companies which operate within the neighbourhood centre in the same scheme.

from Morphet et al. 1994

As local authorities develop an operational understanding of sustainable development, practices will develop further. In particular, there will be a growing convergence between expenditure and environmental management. There are already examples of this through energy saving programmes or purchasing policies, where good environmental practices have also become sound financial management. There will also probably be more overt moves in this direction as Central Government pursues its commitment to green accounting.

Local authorities are also facing other pressures for change which will have implications for the green agenda. The structure and management of U.K. local government is under review. Although it is as yet impossible to determine the final outcome, it seems likely that unitary authorities will emerge within a system of central government regional administration. These new local authorities will probably operate from 1996/7 and will almost immediately be required to subject the majority of their services to competitive tendering. The implications of this dual process are important.

In respect of the review, the introduction of a unitary system may provide an approach at the local level which has easier local definition for the public. At present there is inevitably some confusion of responsibilities. The same will be true of the authorities who will have clearer ownership of the local environment. As indicated above, much of implementation of sustainable development initiatives will be derived at the local level and this will continue notwithstanding the role of central government. National environmental standards have increasingly given way to those derived from the EU, where the role of the local authority is clearly defined as a key actor in the process. In time, as the EU moves to a more regionalised structure, the role of local authorities could become more important as an agent of delivery.

In this role, local authorities may come to press for increased local powers. Indeed as the public's awareness of the Freedom of Access to Environmental Information Regulation, together with potential changes in company disclosure of environmental information become more widely known, then pressure to improve local environmental standards may increase. This could be further enhanced through EU proposals for the introduction of third party rights, which could be particularly important in the environmental field. Thus communities could seek to improve the operational standards of local businesses for example as has happened in Denmark.

Other changes such as the increased control of waste landfill together with fuel taxes may propel more local authorities into waste minimisation and energy production strategies. This will have locally beneficial effects, not least in respect of water quality and habitat protection but also through the supply of lower cost energy.

At present, the lack of coordination between central government bodies and agencies on environmental matters is well known. The review of local government could help to clarify both roles and purpose, not least in strengthening local advocacy roles. Thus local councillors may be able to spend a far greater proportion of their time in campaigning for improved local standards. The increasingly transparent approach to environmental matters at EU, Government and local government levels will also serve to identify responsibilities for action. This could also be reinforced through the EU's proposals for civil liability.

Conclusion

As communities become increasingly involved in environmental issues, whether they be concerned with results of increased road capacity or the loss of green space, the need to live within our environmental means will become more important. Local authorities are concerned to ensure a good quality of life for their residents and an efficient operating environment for their business community. There may be increasing local pressure to achieve improved environmental standards through the LA21 process. Local authorities are providing the framework and community leadership for this approach to sustainable development in addition to their regulatory and monitoring roles. Although they do not, as yet, readily use the term the precautionary principle, it is clear it is one which they are already applying in practice.

References

Commission of the European Communities 1992. Towards Sustainability, The European Commission, Luxembourg.

UWE/Baker Associates 1993. Environmental Appraisal of Development Plans, Doe/HMSO London.

Morphet J., T. Hams, M. Jacobs, R. Levitt, H. Lusser and D. Taylor 1994. Greening Your Local Authority, Longman, Harlow.

Part IV

The International Dimension

Where precaution will ultimately bite is at both ends of citizenship, namely the individual household at the microlevel, and the global household at the planetary level. The more any action depends on the goodwill and understanding of others, the more a binding sense of responsibility for their wellbeing triggers precautionary action. Indeed, James Cameron makes the point that precaution as a legal principle really only came of age in international law. This is because collective agreements succeed only where individual actors suppress their selfish biasses in favour of outcomes that benefit them all right, but only when everybody agrees to the same set of rules. Clearly if an outcome could diminish the life chances of everyone alive now or yet to be born, and if the only way of securing a safeguard against the threat required everyone to agree to the same terms of compliance, then international agreements regarding environmental protection clearly are very important.

But one should beware against simple mindedness or naivete. Dan Bodansky indicates that a litigious setting can distort the basis of the public interest in favour of certain interests at the expense of others. To guild the environmental protection lily when resources or technological inventiveness is being diverted from, say the health needs of the very poor, or the protection of localised ecology so deeply meaningful to residents who may have no other access to greenery, may be doing a nation a disservice. Bodansky's important analysis reminds us that precaution is played and in a pattern of power that does not self evidently advantage those whom it is intended to assist.

Nigel Haigh shows how the emerging European Union has capitalised on the risk aversion that is built into the protection of common property resources such as multi-country airsheds, border rivers and shallow seas. Whenever a collectively owned resource is to be managed by its nation states, the precautionary principle tends to push the margins of protection towards the highest common denominator, not the lowest as is usually the case in negotiated collective agreements. This is partly because of the peculiarity of risk aversion when the outcomes of others can destroy the effort already invested by some in cleanliness or environmental safeguard.

Paradoxically the principle of precaution does not always apply to the more complex notion of burden sharing. True, in a shallow sea such as the Southern North Sea or the Mediterranean, states who have invested in sewage treatment or nutrient removal expect their neighbours to do likewise even if the contribution of the latter is not so environmentally burdensome. In this context burden sharing means equivalence of effort at reaching a collective solution, almost irrespective of the benefits and costs.

But where burden sharing means that some countries should do more to allow others the ecological space they require legitimately to develop without undue environmental constraints, the quality of precautionary mercy is not so universally applied. Thus the European Union as a whole has ratified the UN Framework Convention on Climate Change. This means that it is committed as a 12-nation entity to reducing the total emissions of carbon dioxide, methane and nitrous oxides to 1990 levels by the year 2000. To do this, however, Germany and Britain, and possibly France, need to reduce their emissions by margins greater than 1990-2000 so that the poorer states, notably Greece, Portugal, Spain and Ireland, can increase their greenhouse gas emissions while they take a little longer to shift towards a more sustainable development past. This is the spirit of precaution in the international age, but as yet there is precious little evidence that these heavyweight emission countries are prepared to bear their extra burden. The outcome will depend mightily on the legal competence of the European Union to persuade its member states to toe the line, and on the diplomatic skills of negotiators either to lead or follow public opinion on such matters. This is one of many international areas where the emerging radicalism of the precautionary principle will be sorely tested.

In Australia, as in other federal states such as Germany and Canada and the US, it is possible that the precautionary principle may be involved to give greater political leverage over states rights by central government. Ronnie Harding and Liz

Fisher hint that the recent intergovernmental agreement between the Commonwealth Government and the States invokes an element of common responsibility over resource management and environmental protection that was not so constitutionally obvious before. It also provides greater say for aboriginal peoples over their rights to sacred tribal areas and historically commonly owned resources that remain ambiguous in legal definition. So precaution in Australia may partly be a veil to ensure that all states toe the national line on safeguarding certain aspects of ecological space and critical cultural heritage, and that environmental protection laws have a measure of comparability. The authors reveal another facet of the precautionary principle, namely its role in evening out national and regional treatment of key cultural and environmental principles, both in custom and in law, so that fairness of treatment becomes enshrined in good practice and a more paramount obligation to a greater global good. If that is the case, then precaution has an emerging role that could prove indispensible for constructive intergovernmental relations.

Chapter 12

The Precautionary Principle in US Environmental Law

By Daniel Bodansky

Few things in life are certain - except, of course, death and taxes. If certainty were a requirement for action, we would never do anything. How well we do in life depends in large measure on how successfully we cope with its uncertainties.

International environmental issues are particularly uncertain. Will continued emissions of carbon dioxide and other so-called "greenhouse gases" lead to global warming? Is acid rain responsible for the decline in North American temperate forests? Do driftnets threaten the sustainable management of high seas fisheries? These are some of the many questions for which current science provides no definitive answers.

Although uncertainties about the environment have always existed, their significance as a management issue has grown in recent years, as a result of the changing nature of environmental problems. So long as environmental problems were primarily local, acute and immediate in nature, uncertainties were comparatively small and management decisions straightforward. But as we face increasingly complex, global and long-term hazards, the limits of our scientific knowledge have become more manifest.

In recent years, environmentalists have urged adoption of the so-called "precautionary principle" as a means of coping with uncertainty. Although proponents have had a hard time agreeing on its precise meaning, broadly speaking the precautionary principle says that, with respect to the environment, we should err on the side of caution; we should resolve uncertainties in favor of the environment.

In the United States, the precautionary principle underlay the first wave of federal environmental statutes in the 1970s, one of whose most "striking characteristics" was a "manifest unwillingness to wait for definitive proof" of environmental harm (Percival 1992, 441). The 1970 Clean Air Act, for example, called on regulators to apply "an ample margin of safety" in setting emissions limits for hazardous pollutants (CAA § 112, 42 USC § 7412), while the 1972 amendments to the Federal Water Pollution Control Act (later renamed the Clean Water Act) established the goal of eliminating water pollution altogether (CWA § 101, 33 USC § 1251). Thus, although the United States has often questioned the precautionary principle in international fora, US domestic law has in many respects been precautionary in nature.

The precautionary principle is a useful antidote to the traditional reluctance of governments to act until actual environmental harm has occurred. But US environmental regulation also illuminates the difficulties in implementing a precautionary approach. Consider, for example, the "ample margin of safety" standard in the 1970 Clean Air Act, which required the Environmental Protection Agency (EPA) to use a precautionary, health-based approach in regulating emissions of "hazardous air pollutants" - if necessary by setting a zero emissions standard. The effect of this ostensibly precautionary measure was just the opposite of its intent. EPA viewed it as unreasonably stringent, and, to avoid triggering its application, delayed designating substances as "hazardous." As of the mid-1980s, more than fourteen years after the passage of the Act, EPA had implemented the ample margin of safety standard for only seven substances (Dwyer 1990, 261-62).

Implementation of the Clean Water Act's "no discharge" goal has been similarly problematic. More than two decades after the Act's adoption, we still have little systematic data about the quality of the nation's waters. "[B]ut the best of admittedly poor statistics show essentially no change in water quality since the Clean Water Act took its present form" (Pedersen 1988, 69). As several commentators concluded, "The regulatory experience under the Act has taught that eliminating pollutant discharges into national waters will be far more difficult than the ... Congress thought" (Van Putten and Jackson 1986, 864).

Not only has the precautionary principle not produced the expected results; it has led to a backlash. During the last decade, US environmental law has increasingly stressed risk assessment and cost-benefit analysis, both of which, unlike the precautionary principle, presume that we have sufficient knowledge to measure risks and calculate the appropriate responses. Thus, just as international institutions such as UNEP and the North Sea Conference have begun to discover the precautionary principle, US environmental law has been moving away from it. In part this resulted from the Reagan-era opposition to environmental regulation generally. But in part it reflects a more widespread concern about the perceived over-stringency and inefficiency of many precautionary standards.

As international institutions join the growing bandwagon in favour of the precautionary principle, they could perhaps profit from the chequered US experience. If it is to be more than a slogan, we need to appreciate the complexities of translating the precautionary principle into precautionary action.

What is the Precautionary Principle?

The precautionary principle addresses two problems raised by the prevalence of scientific uncertainty in environmental decision-making. First, uncertainty creates an evidentiary problem: what must we know before taking measures to protect the environment, and with what degree of certainty? Are we justified, for example, in controlling emissions of potentially hazardous substances when there is no evidence of actual harm? Until recently, this was one of the main questions in the ozone debate. Scientific theories predicted that emissions of CFCs would deplete the ozone layer; but actual measurements of ozone depletion were not made until the mid- to late-1980s. The same problem has until now frustrated efforts to respond to the threat of global warming. Moreover, even when evidence of environmental harm is forthcoming, there is still the question, what is causing the harm? How certain must we be that the ozone hole is due to chlorine-loading or that the observed decline in temperate forests is due to acid rain before requiring emissions reductions in CFCs or sulphur dioxide respectively?

Second, uncertainty raises the management question: how should we respond to uncertain risks? This is, of course, not the only issue that must be addressed in managing environmental problems. Even if we had perfect scientific knowledge, considerable management problems would remain. Assume, for example, that definitive evidence was found that acid rain is causing forest decline, or that current levels of carbon dioxide emissions are causing global warming. What regulatory measures would be warranted? The answer is not automatic and would depend on our answers to a number of ancillary questions. What levels of forest decline and global warming are tolerable? How much are we willing to spend on control measures? To what extent should costs and benefits be balanced? These problems of regulatory policy result not from scientific uncertainty but from differing values and differing tolerance levels for environmental harm. The management problem that the precautionary principle addresses is not: how much should we try to prevent or eliminate known environmental harms? Nor does the precautionary principle tell us what levels of environmental risk are "reasonable". Rather, the precautionary principle addresses the issue: what types of regulatory approaches are appropriate given the pervasiveness of environmental uncertainty? Regulatory approaches that minimize the need for information about the causal relations between human activities and environmental harms are precautionary - for example, rules requiring the elimination of all pollution or as much pollution as technologically feasible.

Assessing uncertain risks: when are environmental actions warranted?

The principle of anticipation

Traditionally, environmental regulation in the United States (as elsewhere) depended on proof of actual harm - on "counting the dead bodies" (Percival et al. 1992, 441). For example, restrictions on discharges of mercury were imposed only after the discovery that mercury in fish had caused severe birth defects among children in Minimata, Japan. Claims could be brought under nuisance or trespass law for actual damages; but the law did not generally try to anticipate and prevent environmental harms (Belsky 1984, 6-8). Moreover, "to succeed in [a lawsuit], the plaintiff had to overcome an almost insurmountable burden of proof" (Belsky 1984, 6). He or she had to prove individualised environmental damages, caused by the activities of specific persons or entities. "Even if the plaintiff was successful in a tort action for environmental injury, the victory might not eliminate the harmful activity. Money damages could be awarded and the pollution allowed to continue" (Belsky 1984, 8).

One of the most basic elements of modern environmental statutes is a rejection of this reactive view that actual harm must be proven before undertaking environmental regulation. The 1970 National Environmental Policy Act (NEPA), for example, requires federal agencies to consider the potential environmental impacts of their activities in advance, by preparing an environmental impact statement (NEPA § 102, 42 USC § 4322). Similarly, the Clean Water and Clean Air Acts seek to prevent environmental damage resulting from water and air pollution respectively. Under these statutes, "[r]egulatory action may be taken before the threatened harm occurs; indeed, the very existence of ... precautionary legislation would seem to *demand* that regulatory action precede, and, optimally, prevent, the perceived threat" (Ethyl Corp., 541 F.2d at 13).

Identifying risk

Instead of reacting to actual harms, modern U.S. environmental statutes try to identify and prevent unreasonable *risk* of harm. For example, the House report on the 1977 Clean Air Act Amendments stated that EPA's "duty [is] to assess risks rather than wait for proof of actual harm" (HR Rpt No. 294, 1977, 49). Indeed, according to one EPA administrator, "EPA's primary mission is the reduction of risk" (Ruckelshaus 1984, 10190).

The emergence of this anticipatory, risk-based approach, can be seen in microcosm in the successive appellate court decisions in *Reserve Mining Co. v. EPA*, a mid-1970s case concerning whether to prohibit waste discharges from an iron ore processing plant. At the time of the suit, no harm to the public health had been demonstrated from the discharges. The discharges, however, contained asbestiform fibers similar to fibers known to cause disease in an occupational setting. Initially, a panel of the appellate court declined to prohibit the discharges, stating:

> The discharges may or may not result in detrimental health effects, but, for the present, that is simply unknown.... We do not think that a bare risk of the unknown can amount to proof in this case. Plaintiffs have failed to prove that a demonstrable health hazard exists (Reserve Mining, 498 F.2d at 1083-84).

On review, the full court reversed. The court agreed with the earlier decision that, "in assessing the probabilities ..., it cannot be said that the probability of harm is more likely than not." Nevertheless, the court held that, because "the public's exposure to asbestos fibers ... creates some health risk," this risk justifies "precautionary and preventive measure to protect the public health" (Id. 520)

Risk and uncertainty

Regulating risk is, of course, more precautionary than reacting to actual harm; but risk assessment need not be precautionary in the full sense of the term. Risk is a function of the magnitude and the probability of harm. Although risk involves estimates of probabilities - and hence of uncertainties about whether individual events will occur - we can sometimes have a high degree of confidence about those probabilities and consequently about the aggregate risk posed by an activity (Wilson and Crouch 1987, 267). Russian roulette for example involves a predictable one-in-six chance of death. Uncertainty, in contrast, involves what are sometimes referred to as "second-story probabilities" - that is, estimates of the probability that a given risk assessment is correct. Animal bioassays may indicate that regular saccharine use will produce one additional cancer per one million lifetimes; but what is our confidence level that this risk estimate is correct? If our confidence level is low, then the risks posed by saccharine are not only probabilistic but uncertain. In fact, the variance between high and low risk estimates for saccharine vary by a factor of many millions (Latin 1988, 89). As Latin has observed, these "estimates provide a range of uncertainty equivalent to not knowing whether one has enough money to buy a cup of coffee or pay off the national debt" (Latin 1988, 92).

Risk assessment, unlike the precautionary principle, generally assumes that we can quantify and compare risks. It is information intensive and rational. Moreover, it can and often does take a neutral attitude towards uncertainty. In calculating the likelihood of harm, first- and second-story probabilities are folded together. Thus, a definite risk of one death in one million is viewed as equivalent to a highly uncertain, one-in-one-million risk of one million deaths.

In contrast, the precautionary principle is not neutral towards uncertainty - it is biased in favor of safety. At the extreme, a precautionary approach could involve shifting the burden of proof altogether, placing the burden of proving safety on those proposing potentially harmful activities. Alternatively, it could attempt to bridge gaps in our knowledge by making conservative assumptions, which tend to overestimate risk.

Evidentiary approaches to the precautionary principle

Shifting the burden of proof

A few US environmental statutes address the problem of uncertainty by shifting the burden of proof. Ordinarily, people are free to act as they choose and the government has the burden of showing why that freedom should be limited. Thus, under most environmental statutes, the government has the burden of proving that an activity or product poses a risk and that environmental measures are therefore warranted (APA, 5

U.S.C. § 556(d); Industrial Union Department, AFL-CIO, 448 US at 652-55). In contrast, under burden-shifting statutes, regulators need not show than an activity or product is dangerous; instead, proponents of the activity or product have the burden of establishing "safety." If there is insufficient evidence to decide either way - that is, if there is radical uncertainty - then the activity cannot proceed.

Under the Federal Food, Drug and Cosmetics Act, food additives may not be approved for marketing unless the manufacturer demonstrates that the "proposed use of the food additive, under the conditions of use to be specified, will be safe" 21 U.S.C. § 348(c)(3)(A). In this context, safety has been defined to mean, "reasonable certainty of no harm." 21 U.S.C. §§ 301. Other examples of burden-shifting statutes include the Toxic Substances Control Act, under which the EPA screens new chemicals, 15 U.S.C. §§ 2604-2605; nuclear regulatory statutes that require preapproval of nuclear power plants, 42 U.S.C. § 2131; and the Marine Mammal Protection Act, which requires that applicants for permits to take marine mammals show that the taking will not have adverse effects, 16 USC § 1371; Comm. for Human Legislation v. Richardson, 540 F.2d 1141, 1145 (DC Cir. 1976) ("The Act was deliberately designed to permit takings of marine mammals only when it was known that the taking would not be to the disadvantage of the species."). The "no jeopardy" procedure of the Endangered Species Act, which requires agencies to insure that their actions are not likely to jeopardize the continued existence of any endangered or threatened species, also shifts the burden of proof (ESA § 7(a)(2), 16 USC § 1536). Under this provision, agencies are to give "the benefit of the doubt to the species," and should not proceed in the face of inadequate knowledge (Roosevelt Campobello Int'l Park v. EPA, 684 F.2d 1041, 1049 (DC Cir. 1982)). For a general discussion of burden-shifting statutes, see Huber 1983, 1030-37.

Under the Federal Insecticides, Fungicide and Rodenticide Act (FIFRA), the EPA does not have the burden of introducing evidence that a proposed new pesticide is hazardous; instead, the burden is on manufacturers to establish that the pesticide will not have "unreasonable adverse effects on the environment" (FIFRA § 3(c)(5)(C), 7 USC § 136a(c)(5)(C); EDF v. Ruckelshaus).

Industry must collect data, establish testing protocols and perform tests about the pesticide's health, safety and environmental effects. If an applicant cannot submit adequate evidence, the pesticide will be denied registration automatically. Moreover, should significant uncertainty persist about a pesticide's safety, the manufacturer bears the risk. Unless it can prove that the pesticide will not have "unreasonable adverse effects on the environment," the pesticide may not be registered for use.

Due to the difficulties experienced by EPA in administering the registration process, in 1978 Congress amended FIFRA to allow conditional registration. Under this procedure, EPA may conditionally register new pesticides when safety data is inadequate, if the pesticide is similar to currently registered pesticides, the application is for a new use for an existing pesticide, or the pesticide contains a new active ingredient and the pesticide's use is in the "public interest."

Burden-shifting statutes such as FIFRA illustrate a number of points about the precautionary principle. First, a precautionary approach to risk identification need not imply a precautionary approach to risk management. Although FIFRA addresses the evidentiary problems posed by uncertainty by shifting the burden of proof, it uses an information-intensive balancing test to determine what constitutes an "unreasonable adverse effect on the environment." Under this test, the government must "tak[e] into account the economic, social and environmental costs and benefits of the use of the pesticide" (FIFRA § 2(bb), 7 USC § 136(bb)). Even if a pesticide is likely to cause substantial environmental damage, EPA must approve registration if the applicant can prove that the pesticide's benefits outweigh its harms (40 CFR § 162.11(b)(1)(C)).

Second, burden shifting need not be an all or nothing proposition. The question is, who has what burden of proof on what issue? For example, in proceedings to suspend or cancel existing pesticides (as opposed to registering new ones), the EPA has the initial burden of producing evidence suggesting that a pesticide is unsafe. The legislative history of FIFRA suggests, however, that the burden on EPA is not high. Congress intended any substantial question of safety to trigger the issuance of cancellation notices (EDF v. Ruckelshaus, 439 F.2d at 593). Positive evidence of a hazard is not necessary; instead, cancellation is appropriate whenever there is no adequate assurance of safety (Id. 594). Only after this burden has been met does the burden shift to the manufacturer to establish that its pesticide does not cause an unreasonable risk to the environment (EDF v. EPA, 598 F.2d at 1004, 1012-1018).

Third, although burden shifting is often perceived as the most precautionary approach to environmental regulation, it does not insure against environmental harm. Some very damaging substances - such as DDT and CFCs - were originally perceived as safe and would presumably have been permitted even under a shifted burden of proof.

Finally, where significant uncertainties exist and there is no persuasive evidence about a product's safety, the decision about who has the burden of proof in essence determines the substantive outcome (Rodgers 1980, 225). This makes the initial question critical: when is a precautionary, burden-shifting approach warranted? Many formulations of the precautionary principle advanced at the international level have focused on the gravity of the risk: precaution should be exercised with respect to risks of "serious and irreversible" harm (Second World Climate Conference Ministerial Declaration, 7 Nov. 1990). In essence, these formulations do not shift the burden of proof completely, since some evidence is still necessary that an activity may cause serious and irreversible harm before the burden shifts to the other side to establish safety.

In contrast, US environmental law has tended to shift the burden of proof based, not on the severity of the risk, but on factors such as whether the risk is old or new, familiar or familiar, natural or man-made. New pesticides, food additives and chemicals must be proven safe in order to be licensed for use, while existing pesticides, additives and chemicals are presumed safe (Huber 1983). Natural carcinogens are tolerated, while synthetic compounds are subject to strict scrutiny. Although some might argue that new or artificial substances are inherently more risky than existing ones, the new-old/artificial-natural distinctions appear to be based, not on comparative assessments of the magnitude of the risks, but rather on the perception that mitigating old risks is more costly than excluding new ones (Huber 1983, 1054).

Ironically, however, this selective burden shifting may actually produce greater long-term harm than an unshifted burden of proof, by preventing the introduction of new activities or products which, while not risk free, are better than what they would replace. Requiring proof that nuclear power plants are completely safe, for example, prevents the replacement of coal plants that contribute to global warming and acid rain. Similarly, pre-screening new drugs for safety inhibits their introduction and arguably has caused more deaths than open access/liability regimes such as England uses (Johnson 1980, 18).

Reduced evidentiary standards

In contrast to FIFRA and the FDCA, most US environmental statutes do not shift the burden of proof. Instead, they predicate agency action upon a showing of risk. The question is, what standard of proof must agencies meet? How certain must we be that an activity is risky before taking action?

Generally, US law does not require agencies to find that a "significant risk exists with anything approaching scientific certainty" (Industrial Union Dept., AFL-CIO). In this respect, statutes such as the Clean Air Act and the Clean Water Act conform with those formulations of the precautionary principle which state, "lack of full scientific certainty should not be used as a reason for postponing measures to prevent environmental degradation" (Bergen Ministerial Declaration on Sustainable Development in the ECE Region, 14 May 1990).

For example, in an early case interpreting the Clean Air Act, the District of Columbia Court of Appeals upheld an EPA regulation requiring reductions in lead additives in gasoline, despite what it acknowledged was a lack of "hard proof of any danger" (Ethyl Corp. v. EPA). The evidence indicated that lead in high concentrations is toxic and can be absorbed into the body from the ambient air, and that gasoline emissions account for 90 percent of airborne lead. But uncertainties persisted about the sources of human exposure and the exposure levels that are dangerous. In upholding the agency action, the court commented:

> Undoubtedly, certainty is the scientific ideal - to the extent that even science can be certain of its truth. But certainty in the complexities of environmental medicine may be achievable only after the fact.... Awaiting certainty will often allow for only reactive, not preventive regulation.... (Ethyl Corp., 541 F.2d at 24-25).

The court then went on to find that the Clean Air Act, which authorises EPA to regulate gasoline additives whose emission products "will endanger the public health or welfare," takes a precautionary approach to the problem of scientific uncertainty:

> .... Case law and dictionary definition agree that endanger means something less than actual harm.... A statute allowing for regulation in the face of danger is, nec essarily, a precautionary statute....
>
> Where a statute is precautionary in nature, the evidence difficult to come by, uncertain or conflicting because it is on the frontiers of scientific knowledge, ... we will not demand rigorous step-by-step proof of cause and effect. Such proof may be impossible to obtain if the precautionary purpose of the statute is to be served (Ethyl Corp., 541 F.2d at 13, 28).

Although different statutes use different terms to describe the standard of proof for regulatory action, these standards generally require less than scientific certainty of harm. The Toxic Substances Control Act, for example, allows EPA to regulate chemicals if there is a "reasonable basis to conclude" that the chemical "presents or will present an unreasonable risk of injury to health or the environment" (TSCA § 6(a), 15 USC § 1605(a)). Similarly, the Clean Air Act allows regulation of gasoline additives that "may reasonably be anticipated to endanger the public health or welfare" (CAA § 211(c)(1), 42 USC § 7545(c)(1)). Other statutes allow regulation on the basis of the "best scientific evidence available" (MMPA 16 USC § 1373; ESA § 7, 16 USC § 1536(a)(2)). All of these standards allow regulation even when the evidence is incomplete or ambiguous.

Interestingly, however, despite these relaxed standards of proof, agencies have often been unable or unwilling to take regulatory action. For example, under TSCA, EPA has regulated only six chemicals, in part due to lack of information. For instance, no toxicity information at all is available for more than three-quarters of the thousands of chemicals currently in use (Percival 1992, 508), and developing an assessment of a single chemical on average takes three years (Dwyer 1990, 138). After reviewing implementation of several environmental statutes, one commentator concluded that the decision-making process "consistently fails to produce regulatory action whenever substantial uncertainty exists" (Flournoy 1991, 337-338). Thus, while reversing the burden of proof may stifle new, potentially benign activities and products, leaving even a reduced burden of proof on regulatory agencies may result in inaction.

Use of conservative evidentiary presumptions

US environmental law is also precautionary in using conservative evidentiary presumptions that tend to overestimate risk. Examples of conservative assumptions include linear, no-threshold dose-response curves and extrapolating from substances whose risks are known to related substances whose risks are unknown. In some cases, a statute itself establishes an evidentiary presumption. For example, under the Delaney Amendment, if a food additive causes cancer in animals, this creates an irrebuttable presumption that the additive is unsafe (21 U.S.C. § 348(c)(3)(A)). Other evidentiary presumptions have been created by regulation. OSHA regulations, for example, mandate the use of no-threshold dose-response curves for carcinogenic substances (close to a "worst case" model) and permit inferences of carcinogenic hazard from one or more positive animal tests (29 C.F.R. § 1990.143).

The use of conservative evidentiary presumptions, even in the absence of statutory authorisation, has been sanctioned by the US Supreme Court. As it concluded in the *Benzene* case, "[S]o long as [assumptions] are supported by a body of reputable scientific thought, [agencies are] free to use conservative assumptions in interpreting the data... risking error on the side of overprotection rather than underprotection" (Industrial Union Dept., AFL-CIO, 448 U.S. at 656). Relying on this decision, the DC Circuit Court of Appeals in *Public Citizen Health Research Group v. Tyson* upheld OSHA's use of animal studies to predict human health effects and of a no-threshold, linear dose-response curve. In approving the use of these assumptions, the Court said:

> While nothing can be *known* (in the sense of scientific certainty) at this time about the precise biological responses at low exposure levels, estimation techniques can provide a reasonable prediction....
>
> To the extent [the plaintiff's] argument asserts that OSHA cannot make any assumptions, even if they are supported by scientific thought, Congress has clearly come to the opposite conclusion. If Congress had intended to require the agency to "prove" all of its assumptions, Congress would not have allowed the agency to rely on the "best available evidence" and the "latest available scientific information."

In *EDF v. EPA*, the court also approved extrapolations from data about familiar substances to substances whose properties are less well understood.

Uncertainty not only makes it difficult to identify and assess environmental risks; it also complicates the management problem of determining the appropriate response. According to the precautionary principle, if environmental impacts are uncertain, then our management strategies should not depend on being able to predict environmental harm, but instead should seek to reduce the risk of harm by reducing the overall impact of human activities on the environment. In this respect, the precautionary principle differs from information-dependent management strategies such as cost-benefit balancing or the assimilative capacity approach.

Rejection of the assimilative capacity approach

Prior to the 1970s, regulatory agencies in the United States typically used an "environmental quality" approach to environmental management. Regulators first calculated the "acceptable" level of pollution for a given body of water or air and then allocated discharges among pollutant sources (Van Putten and Jackson 1986, 867). Although this approach in theory makes environmental and economic sense, it depends on having accurate scientific information about the "assimilative capacity" of the environment - that is, about the level of discharges that can safely be absorbed.

In enacting the 1972 Federal Water Pollution Control Act, Congress rejected the assimilative capacity approach, for essentially precautionary reasons. In Congress' view, the assimilative capacity approach "assumes more knowledge about our complex ecosystem than we actually have" (HR Rpt No. 911, 1972). In contrast, the FWPCA is based "on the hard-nosed assessment of our scientific ignorance: `we know so little about the ultimate consequences of injection of new matter into water that [the Act requires] a presumption of pollution ....'" (Weyerhaeuser Co. v. Costle, 590 F.2d at 1043). It attempts to replace standards that focus on the tolerable effects of water pollution with standards that focus on pollution's preventable causes (EPA v. California State Water Resources Board, 426 US at 202).

No harm rule

The most extreme response to the problem of uncertainty is to try to eliminate the risk of harm altogether - for example, by banning all discharges of pollutants into the environment. An example of this approach is the "zero discharge" goal established by the 1972 Federal Water Pollution Control Act (CWA § 101(a)(1), 33 USC § 1251 (a)(1)). In contrast to the assimilative capacity approach, the "zero discharge" goal avoids the need for scientific information about whether a given discharge will cause environmental harm. All discharges of pollutants are presumed harmful and must be eliminated.

The Endangered Species Act establishes a similarly absolutist, "no harm" rule - again for precautionary reasons. Once a species is designated as endangered or threatened, then the Endangered Species Act requires virtually total protection. In justifying this rule, Congress explained:

> Who knows, or can say, what potential cures for cancer or other scourges, present or future, may lie locked up in the structures of plants which may yet be undiscovered, much less analyzed? ... Sheer self-interest impels us to be cautious. The institutionalization of that caution lies at the heart of the [Endangered Species Act] (HR Rpt No. 93-412, 1973).

In *TVA v. Hill*, the Supreme Court held that this policy of "institutionalized caution" made it "abundantly clear that the balance has been struck in favor of affording endangered species the highest of priorities."

These absolutist provisions in US environmental law have been heavily criticised. Many commentators argue that the provisions are infeasible, since we can never eliminate emissions or risks completely. Concentrations of chemicals at sufficiently low levels may escape detection currently, leading to claims that discharges have been reduced to zero. But as our instrumentation improves, detection at lower and lower concentrations becomes possible.

Moreover, as economists are fond of noting, "going the last mile" in pollution reduction can be tremendously expensive, since the marginal cost of abatement tends to rise sharply as we approach the goal of zero emissions, in return for only small improvements in environmental quality (Breyer 1993). Indeed, in some cases implementation of a zero emissions standard may be possible only by shutting down entire industries. For example, in *NRDC v. EPA*, 824 F.2d at 1154 it was alleged that a zero-emissions standard for non-threshold pollutants would result in the elimination of such activities as coal burning power plants, steel manufacturing, and the refining, storage and dispensing of petroleum products. While overregulation may be a rational response to uncertainty, it is not rational when we are reasonably certain that the costs exceed the benefits. Moreover, as one commentator notes, "Demanding perfection now, without compromise, delays real progress" (Dwyer 1990, 281).

Margin of safety standards

Both the Clean Air Act and the Clean Water Act originally required that the EPA apply an "ample margin of safety" in setting emissions standards for hazardous substances (CAA § 112(d)(4), 42 USC § 7412(d)(4); CWA § 307, 33 USC § 1317(a)(4)). Similarly, under the Clean Air Act, EPA must apply an "adequate margin of safety" in setting national ambient air quality standards (CAA § 109, 42 USC § 7409).

In applying these health-based standards, courts have held that EPA should "err on the side of caution" (Lead Industries Assn, 647 F.2d at 1155). As one court noted, "Congress' directive ... to allow an 'adequate margin of safety' alone plainly refutes any suggestion that the [EPA] Administrator is only authorised to set primary air quality standards which are designed to protect against health effects that are known to be clearly harmful" (Lead Industries Assn, 647 F.2d at 1155). Another court similarly found that the "margin of safety" test was "intended to provide protection against hazards which research has not yet identified" (EDF v. EPA, 598 F.2d at 81). The court allowed EPA to establish very stringent emission standards for substances whose dangers were not well established, based on extrapolations from data about more familiar substances (EDF v. EPA, 598 F.2d at 83).

Although the margin of safety approach seeks to allow regulation in the face of uncertainty, implementation has proved difficult. Despite the acceptance of relaxed evidentiary standards, setting national ambient air quality standards (NAAQS) at levels that provide an adequate margin of safety has been riddled with questions:

> Each step in the process is difficult and controversial. Scientific data are often lacking or inconsistent. EPA often has to interpret very limited evidence of adverse health effects based on data drawn from a tiny portion of the population exposed to certain pollutants. These health effects may vary depending on both the magnitude and the duration of exposures. The very idea of a health effect is also not fixed. Is a "health effect" any detectable change in blood chemistry, or only changes proved to have an adverse effect on bodily functions? What populations should be used as the measure of effects, given that small children and the elderly may be more susceptible to effects of air pollution? Should it matter that most human exposure to a particular air pollutant is from non-air sources? What constitutes a margin of safety if there is no known threshold for a particular pollutant? ....
>
> The regulatory burden involved in establishing a NAAQS is so demanding that EPA has strong incentives to avoid making frequent changes in such standards, much less to promulgate new ones (Percival et al. 1992, 770-771).

Implementation of the highly precautionary, ample margin of safety standard has proved even more problematic. As one commentator has observed, "[S]etting emission standards for hazardous air pollutants is an enormously complicated political and scientific task that cannot be accomplished simply by commanding an agency to adopt emission standards that provide an ample margin of safety" (Dwyer 1990, 250).

Although the standard is less stringent than the zero emissions rule (since "safety" does not mean "risk free") (NRDC v. EPA, 824 F.2d at 1148), it is still quite absolutist. Thus, even after EPA found that vinyl chloride is a "non-threshold pollutant" - that is, a pollutant that "appears to create a risk to health at all non-zero levels of emissions" - the DC Circuit Court of Appeals declined to require that emissions be eliminated. EPA must initially determine what level of emissions is "safe", without regard to cost or feasibility. Only after safety is assured may EPA consider costs and feasibility in defining an "ample" margin of safety (NRDC v. EPA, 824 F.2d at 1165-1166).

Because of these potentially enormous implementation costs, EPA has been reluctant to trigger application of the standard by listing pollutants as toxic (Houck 1991, 10535). The impasse was finally resolved for the Clean Water Act by a judicial settlement, under which EPA agreed to list nearly 130 chemicals as toxic, in exchange for authorisation to consider economic and technological considerations in defining best available control technologies (NRDC v. Train, 8 Env't Rep. Cas. (BNA) 2120 (Dist. DC 1976)). The 1990 amendments to the Clean Air Act made similar changes. The amendments set forth a list of hazardous air pollutants, but explicitly allow EPA to consider the cost of achieving emissions reductions in setting emissions standards (CAA, 42 USC § 7412(d)(2)).

Best available technology

Best available technology (BAT) standards provide an alternative means of implementing a precautionary approach. They require pollution to be reduced, not because harm can be demonstrated, but simply because it is technologically and economically feasible to do so. Thus, they do not depend on evidence of cause and effect relations between polluting activities and environmental harm.

Both the Clean Air and Clean Water Acts include "best available technology" requirements. Under the Clean Water Act in particular, industry is required to introduce progressively stricter pollution control technologies. The 1972 Act required existing polluters, as a first step, to adopt the "best available technology economically achievable" and new polluters to use the "best available demonstrated control technology." Subsequently, existing polluters were to upgrade their abatement efforts by adopting the "best available technology economically achievable."

Implementation of BAT requirements, however, has proven difficult. Indeed, one commentator goes so far as to describe the development of technology standards as the "most Herculean task ever imposed on an environmental agency" (Houck 1991, 10537). While BAT standards do not depend on scientific information about environmental harms, they do require technical information about alternative abatement technologies, as well as about the industry being regulated - information that quickly becomes outdated. In adopting these standards, we have, "[f]or better or worse, ... shifted our faith from science to engineering" (Houck 1991, 10536).

Although the process of adopting technology standards has improved as EPA has acquired more experience, "it remains extraordinarily cumbersome and data-intensive" (Percival 1992, 898-899). More than twenty years after enactment of the Clean Water Act, most industrial dischargers of toxic pollutants still are not covered by any standard (Id. 912).

Best available technology standards have also been heavily criticised as inefficient. Critics argue that the standards waste money by "ignoring geographic variations in pollution effects;" tend to impose stricter requirements (and therefore higher costs) on new products; and do not encourage (and may actually discourage) the "development of new, environmentally superior strategies" (Ackerman and Stewart 1988, 173-175).

Finally, BAT standards have been applied unevenly. Some industries have been subjected to very strict, essentially zero-discharge standards; others have been allowed to continue polluting, using technology well below the best available. "The disparity in these standards reflect nothing more starkly than a disparity in [political] clout" (Houck 1991, 10539).

Conclusions

What lessons can we draw from the US experience in attempting to adopt a precautionary approach? The main lesson is the difficulty of implementing the precautionary principle. The precautionary principle says that we should err on the side of caution. But it does not answer the difficult questions that must be addressed in actual environmental decision-making: Should we always take a precautionary approach, no matter how small the likelihood of harm? And, if not, what level of harm must be shown, and with what degree of certainty? Moreover, how much should we err in favor of the environment? For example, should we reduce environmental risks, even if that means shutting down entire industries? These are the types of questions that US environmental agencies have had to wrestle with over the last twenty years - not very consistently and with only limited success.

Shifting the burden of proof, or requiring the elimination of all pollution, is the simplest way of coping with uncertainty. But unless we want to stop everyone from doing everything, neither approach provides a general solution. No matter how cautious we are, we cannot always require proof of safety as a condition for action, not least because safety is even more difficult to establish than harm. Harm at least can be shown after the fact. But safety is in essence a negative (i.e., no harm), and proving a negative is, as we know, impossible. For example, even when products appear to be safe, they may later turn out to have harmful effects. Shifting the burden of proof or requiring zero discharges can be done only selectively - most likely for activities that lack a political constituency and thus are particularly vulnerable to prohibition (ocean incineration, introduction of new pesticides, nuclear power, and so forth).

In contrast, relaxed standards or proof have been largely ineffectual. For many environmental risks, there is so little information that even a relaxed evidentiary standard is difficult to meet. And even when some evidence exists, the administrative burdens of gathering that evidence and using it to justify regulatory decisions often require more resources than the EPA possesses.

Technology standards have been perhaps the most effective response to uncertainty. Yet these standards are far from unproblematic: they are extraordinarily difficult to develop, quickly become outdated, and are economically inefficient. Moreover, they have had only limited success in preventing pollution. More than twenty years after passage of the Clean Water Act, there has been little measurable improvement in the quality of US waters.

What, then, are we to do? First, in managing environmental problems, we need to begin with a recognition of the incompleteness of our knowledge. The precautionary principle reflects no more than simple prudence when it states that lack of full scientific certainty is not an excuse for failing to take action to protect the environment.

Second, while absolute rules have an emotional appeal, there is no avoiding the need for a comparative approach to the problem of environmental risk. Given limited resources for environmental protection, we need to decide how to allocate them most effectively. While we may not be able to do this well, given our limited information, the alternative is even worse - "simply regulating to the hilt whatever pollutants or problems happen to get on the regulatory agenda" (Ackerman and Stewart 1988, 175).

Third, in deciding whether to take action, we need to consider a variety of factors -not only whether an activity or product has potentially serious effects (which, of course, itself may be highly uncertain), but also the likelihood of harm, the costs of taking action, and the probability of new information that will reduce uncertainties.

The difficulties in addressing uncertainty are highlighted by several aphorisms that all appear common sense, but point in different directions: an ounce of prevention is worth a pound of cure; look before you leap; nothing ventured, nothing gained; and the best can be the enemy of the good.

When uncertainties exist, none of our options are risk free. Simple rules promise simple answers. But, in the end, there may be no practical alternative to the imperfect, difficult, often dissatisfying task of muddling along.

Abbreviations

CAA Clean Air Act, 42 USC §§ 7401-7642

CWA Clean Water Act, 33 USC §§ 1251-1387

EPAUS Environmental Protection Agency

ESA Endangered Species Act, 16 USC §§ 1531-1544

FDCA Food, Drug and Cosmetic Act, 21 USC § 301-392

FIFRA Federal Insecticide, Fungicide and Rodenticide Act, 7 USC §§ 136-136y

FWPCA Federal Water Pollution Control Act (renamed Clean Water Act)

MMPA Marine Mammal Protection Act, 16 USC § 1361-1407

NEPA National Environmental Policy Act, 42 USC §§ 4321-4370

OSHA Occupational Safety and Health Administration

TSCA Toxic Substances Control Act, 15 USC §§ 2604-2654

References

Cases

Environmental Defense Fund v. EPA, 548 F.2d 998 (DC Cir. 1977), cert. denied 431 US 925 (1978)

Environmental Defense Fund v. EPA, 598 F.2d 62 (DC Cir. 1978).

Environmental Defense Fund v. Ruckelshaus, 439 F.2d 584 (DC Cir. 1971).

EPA v. California State Water Resources Board, 426 US 200 (1976).

Ethyl Corp. v. Environmental Protection Agency 541 F.2d 1 (DC Cir. 1976) (en banc).

Hercules Inc. v. EPA, 598 F.2d 91 (DC Cir. 1978).

Industrial Union Department, AFL-CIO v. American Petroleum Institute, 448 US 607 (1980).

Lead Industries Assn v. EPA, 647 F.2d 1130 (DC Cir. 1980).

Natural Resources Defense Council v. EPA, 824 F.2d 1146 (DC Cir. 1987) (en banc).

Public Citizen Health Research Group v. Tyson, 796 F.2d 1479 (D.C. Cir. 1986).

Reserve Mining v. EPA, 498 F.2d 1073 (8th Cir. 1974), reversed by 514 F.2d 492 (8th Cir. 1975) (en banc).

TVA v. Hill, 437 US 153 (1978).

Books and Articles

Ackerman, B. and Stewart, R. 1988. Reforming environmental law: the democratic case for market incentives. Columbia Journal of Environmental Law, 13, 171.

Belsky, M. 1984. Environmental policy law in the 1970s: shifting back the burden of proof. Ecology Law Quarterly, 12, 1-88.

Breyer 1993. Breaking the Vicious Circle: Toward Effective Risk Regulation. Harvard University Press, Cambridge.

Clark, W. 1980. Witches, floods and wonder drugs: historical perspectives on risk management. In R. Schwing and W. Albers (eds.) Societal Risk Assessment: How Safe Is Safe Enough. Plenum Press, New York, 287-313.

Dwyer, J. 1990. The pathology of symbolic legislation. Ecology Law Quarterly 17, 233-316.

Flournoy, A. 1991. Legislating inaction: asking the wrong questions in protective environmental decisionmaking. Harvard Environmental Law Review 15, 327-391.

Houck, P. 1991. The regulation of toxic pollutants under the clean water act. Environmental Law Reporter 21, 10528-10560.

Huber, P. 1983. The old-new division in risk regulation. Virginia

Law Review 69, 1025-1107.

Johnson, P. 1980. The perils of risk avoidance. Regulation, May/June, 15-19.

Latin, H. 1988. Good science, Bad regulation and toxic risk assessment. Yale Journal on Regulation 5, 89-148.McCarey, M. 1977. Pesticide regulation: risk assessment and the burden of proof. George Washington Law Review 45, 1066-1094.

Pedersen, W. 1988. Turning the tide on water quality. Ecology Law Quarterly 15, 69-102.

Percival, R., Miller, A., Schroeder, C. and Leape, J. 1992. Environmental regulation: law, science and policy. Little, Brown and Co., Boston.

Rodgers, W. 1980. Benefits, costs and risks: oversight of health and environmental decisionmaking. Harvard Environmental Law Review 4, 191-226.

Ruckelshaus, W. 1984. Risk in free society. Environmental Law Reporter 14, 10190-10194.

Van Putten, M. and Jackson, B. 1986. The dilution of the Clean Water Act. Journal on Law Reform 19, 863-901.

Von Moltke, K. 1987. The Vorsorgeprinzip in West Germany Environmental Policy. Institute for European Environmental Policy, Bonn.

Wilson, R. and Crouch, E. 1987. Risk assessment and comparisons: an introduction. Science 236, 267-270.

Chapter 13

The Introduction of the Precautionary Principle into the UK

By Nigel Haigh

"Environmental policy must evolve on the basis of sound science, informed debate, foresight and a proper balance between development and conservation. We accept the precautionary principle".

The Minister of State for the Environment, Lord Caithness, speaking in Parliament, 13 January 1988.

Introduction

The Precautionary Principle entered the language of environmental policy in Britain only in the mid 1980s. Mr. Waldegrave, the Minister of State for the Environment at the time noted that quite a number of serious scientists were talking about the possibility of a serious catastrophic event in connection with the ozone layer. As a consequence, he continued, most of the advanced countries of the world have taken the view that precautionary measures should be taken, perhaps in advance of scientific consensus" (Waldegrave, 1986). The exact status of this as a principle for the making and administration of policy nevertheless remains uncertain because this has never been spelt out by the Government in any detail. The principle is now stated in the Treaty of Maastricht as a principle under which EC policy is to be made, and the principle has been embodied in some British legislation. Whether it is or should be a principle of science is another question altogether. This has been the subject of heated discussion in the New Scientist following the publication of a controversial article on "green science" by Wynne and Mayer (1993).

Perhaps for the same reason that there is no written constitution in Britain, the British have always been reluctant to enunciate principles as a guide to government policy. The reason that the precautionary principle is now recognised in Britain can be attributed to the international character of environmental policy and the fact that Britain is a party to a number of international declarations or agreements which have included the principle in one form or another.

As with many other principles, the influence of the precautionary principle in any particular set of circumstances is not always clear. Principles sometimes do conflict with each other and no one principle can therefore be considered in isolation. The principles of liberty and of equality - two of the three slogans of the French Revolution - provide but one example of conflicting principles which require each to be modified on occasion to take account of the other. The same is likely to be true whenever an attempt is made to apply the precautionary principle.

This chapter briefly describes the precautionary principle as it first appears in Germany, then in international declarations and conventions, and then in the European Community. It concludes with its introduction into Britain and some comments are made on the meaning of the official British statements.

German origins

In a report prepared for the Royal Commission on Environmental Pollution in 1987, Konrad von Moltke (1988) discussed the principle in German environmental policy and explained that it was first enunciated by the German Federal Government in 1976 under the name of the *Vorsorgeprinzip* using these words:

> "Environmental policy is not fully accomplished by warding off imminent hazards and the elimination of damage which has occurred. Precautionary environmental policy requires furthermore that natural resources are protected and demands on them made with care".

In the early 1980s discussion of the *Vorsorgeprinzip* was relatively muted in Germany although the German Council of Experts on the Environment discussed it in a special report on the North Sea in 1980. It is possible that the reason the debate became more animated in the mid 1980s was the sea change in German environmental policy that took place following confirmation of dramatic forest damage in Germany. von Moltke argues that the *Vorsorgeprinzip* then provided a justification for action on air pollution additional to the measures taken before.

In 1986 the Federal Government issued 'Guidelines' on *Vorsorge* discussing the subject at length. However, the meaning of the *Vorsorgeprinzip* cannot be said to be easily understood. It has to be distinguished from the pre-existing concept of *Gefahrenabwehr* or protection against risks. The essential difference is the identifiability of a given risk. Public authorities are clearly obliged to act to protect against identifiable risks. The *Vorsorgeprinzip* raises the need to act against risks which are not (yet) proved, or even the need to act in the absence of risk (for example maintaining an environmental resource undisturbed). In deciding to take action public authorities in Germany are bound by principles of administrative law including the principle of the proportionality of administrative action to the achievement of a prescribed goal, and the principle of prohibition of excessive actions. Action taken following the *Vorsorgeprinzip* thus requires a balancing of the risks, costs and benefits.

In practice in Germany, *Vorsorge* is often taken to be synonymous with emission standards in accordance with the state of technology, as, for example, in the air pollution legislation which states:

> 'Installations subject to authorisation are to be constructed and operated in such as a manner that ... 2. Precaution is taken against damaging environmental effects, in particular by means of measures for the control of emissions in accordance with the state of technology.'

International declarations and conventions

A number of international declarations or conventions relating to the precautionary principle to which the UK is a party are listed in Table 1.

The first appearance of the principle internationally (Items 1.1 to 1.3) concerns a particular problem (protection of the ozone layer) which involved restricting emissions of specific substances (CFCs and other ozone depleting substances). At that time (1980 to 1987) it had not yet been established conclusively that CFCs were indeed responsible for depletion of the ozone layer.

The principle then appears more broadly (Items 1.4, 1.5 and 1.6) in statements concerning the North Sea made between 1987 and 1990. Here application of the principle is restricted to the most dangerous substances entering the North Sea. The principle is stated to mean that it is appropriate to take action even when there is no scientific evidence to prove a causal link between emissions and effects.

The Bergen Declaration (Item 1.7) is the first general statement of the precautionary principle made by Ministers in an international declaration. That declaration was made at a conference of Ministers from 34 countries organised in 1990 by the Norwegian Government in cooperation with the UN Economic Commission for Europe. It was part of the follow up to the Brundtland Report and was intended to prepare for UNCED in Rio de Janeiro in 1992. The principle is there said to be required to achieve sustainable development. The point is made that it goes beyond prevention by requiring anticipation. Again lack of scientific certainty is not to be used for postponing measures to prevent environmental degradation, but this is conditional on the existence of threats of serious or irreversible damage. Precautionary action is therefore not always appropriate: it is justified only if the threat is sufficiently serious, i.e. it is qualified by the principle of proportionality.

Items 1.8 and 1.9 show that the precautionary principle is recognised by both the OECD and EC. The position in the EC is discussed more fully below.

The principle was adopted at UNCED in Rio de Janeiro (Item 1.10) by a large number of countries including for the first time developing countries. A further qualification is here introduced. The principle is to be applied by States only 'according to their capabilities' implying that poorer countries might not have to apply the principle so rigorously.

A fairly recent statement of the principle (Item 1.12) relates to the North Sea and North East Atlantic. It differs from earlier statements relating to the North Sea (Items 1.4, 1.5 and 1.6) in not being restricted to particularly dangerous substances. It applies also to damage to amenities. In other words, the degree of risk implied by the proportionality principle before action is appropriate appears to have been enlarged.

Almost certainly the precautionary principle will continue to be stated using slightly different words on different occasions so that it is likely to be interpreted differently depending on the country or international organisation relying on it.

The European Community

From the date of its entry into force (1 November 1993), the Treaty of Maastricht requires Community policy on the environment to be based on the precautionary principle (see Item 8). But even before that date the principle has influenced EC policy so its history is worth tracing.

The Treaty of Rome that came into effect in 1957 had no reference to the environment, and it was not until the Single European Act amended the Treaty in 1987 that environmental policy was expressly provided for. This did not prevent the EC adopting an action programme on the environment in 1973 which resulted in a large number of items of legislation, some of which incorporate the precautionary principle (see Haigh, 1992).

The Single European Act introduced new Articles relating to the environment which set out certain principles, but without referring to the precautionary principle.

Article 130r (1) set out three objectives of action by the EC relating to the environment:

- to preserve, protect and improve the quality of the environ ment

- to contribute towards protecting human health

- to ensure a prudent and rational utilisation of natural resources

Article 130r (2) stated that EC action relating to the environment should be based on three principles:

- that preventative action should be taken

-t hat environmental damage should as a priority be rectified at source

- that the polluter should pay

Article 130r (3) required EC action to take account of four factors:

- available scientific data

- environmental conditions in the various regions of the EC

- the potential benefits and costs of action or lack of action

- the economic and social development of the EC and the balanced development of its regions

The distinction between the precautionary principle and the principle of prevention is emphasised by the Maastricht Treaty which includes several revisions to Article 130r. One of these is the insertion of the precautionary principle in addition to the principles of prevention and of rectifying damage at source. This must imply that the precautionary principle means something more than the other two.

Until the Maastricht Treaty was ratified, one had to look to Council Resolutions for any agreed EC statements on the precautionary principle.

The Council Resolution on the fifth Action Programme adopted in December 1992 referred to the European Council's Declaration at Dublin of 1990 (known as 'the Environmental Imperative') and included these words in the preamble:

> Whereas the Declaration of the Heads of State and Government,meeting in Council on 26 June 1990, calls inter alia for a further action programme on the environment to be elaborated on the basis of the principles of sustainable development, preventive and precautionary action, and shared responsibility' (emphasis added).

The fifth Action Programme itself, states (Chapter 2) that:

> 'In accordance with the European Council's Declaration, "The Environmental Imperative", the guiding principles for policy decisions under this Programme derive from the PRECAUTIONARY APPROACH and the concept of SHARED RESPONSIBILITY, including effective implementation of the "Polluter Pays Principle" (capitals in the original).

The fifth Action Programme however does not go on to explain what is meant by the precautionary approach.The fourth Action Programme of 1987 did not use the words precautionary principle. Nor did the earlier Programmes, although the first

Action Programme of 1973 had enunciated a set of eleven principles which included (to paraphrase):

- the polluter pays principle

- the principle of prevention: it is better than cure

- the principle that environmental effects should be taken into account at the earliest possible stage in decision making

- the principle that exploitation of natural resources which causes significant damage to the ecological balance must be avoided.

The last three principles are closely related to the precautionary principle so that it can be argued that some elements were present. However, the words 'precautionary principle' only formally entered the language of EC environmental policy with the Dublin Declaration in 1990 and the fifth Action Programme of 1992 and only because a legal obligation when Maastricht entered into force in November 1993.

The introduction of the precautionary principle into the EC Treaty and Action Programme can be seen to follow its development elsewhere. The principle was not yet sufficiently accepted for it to have been introduced into the Single European Act when it was being drafted in 1985 despite its earlier adoption in Germany. By the time of the Dublin Declaration in June 1990, the principle had been endorsed one month earlier at Bergen (Item 1.5). Its introduction in 1991 during the drafting of the Maastricht Treaty and fifth Action Programme then followed.

The practical effects of the Maastricht Treaty's requirement for EC environmental policy to be based on the precautionary principle remains to be seen. Since the principle has already been relied upon in EC policy, it can be argued that the change will not be dramatic. The earliest example of an explicit reference in EC legislation to a precautionary measure is to be found in the EC Council Decision of April 1980 on CFCs (see

Item 1.1). An EC Commissioner has also asserted that the setting of the maximum admissible concentrations for pesticides in drinking water at the limit of detection in Directive 80/778 of July 1980 was an early example of the precautionary principle. Since the Commission is now proposing to amend the drinking water Directive, and amendment of the pesticides parameter has considerable economic and environmental consequences, the negotiations are bound to involve discussion of the precautionary principle.

Other examples of the precautionary principle being embodied in EC legislation are Directive 79/831 on the testing of new chemicals before they are marketed and Directives 90/219 and 90/220 concerning genetically modified organisms. These three Directives are concerned with taking measures because of potential or unknown risks. Directive 90/219 makes the point in its preamble where it says that 'whereas the precise nature and scale of risks associated with genetically modified organisms are not yet fully known ...'.

Now that the Maastricht Treaty is ratified the precautionary principle will apply to a British Minister when, as a member of the Council, he contributes to the formulation of EC policy by agreeing the form of words in an item of EC legislation. It is however qualified by a need to balance the benefits and costs of action or lack of action. The principle applies to Community policy and does not apply to any aspects of purely national policy which are not part of EC policy. For example much of British planning legislation is not covered by any EC legislation and for that reason cannot be regarded as part of EC policy.

Britain - the theory

The earliest statement in Parliament by a Minister that the Government accepted the precautionary principle was made by the Earl of Caithness in a debate in the House of Lords in January 1988. That statement and subsequent official British statements are quoted in Table 2.

Two months earlier Britain had already accepted the precautionary approach when it agreed to the declaration of the Second Conference on the North Sea in November 1987. It was Germany that had pressed for its inclusion in that declaration. The subtle shift from the word 'approach' to the word 'principle' may or may not have been inadvertent, but it is interesting that although the words 'precautionary approach', 'precautionary action' and 'precautionary policy' appear in subsequent official publications the words 'precautionary principle' do not appear again until the 1990 White Paper *This Common Inheritance: Britain's Environmental Strategy* (Item 2.6). The White Paper started with a chapter headed 'First Principles' and so provides one of the rare occasions when the British Government has enunciated a set of principles. Precautionary action was accordingly elevated to a principle in the White Paper despite the absence of much domestic debate on the subject of principles.

The White Paper is one of the most authoritative interpretations provided by the British Government on the subject, though earlier contributions are useful in helping to clarify its meaning. The statement is nothing like as complete a discussion as the German 'Guidelines' of 1986, but the following points can be made about its meaning:

1. The principle applies to Government action. None of the statements say explicitly that it applies to action by other administrative bodies (e.g. local authorities) or indeed to bodies completely outside Government (e.g. industrial companies) whose actions affect the environment.

2. Action under the principle is subject to the condition that there is a significant degree of risk. Benefits and costs also have to be balanced. This is the 'proportionality' principle which has to be made explicit in Britain in contrast to Germany where it appears in the constitution and can be taken for granted.

3. The distinction between 'prevention' and 'precaution' is not made very clear in the White Paper (Item 2.6) nor in one of the brochures which preceded it (Item 2.3) but the distinction is

emphasised in the 1989 brochure (Item 2.4) where precautionary action is seen as going beyond prevention. In yet another brochure (Item 2.5) 'precautionary policy' is identified with 'anticipatory policy' which again distinguishes it from prevention of known harm.

4. A brochure of 1989 (Item 2.4) gives examples of precautionary action, namely curbs on CFCs to protect the ozone layer and the reduction by half of discharges of dangerous substances to the North Sea. In both these examples a causal connection had not at the time been proved between emissions and effects. Now that a scientific consensus exists that CFCs are indeed the cause of depletion of the ozone layer, the steps being taken should properly now be called preventative rather than precautionary.

5. The White Paper (Item 2.6) discusses precautionary action in the context of limiting the use of potentially dangerous materials and the spread of potentiality dangerous pollutants but does not limit it to the field of pollution. The next paragraph broadens the action to cover wastage of natural resources and "bequeathing a burden of environmental debts tomorrow". This certainly covers pollution but can presumably apply to loss of flora and fauna and their habitats from other causes and conceivably also to loss of cultural assets (landscape, historic sites) though these are not expressly stated as being covered (but see point 6 below).

6 .The link between sustainable development and the precautionary principle is not made explicitly in the White Paper, though it is in one of the brochures (Item 2.5) as it is in the Bergen Declaration (Box 13.1, Item 1.7). If the precautionary principle is interpreted in Britain as linked to sustainability, then presumably it applies not just to pollution but also to protection of fauna and flora and their habitats which are affected by changes in land use as well as by pollution.

There is clearly a need for a more complete statement by the British Government as to what it understands by the precautionary principle. Particular points that need clarification are inter alia to what extent the principle applies to more than pollution control, and whether it applies to action by administrative bodies and public or private companies. These themes were partially addressed in the most complete statement on sustainable development issued by the Government in January 1994 (Department of the Environment, 1994). There the Government quoted the Rio Declaration on the precautionary principle (see Item 1.10 in Box 13.1), and stated

> "This wording is a useful reminder that the principle can be applicable to all forms of environmental damage that might arise; nor should it apply only to actions of Government"

This is an important clarification, and suggests that the precautionary principle is at least eligible for a fairly wide interpretation in current affairs.

Britain - the practice

There are not that many examples of the precautionary principle applied in practice in Britain. The two examples given in a Department of the Environment brochure (Item 2.4) have already been mentioned: restrictions on CFC production and on discharges of dangerous substances to the North Sea. Another example is the Government's decision announced at the third North Sea Conference at the Hague in 1990 to stop dumping sewage sludge at sea. What can also be regarded as a practical example, even before the principle was stated, was the decision taken by the Government in April 1983 that lead should be removed from petrol. This was done under the pressure of public opinion and following a report from the Royal Commission on Environmental Pollution. It is interesting that this decision was made in Britain, which did not then subscribe to the principle, before it was made in Germany even though the principle was by then already recognised there. When it comes to political action, public pressure is as likely to count as much as, or more than, principle.

The control of genetically modified organisms is one area going beyond traditional pollution control where, as a result of EC legislation, the precautionary principle is embodied in UK legislation. Part VI of the Environmental Protection Act 1990 states that it is "for the purpose of preventing or minimising any damage to the environment which may arise from the escape or release from human control of genetically modified organisms". In other words, the risk may not be known for certain. The Act places obligations on persons who intend to release or market genetically modified organisms to carry out risk assessments and notify the authorities, and as a result the precautionary principle has been transformed by legislation so as to apply to given persons in given circumstances and not just to Government when making policy. This could be the pattern for its future extension to apply to more than action by Government.

The precautionary principle is often taken to be synonymous with the setting of emission standards from industrial plant based on what is technically achievable (best available technology). As is pointed out in Chapter 2, this is how it is often seen in Germany. If this is so then it can also be argued that the precautionary principle has existed in Britain for over 100 years for aspects of air pollution control. The Alkali Act 1874 required that emissions of noxious gases from certain plants should be prevented, using the best practicable means, without any need to demonstrate that the gases were actually causing harm in any particular case. The Environmental Protection Act 1990 now extends this requirement to discharges to water as well as to air of 'prescribed substances'. To argue that this is an embodiment of the 'precautionary principle' rather than the 'principle of prevention' is to show how difficult it is to distinguish between them. If it is known that the substances will cause harm before action is taken then the principle of prevention is being applied and precaution is not involved. If the substances are not known to cause any harm in a particular case but might cause harm, and action is taken, then it is the precautionary principle that is being applied. It needs to be recognised that the precautionary principle only applies when there is uncertainty. Once the uncertainty is removed then precaution is no longer the right word. Since there is likely to be uncertainty about when uncertainty disappears there will also be uncertainty about whether to talk of the principle of precaution rather than of prevention.

Possibly the most important example of the application of the precautionary principle concerns the greenhouse effect leading to global warming and climate change. It is not known with absolute certainty is how serious the build up of greenhouse gases will be, and whether for example carbon dioxide will be dissolved in sea water to a sufficient extent to offset a certain increase in emissions. The decision by the EC Member States collectively to curb emissions of CO_2 and the decision by the British Government to do the same are examples of the precautionary principle being applied. The British White Paper of 1990 made this clear when it talked about the need to narrow the uncertainties and then said: "but in the meantime, the risks clearly justify action to begin to reduce greenhouse gases, so that the problem is contained while the longer-term analysis continues". The debate about further action to counter climate change is guaranteed to focus further attention on the principle.

Whether the precautionary principle should be a principle of science is a matter that the scientific community will want to resolve for itself, but there is nothing in UK Government statements to suggest that it is thought of in that way. The principle, as it is understood by Government, must nevertheless now influence scientists when they give advice for the making of policy because they will know that the Government is guided by the principle as they take their decisions.

References

Haigh, N. 1992. Manual of Environmental Policy: The EC and Britain. Longman, Harlow.

von Moltke, K. 1988. The Vorsorgeprinzip in West German environmental policy. 12th Report of the Royal Commission on Environmental Pollution, HMSO.

Waldegrave, W. 1986. Assessment in a political context. In. G. Conway (ed) The Assessment of Environmental Problems. Imperial College for Environmental Technology.

Wynne, B. and Meyer, S. 1993. How science fails the environment. New Scientist, 5 June, 33-35.

Box 13.1

INTERNATIONAL DECLARATIONS, CONVENTIONS, TREATIES AND OTHER STATEMENTS RELATING TO THE PRECAUTIONARY PRINCIPLE TO WHICH THE UK IS A PARTY[1]

1.1 EC Council Decision 80/372 concerning CFCs in the Environment - April 1980

"Whereas, in accordance with the common position of Member States of 6 December 1978 and in accordance with recommendation III of the Munich Conference, a significant reduction should, as a precautionary measure, be achieved in the next few years in the use of chlolofluorocarbons giving rise to emissions."

1.2 Vienna Convention for the Protection of the Ozone Layer - March 1985

"*Mindful also* of the precautionary measures for the protection of the ozone layer which have already been taken at the national and international levels."

1.3 Montreal Protocol on Substances that Deplete the Ozone Layer - September 1987

"Determined to protect the ozone layer by taking precautionary measures to control equitably total global emissions of substances that deplete it, with the ultimate objective of their elimination on the basis of developments in scientific knowledge, taking into account technical and economic considerations."

1.4 Second Conference on the North Sea - London - November 1987

Box 13.1 continued

"Accepting that in order to protect the North Sea from possibly damaging effects of the most dangerous substances, a precautionary approach is necessary which may require action to control inputs of such substances even before a causal link has been established by absolutely clear scientific evidence."

1.5 PARCOM Recommendation 89/1 - 22 June 1989

"The Contracting Parties to the Paris Convention for the Prevention of Marine Pollution from Land-Based Sources:

ACCEPT the principle of safeguarding the marine ecosystem of the Paris Convention area by reducing at source polluting emissions of substances that are persistent, toxic and liable to bioaccumulate by the use of the best available technology and other appropriate measures. This applies especially when there is reason to assume that certain damage or harmful effects on the living resources of the sea are likely to be caused by such substances, even where there is no scientific evidence to prove a causal link between emissions and effects ("the principle of precautionary action")."

1.6 Third Conference on the North Sea - The Hague - March 1990

"The participants adopted the following premises as a basis for their future work. They:

-will continue to apply the precautionary principle, that is to take action to avoid potentially damaging impacts of substances that are persistent, toxic and liable to bioaccumulate even when there is no scientific evidence to prove a causal link between emissions and effects."

1.7 Bergen Ministerial Declaration - May 1990

"In order to achieve sustainable development, policies must be based on the precautionary principle. Environmental measures must anticipate, prevent and attack the causes of environmental degradation. Where there are threats of serious or irreversible damage, lack of full scientific certainty should not be used as a reason for postponing measures to prevent environmental degradation."

1.8 OECD Council Recommendation C(90)164 on Integrated Pollution Prevention and Control - January 1991

The Recommendation is accompanied by Guidance which is an integral part of the Recommendation. It lists some essential policy aspects including:

> "the absence of complete information should not preclude precautionary action to mitigate the risk of significant harm to the environment."

1.9 The Treaty of Maastricht - signed February 1992 (in force from November 1993)

> "Community policy on the environment shall aim at a high level of protection taking into account the diversity of situations in the various regions of the Community. It shall be based on the precautionary principle and on the principles that preventive action should be taken, that environmental damage should as a priority be rectified at source and that the polluter should pay. Environmental protection require ments must be integrated into the definition and implemen tation of other Community policies."

1.10 United Nations Conference on Environment and Development (UNCED) - Agenda 21 - Rio de Janeiro - June 1992

Principle 15 reads as follows:

Box 13.1 continued

"In order to protect the environment, the precautionary approach shall be widely applied by States according to their capabilities. Where there are threats of serious or irrevers ible damage, lack of full scientific certainty shall not be used as a reason for postponing cost-effective measures to prevent environmental degradation."

1.11 Framework Convention on Climate Change - June 1992

Article 3 on 'Principles' includes:

"the parties should take precautionary measures to anticipate, prevent or minimize the causes of climate change and mitigate its adverse effects. Where there are threats of serious or irreversible damage, lack of full scientific certainty should not be used as a reason for postponing such measures ..."

1.12 Convention on Protection of the Environment of the North East Atlantic - Paris - signed September 1992

"The Contracting parties shall apply:

a) the precautionary principle, by virtue of which preventive measures are taken when there are reasonable grounds for concern that substances or energy introduced, directly or indirectly, into the marine environment may bring about hazards to human health, harm living resources and marine ecosystems, damage amenities or interfere with other legitimate uses of the sea, even when there is no conclusive evidence of a causal relationship between the inputs and the effects."

Box 13.2

OFFICIAL STATEMENTS IN BRITAIN RELATING TO THE PRECAUTIONARY PRINCIPLE[2]

2.1 The Minister of State for the Environment (the Earl of Caithness) speaking in a debate on the environment in the House of Lords, 13 January 1988 (Official Report Col 1311)

"Environmental policy must evolve on the basis of sound science, informed debate, foresight and a proper balance between development and conservation. We accept the precautionary principle."

2.2 "Inputs of Dangerous Substances to Water: Proposals for a Unified System of Control" - Department of the Environment/ Welsh Office, July 1988

"In addition, for those substances which represent the greatest threat to the environment, the Government considers it is necessary to go further by seeking to minimise inputs to all parts of the environment as part of a more precautionary approach to water pollution".

2.3 " Protecting Your Environment: A Guide", brochure published by the Department of the Environment, July 1988

"The Government's aim in environmental protection policy is to prevent undue risks to human life and health now and in the future and to maintain the resources necessary to support man and his activities. Important related objectives are the protection of the natural environment and the improvement of public amenity.

The principles underlying this approach to pollution control are the need to:

Box 13.2 continued

* base decisions on the best available scientific foundation

* adopt a preventive, precautionary approach

* set realistic goals for environmental quality

* take technical feasibility and economic considerations into account in reaching decisions

* recognise interactions between different sectors of the environment, and dispose of wastes - which industrial society inevitably produces - according to the 'best practicable environmental option'

* recognise the international dimension to many environmental problems, and to take international remedies accordingly

* inform the public about the state of the environment and to take public feelings into account in developing environmental policy."

2.4 'Environment in Trust' brochure published by the Department of the Environment - March 1989

This brochure includes a section with three headings: *The Polluter Pays Principle*, *Prevention* and *Precaution*. The latter two read as follows:

"Prevention

The Government believe that in environmental protection,

prevention is better than cure. All environmental protection policy is aimed at the prevention of damage.

Precaution

Within this preventative approach the Government will take precautionary action when the risks justify it, even if scientific knowledge is not complete."

The brochure then gives two examples of precautionary action: the ceiling put on CFC production in the EC in 1980, and the decision to reduce by half the discharge of dangerous substances into the North Sea by 1995.

2.5 "Sustaining our Common Future" - A Progress Report by the UK on Implementing Sustainable Development, Department of the Environment, September 1989

2.6 White Paper "This Common Inheritance: Britain's Environmental Strategy" presented to Parliament, September 1990, Cm 1200

Chapter 1 of the White Paper is headed 'First Principles'. It includes a heading 'Precautionary Action' in which the following passage appears:

"1.18. Where the state of our planet is at stake, the risks can be so high and the costs of corrective action so great, that prevention is better and cheaper than cure. We must analyse the possible benefits and costs both of action and of inaction. Where there are significant risks of damage to the environment, the Government will be prepared to take precautionary action to limit the use of potentially dangerous materials or the spread of potentially dangerous pollutants, even where scientific knowledge is not conclusive, if the balance of likely costs and benefits justifies it.

Box 13.2 continued

This precautionary principle applies particularly where there are good grounds for judging either that action taken promptly at comparatively low cost may avoid more costly damage later, or that irreversible effects may follow if action is delayed".

1.19. This is similar to the responsible approach which the Government adopts on financial policy. Just as we believe that it is irresponsible for Governments to be extravagant with taxpayers' money, so we see even stronger arguments against wasting the world's, or this country's natural resources and bequeathing a burden of environmental debts tomorrow. We must have development and growth in the world but they must be sustainable. It is scarcely surprising that young people show so much sensitive interest in environmental matters. Much of the debate, after all, is about the state of the world which they will inherit. We must ensure that they are not disappointed by basing our actions on sound science and by taking precautionary action where justified."

2.7 Royal Commission on Environmental Pollution - 16th Report - "Freshwater Quality" - June 1992

Para 1.24 starts:

"Fifthly, a precautionary approach to pollution control should be maintained". (The paragraphs then refer back to the 12th Report and Dr von Moltke's paper).

2.8 UK Strategy for Sustainable Development - Consultation Paper - Department of the Environment - July 1993

Para 1.20 reads:

"... Where appropriate (for example, where there is uncertainty combined with the possibility of the irreversible loss of valued resources), actions should be based on the so-called 'precautionary principle' if the balance of likely costs and benefits justifies it. Even then the action taken should be in proportion to the risk".

[1] This list is illustrative and is not necessarily complete. Emphasis has been added whenever the word precautionary appears.

[2] This list is not necessarily complete. Emphasis has been added whenever the word precautionary appears

Chapter 14

The Precautionary Principle in Australia

By Ronnie Harding and Liz Fisher

Introduction and background

The precautionary principle has been widely discussed in Australia over the past eighteen months. A number of recent events and associated influences can be identified as likely causes, though the full story is not known.

Domestically, important recent developments in environmental management including the Intergovernmental Agreement on the Environment and the Ecologically Sustainable Development (ESD) discussion process, have prescribed 'precaution' as a centrally important principle. Internationally, the UNCED-associated events and international agreements incorporating the precautionary principle have been important influences, particularly since Australia has long prided itself as being a conscientious international actor. As well, sections of the environmental lobby in Australia have been persuasive in attempting to focus attention on the relevance of the principle.

Australia's relatively undeveloped and unique combination of natural resources must also be seen as providing an important context influencing the adoption of, and responses to, the precautionary principle. The extraordinary diversity of ecosystems, which are unique on the world stage, and not well understood scientifically, has meant both that uncertainty regarding consequences of development is rife and that impacts are likely to be perceived as significant. Hence not only is the need to apply precaution triggered, but the concern of the environment lobby is aroused, leading to political pressure. Simultaneously, Australia's richness in mineral and biological resources for exploitation has led to concern during extractive industries that imposition of the precautionary principle will lead to a lessening of resource security at best and cessation of certain development projects at worst. In short, sections of industry and government are alarmed, whilst environmental groups are exuberant over the precautionary debate in Australia. The precautionary principle has captured power politics.

The intergovernmental agreement on the environment

For at least the past ten years there has been much conflict in Australia between the Commonwealth and the States over environmental management control. A brief description of the origins of this in terms of the Constitution and recent politics is given by Farrier (1993). The case of the Gordon-below-Franklin dam in the early 1980s heralded a decade of conflict stemming from Commonwealth 'interference' in what had previously been treated as, primarily, state matters. The Intergovernmental Agreement on the Environment (IGAE) is a response both to this conflict, and also to pressure from both industry and environment groups for more uniform and certain standards providing not only better environment protection, but a more certain environment for business and government decision-making.

The IGAE was signed in May 1992 by the Prime Minister, all State Premiers, Territory Chief Ministers and the President of the Local Government Association. Although not legally binding it sets up a framework for environmental management throughout Australia involving more precise delineation of the roles of different levels of government operating within general policy guidelines.

The precautionary principle is one of four guiding principles in the IGAE. The principle is stated in Section 3.5.1 of that document, as follows:

> Where there are threats of serious or irreversible environ mental damage, lack of full scientific certainty should not be

used as a reason for postponing measures to prevent environmental degradation.

In the application of the precautionary principle public and private decisions should be guided by:

i) careful evaluation to avoid, wherever possible, serious or irreversible damage to the environment; and

ii) an assessment of the risk weighted consequences of various options.

Intergovernmental Agreement on the Environment, May 1992, para 3.5.1

Hence, the precautionary principle, among others, is to be a guiding principle for informed 'policy making and program implementation' by *all levels of government* in Australia (IGAE 1992: para 3.1) *across a very wide range of environmental management concerns*.

The reason for the inclusion of the precautionary principle in the IGAE is not recorded but it seems that a combination of domestic (the ESD process) and international influences were responsible.

Over a two year period from 1990 a formal government-organised discussion process on ESD took place in Australia. 'Dealing cautiously with risk and irreversibility' was one of a number of principles and goals which underpinned the discussions. This process must be credited with playing a major role in raising the level of debate on environmental policy issues in Australia and with facilitating the incorporation of relevant *principles* (such as the precautionary principle) in environmental policy and legislation (see ESD Working Groups, 1991 and ESD Working Group Chairs, 1992).

Since the IGAE is not legally binding, there may reasonably be cynicism regarding its worth. Moreover, in relation to its inclusion of the precautionary principle the many 'let-out' phrases in section 3.5.1 of the IGAE may serve to reinforce that cynicism. But there are indications that the IGAE *is* influencing policy and legislation within the states.

Concurrent with the development of the IGAE the New South Wales Government was drafting legislation to establish the NSW Environment Protection Authority. The resulting Act - *The Protection of the Environment Administration act* 1991, contains the precautionary principle in its Section 6(2). Whilst the preparation of the IGAE was certainly influential in the drafting of the POE Act, it is clear that there was also much pressure from the environment groups in NSW for inclusion of the precautionary principle.

While most states at present do not have the precautionary principle in either their environmental legislation or policies many are considering it. For example proposed amendments to the Water Licensing and Water Administration Acts in NSW include the precautionary principle as does the Environment Protection Bill 1993 in South Australia.

However, inclusion of the precautionary principle in legislation, per se, may mean little. The test of effectiveness comes through demonstration of its application, and upholding of the need for such application by the courts. Moreover, effectiveness would additionally need to be considered in terms of *interpretation* of the principle, and whether similar judgements would have been made in the absence of the principle on the basis of, for example, balance of probabilities. So far we have little evidence to make such judgements although the principle has been used in recent legal processes.

Alan Stewart, an assessor on the NSW Land and Environment Court, in October 1993 referred to the precautionary principle in dealing with scientific evidence in the case of *Simpson v. Ballina* involving an appeal for a rural subdivision which could have caused pollution to an adjoining creek. The case of *Queensland Nickel Management Pty Ltd v. The Great Barrier Reef Marine Park Authority and Ors*, which involved the establishment of an offshore nickel loading facility, was heard between July 1991 and April 1992 by the Federal Administrative Appeals Tribunal and involved considerable discussion of the precautionary principle (Prokuda 1993). No judgement was given in this case since a settlement occurred at the conclusion of evidence.

Most recently and most significantly, application of the precautionary principle was central to Justice Stein's decision in the case of *Leatch v. Director-General National Parks and Wildlife Service and Shoalhaven City Council* in the Land and Environment Court of NSW on 23 November 1993. This case involved a merit appeal against a decision by the NP and WS to grant Shoalhaven Council a licence to 'take or kill' endangered fauna (the Giant Burrowing Frog and the Yellow-bellied Glider) as a result of construction of a road. Justice Stein found a dearth of knowledge in relation to possible impacts of the road building on these species, and whilst there is no express provision in the *National Parks and Wildlife Act* to consider the precautionary principle, he concluded that application of a precautionary approach was not an extraneous matter to the case, and hence was relevant to his deliberations. A key reason for upholding the appeal was consideration of precaution in relation to the high level of uncertainty regarding effects on the Giant Burrowing Frog, coupled with the availability of an alternative route for the road.

The influences for consideration of precaution in these legal processes seem to have been wide. Justice Stein, for example, referred to international agreements as well as to domestic legislation and policies.

It may also turn out to be significant that the National Strategy for Ecologically Sustainable Development (ESD) (Commonwealth of Australia 1992) includes the precautionary principle as a guiding principle. Such inclusion suggests that application of precaution is implicit in any statement of ESD in legislation. As well, a number of policy documents include the precautionary principle as part of the definition of ESD. Inclusion of reference to ESD in legislation and policy in Australia is becoming commonplace and hence we may assumed by implication an equally common reference to the precautionary principle. As one example the *Local Government Act 1993* (NSW), requires local councils to consider ESD measures. The placement of ESD and by inference, the precautionary principle, in legislation governing this grass roots level of environmental management, we regard as being most significant in terms of its potential to influence public norms and expectations.

However, the extent of commitment of at least the Commonwealth government to the principle must be doubled. During the latter stages of the development of the ESD strategy, resource economist, Michael Young of the CSIRO, was commissioned by the Department of Prime Minister and Cabinet, which was coordinating the ESD process, to produce a report on 'the concept of intergenerational equity and the role of the precautionary principle and the use of the discount rate in government decision-making'. Young's report (1993) provides an excellent overview of the implications of application of these principles and tools, very much from an economist's perspective. However, it appears that the officials responsible for the National Strategy for ESD decided not to give prominence to these issues since Young's report is not included in the *Compendium of ESD Recommendations*.

A conference on the Precautionary Principle organised by the Institute of Environmental Studies at the University of New South Wales on 20-21 September 1993 provided an interesting measure of interest in the application of the precautionary principle in Australia. Familiarity with the precautionary principle varied enormously among participants. Some had not heard of the principle before receiving the conference brochure, and surprisingly, these included people from government departments operating within the IGAE. At the same time it was clear that there had been considerable discussion of the principle *within* many government departments, environment groups, industry 'umbrella' organisations (such as the Australian Chamber of Manufacturers) and individual companies.

Within industry groups it is probably reasonable to distinguish between manufacturing industries and those involved in resource extraction in relatively 'natural' ecosystems. For the reasons indicated earlier, the latter seem most concerned by the precautionary principle. There has been a history of bitter conflict in Australia between resource extraction industries such as mining and forestry, which are significant in Australia's export earnings, and the environment lobby. For these industries the precautionary principle holds the threat of providing a new generation of weaponry for their opponents in the environmental battlefield; namely that the principle would provide justification for a 'zero risk/do nothing' approach to development decisions.

Some groups have been keen to emphasise that the principle of precaution is not new in environmental management - so why all the fuss? Brian Robinson (1993), Chair of the Victorian EPA, sees the philosophy enshrined in the precautionary principle as 'simple commonsense' and the definition of the principle in the IGAE 'as an articulation of common practice by both regulatory agencies and industry' in Victoria. A common concern expressed by government and industry environment managers (Corbyn and Niland 1993; Drake 1993; Robinson 1993; Strauch 1993) is that the precautionary principle should not be 'taken out of context'. That is it should not be separated from the clauses in the IGAE which refer to 'wherever practicable', 'serious or irreversible damage' and 'assessment ... of various options', as well as the broader principles of ESD which refer to cost-effectiveness and the need for a 'strong, growing and diversified economy. As well, industry is particularly concerned that 'vaguely worded or incomplete definitions of this principle appearing in legislation' will not only increase uncertainty regarding development decisions on the basis of environmental criteria, but also possibly lead to costly court challenges and result in investors going elsewhere (Drake 1993). As indicated above, 'resource security' for industry has been a major issue in Australia for some time.

Hence much of the discussion at government and industry level has been directed at defining practical application of the precautionary principle in a manner which does not unreasonably affect economic development and particularly does not increase uncertainty for investors. For many in this group the precautionary principle requires no changes to environmental practice and decision making since we are already operating precautiously.

In contrast some academic and community group commentators have argued that the precautionary principle is not 'just another name for risk assessment', but that it requires that much greater attention be given to the 'nature of uncertainty' and to the social construct of scientific information (Dovers and Handmer 1993; Harding and Fisher 1993; Young 1993) in environmental decision making. Further, for some its practical application cannot be prescribed by *definition* and hence must rely on determination of a *process* for decision making which puts decision on 'how much' precaution into the hands of a wider set of stakeholders than at present (Dovers and Handmer 1993; Harding and Fisher 1993). For these commentators application of the precautionary principle will require significant review of public participation in environmental management.

Conclusions

It is still too early to judge the role that the precautionary principle will play in Australian environmental management. Much consideration of this question has revolved around the legal standing of the principle and the manner in which it is likely to be interpreted in policy (i.e. '*how* precautionary'). Whilst we await specific cases to indicate these directions, the recent decision by Justice Stein must be seen as a benchmark in relation to application of the principle through the courts.

Whatever the immediate outcome in these arenas, we believe that the institutionalisation of precaution in law and policy will play a most significant role in changing community expectations regarding environmental management practice. In the long term it may be the political influence deriving from this which is seen as of most significance.

References

Commonwealth of Australia 1992. National Strategy for Ecologically Sustainable Development. AGPS, Canberra.

Corbyn, L. and Niland, J. 1993. The precautionary principle. A NSW status report. Paper presented to the Precautionary Principle Conference, Institute of Environmental Studies, University of New South Wales, Sydney, Australia, 20-21 September 1993.

Dovers, S.R. and Handmer, J.W. 1993. Ignorance and the precautionary principle: towards an analytical framework. Paper presented to the Precautionary Principle Conference, Institute of Environmental Studies, University of New South Wales, Sydney, Australia, 20-21 September 1993.

Drake, G. 1993. Precautionary principle: a mining perspective. Paper presented to the Precautionary Principle Conference, Institute of Environmental Studies, University of New South Wales, Sydney, Australia, 20-21 September 1993.

Ecologically Sustainable Development Working Groups 1991. Final Reports (9 separate sectoral reports), AGPS, Canberra.

Ecologically Sustainable Development Working Group Chairs 1992. Intersectoral Issues Report. AGPS, Canberra.

Farrier, D. 1993. The Environmental Law Handbook. Planning and Land Use in New South Wales, 2nd edition, Redfern Legal Centre Publishing, Redfern, NSW.

Harding, R. and Fisher, L. 1993. A transdisciplinary approach to the precautionary principle. Paper presented to the Precautionary Principle Conference, Institute of Environmental Studies, University of New South Wales, Sydney, Australia, 20-21 September 1993.

Prokuda, H. 1993. The precautionary principle - a case study. Paper presented to the Precautionary Principle Conference, Institute of Environmental Studies, University of New South Wales, Sydney, Australia, 20-21 September 1993.

Robinson, B. 1993. Victorian EPA - Viewpoint on the precautionary principle. Paper presented to the Precautionary Principle Conference, Institute of Environmental Studies, University of New South Wales, Sydney, Australia, 20-21 September 1993.

Strauch, R. 1993. Precautionary principle. A manufacturing industry view. Paper presented to the Precautionary Principle Conference, Institute of Environmental Studies, University of New South Wales, Sydney, Australia, 20-21 September 1993.

Young, M.D. 1993. Combining intergenerational equity, the precautionary principle and the maintenance of natural capital. Paper presented to the Precautionary Principle Conference, Institute of Environmental Studies, University of New South Wales, Sydney, Australia, 20-21 September 1993. First published in March 1993 as For Our Children's Children. Some practical implications of intergenerational equity, the precautionary principle, maintenance of natural capital and the discount rate. Working document 93/5 A.M.N.R.S Program, Division of Wildlife and Ecology, CSIRO, Canberra.

Chapter 15

The Status of the Precautionary Principle in International Law

by James Cameron

Introduction

The precautionary principle has evolved into a general principle of environmental protection at the international level. The question this paper asks is what is its status in international law? Two further questions follow, firstly, what binding legal treaties are there which create obligations to follow the precautionary principle, and secondly, is there sufficient evidence of the emergence of a customary international law rule requiring the adoption of the principle for those States which have not signed and ratified the relevant Treaties?

Treaties are agreements between states to achieve certain objectives through the voluntary assumption of obligations. They are essentially contractual in nature and remain the primary source of international law. Custom is recognised as a source of international law in Article 38(1) of the Statute of the International Court of Justice instructing the Court to apply "international custom, as evidence of a general practice accepted as law".It is important to note also that a treaty may itself give rise to the confirmation or expression of a customary rule which would extend beyond its signatories. (*North Sea Continental Shelf Cases* FRG v. Denmark; FRG v. The Netherlands ICJ Reports 1969 Pg.3)

Crucial to the identification of a source of international legal obligation, in this context, is the determination of the point at which a pattern of legislative or expository behaviour crystallizes into a customary rule which states feel bound to follow themselves and which they wish to see applied to other states. This involves both the recognition that a state is acquiescing in the practice (state practice) and has accepted the particular practice on the basis of a legal obligation (*opinio juris*) and not merely of comity or goodwill to other States. As Birnie and Boyle (1992) state "the identification of customary law always has been and remains, particularly problematical, requiring the exercise of skill, judgement, and considerable research."

What states do matters most, but what they say is also of use in identifying custom. In a world where they are myriad sources of many-layered obligations and where law and politics are wedded it is mighty hard to find customary rules that really bind let alone enforce them in tribunals. Governments are very adept at avoiding obligation. However three facets of the inquiry into the existence of a rule seem to my mind to be most important:

(1) the pattern of discourse, at the international level, in the subject matter area where the rule is said to operate;

(2) the application of the principle in international practice;

(3) the implementation of international agreements into national law and policy which give effect to the rule.

So far as discourse is concerned, the precautionary principle scores extremely well. International practice is evident and developing. Implementation is happening but it is patchy and poorly distributed amongst nations and subject-matter areas.

Writers

There are colleagues who remain sceptical about the precautionary principle having any binding legal effect at the time of writing their particular work. Birnie and Boyle (1992) for example, put their concerns in this way:

> "Despite its attractions, the great variety of interpretations given to the precautionary principle, and the novel and far-reaching effects of some applications suggest that it is not yet a principle of international law. Difficult questions concerning the point at which it becomes applicable to any given activity remain unanswered and seriously undermine its normative character and practical utility, although support for it does indicate a policy of greater prudence on the part of those states willing to accept it."

This is a view shared by Dan Bodansky (1991), who believes the principle is "too vague" for adoption as a regulatory standard. He goes on to state therefore that:

> "It is appropriate to take a cautious attitude towards the precautionary principle. We may wish to adopt it as a general goal. But it would be a mistake to believe it will resolve the difficult problems of international environmen tal regulation or prevent new hazards from emerging in the future."

Lothar Gundling (1990), whilst recommending the adoption of the precautionary principle as a legal obligation, felt compelled to conclude that the abundance of non-binding instruments which refer to the principle and the lack of binding treaties meant that further "law creating acts" were "necessary". Since then as the materials below set out some of those acts can be identified, although there remains the problem of the mixed pedigree of the instruments which carry the precautionary principle.

Gunther Handl (1990) argues that "State practice, resolutions of international organisations and other pertinent idicia point to the emergence of community expectations that, at least as matter of international policy activities potentially affecting the environment be subject to constraint." However, he continues, "at present the precautionary principle is not a term of art. The principle's exact political, and *a fortiori*, legal implications remain elusive".

Freestone (1991), on the other hand, asks:

> "Would it be reasonable today (in the current state of law) to presume that a state which has participated in the endorsement of the precautionary principle in a particular sector would be held liable in the future for causing harm (whether to neighbours or commons) for activities in that sector which today are strongly suspected (but not proven) to cause substantial harm?"

His assessment is that "the evidence suggests that the answer may well be affirmative." He concludes:

> "At present this is probably arguable on a sector by sector basis, but if present trends continue this may be a general requirement of environmental law in the not too distant future."

De La Fayette (1991) commenting on the Second North Sea Conference, has observed that:

> "it [the precautionary principle] has become the fundamen tal norm underlying the practical measures taken then and at the Third Conference.In adopting the precautionary principle, States have recognized that it is necessary to take action to reduce pollution in the sea even before there is positive scientific evidence that damage has occurred or will occur ... In recent years, this approach has become crucial to actions now being taken or proposed in other aspects of environmental protection, such as global warming and the destruction of the ozone layer."

All of these writings see a policy developing, or emerging, into a rule but cannot quite bring themselves to find obligation which would render illegal State conduct in breach of the principle. In addition they all pre-date UNCED.

I cannot share in the concern about the principle in respect of vagueness and/or generality. The precautionary principle is a general principle. To say so says nothing about its legal effect. At the international level it is not intended to be a command and control-type regulatory standard. Secondary legislation, whether at the national or international level is needed to take the principle and apply it to a particular procedure or discipline. Again, this does not in any way deny its legal effect as a general principle. If those that argue that its generality or elusiveness is a bar to its having legal effect are right what can they say about binding legal agreements which refer to the principle ? Must you ignore the principle on the grounds that though you, as a state party agreed to this particular form of words you are not certain what they mean? I have set out fully elsewhere (Cameron, 1994), my reasoning for the argument that there is a core meaning to the precautionary principle and that it is manifestly implementable through a variety of operationalizing procedures.

As the title of this book suggests, it is the interpretation of the precautionary principle which counts. In my view it can be argued that the precautionary principle is not only capable of having legal effect (rather than policy guidance) but does have legal effect. This is so not only in respect of international agreements which have been ratified, such as the UN Framework Convention on Climate Change, but also generally in respect of decisions taken in cases, such as marine pollution or radioactive waste management, where the principle has been cited consistently and with a conviction that the correct course of action is to apply.

My reservations concern the universality of the principle. If, as I argue there is, in certain fields of environmental concern, such as marine pollution, a duty to follow the general principle of precautionary action, is it a duty which binds all states ? It might be argued that developing countries who are not parties to many of the agreements referred to below may be less likely to accept the binding nature of the principle than, say the Nordic countries. The force of that argument is necessarily limited, since the UN Conference on Environment and Development (UNCED) in my view UNCED universalized the principle. Two Conventions, containing many developing country signatories and ratifications, numerous reference in Agenda 21, and Principle 15 of the Rio Declaration have elevated the principle onto the truly international plane. From my point of view UNCED was the crystallizing moment in the development of the principle from one that was emerging as to one that is legally binding.

Explicit precautionary language - (some examples)

The earliest explicit references to the precautionary principle were contained in domestic West German legislation in the early 1970s. This history is well documented by Sonja Boehmer Christiansen in Chapter 2. At the international level, the rise of explicit precautionary discourse has only been evident in the latter part of the 80s. By 1990, the U.N. Secretary-General was able to report that the precautionary principle "has been endorsed by virtually all recent international forums." A fuller analysis of all these precautionary references are contained in Cameron and Abouchar (1991) and in Cameron and Wade-Gery (1992) See also Handl (1990), Gundling (1990), Nollkaemper (1991), Hey (1991); Freestone (1991) . Many of the citations are annexed to Nigel Haigh's Chapter. Therefore the following may be considered edited highlights.

The earliest international agreement to employ explicitly precautionary discourse is widely accepted to be the Ministerial Declaration of the Second International Conference on the Protection of the North Sea, issued in London in November 1987. In this, the Ministers accepted, inter alia, that:

> "... in order to protect the North Sea from possibly damaging effects of the most dangerous substances, a precautionary

approach is necessary which may require action to control inputs of such substances even before a causal link has been established by absolutely clear scientific evidence."

The 1989 Nordic Council's Conference on the Pollution of the Seas points to the range of variables that are relevant in answering this question:

"... the need for an effective precautionary approach, with that important principle intended to safeguard the marine ecosystem by, among other things, eliminating and prevent ing pollution emissions where there is reason to believe that damage or harmful effects are likely to be caused, even where there is inadequate or inconclusive scientific evidence to prove a causal link between emissions and effects."

In this case, the precautionary principle is invoked for the advancement of a particular end (the safeguarding of the marine ecosystem), and this end is to be attained by particular means (the elimination and prevention of pollution emissions).

The Treaty of European Union (Maastricht)

"The Community policy on the environment ... shall be based on the precautionary principle and on the principles that preventive action should be taken, that environmental damage should as a priority be rectified at source and that the polluter should pay. Environmental protection requirements must be integrated into the definition and implementation of other Community policies."

UNCED

Principle 15 of he 1992 Rio Declaration on Environment and Development states:

> "Where there are threats of serious or irreversible damage, lack of full scientific certainty shall not be used as a reason for postponing cost-effective measures to prevent environ mental degradation."

The 1992 U.N. Framework Convention on Climate Change states that:

> "The Parties should take precautionary measures to antici pate, prevent or minimise the causes of climate change and mitigate its adverse effects. Where there are threats of serious or irreversible damage, lack of full scientific cer tainty should not be used as a reason for postponing such measures, taking into account that policies and measures to deal with climate change should be cost effective so as to ensure global benefits at the lowest possible cost."

The Biodiversity Convention signed at the United Nations Conference on Environment and Development does not specifically refer to the precautionary principle in its operative provisions. However, the Preamble notes that:

> "...where there is a threat of significant reduction or loss of biological diversity, lack of full scientific certainty should not be used as a reason for postponing measures to avoid or minimise such a threat".

A connection has been made between this treaty language and national policy. In his foreword to the UK Government's response to the Framework Convention on Climate Chnage (HM Government 1994, 3) John Major the Prime Minister is unequivocal in his support for the Framework Convention which includes the precautionary principle. The underlying tone of his introduction is of acceptance of the principles put forward and the desire to achieve these. As he states:-

> 'each of us recognised the daunting challenge ... and the need

for precautionary action to be taken...The threat of climate change cannot be tackled by any one group or group of countries in isolation; it requires a global response'

The UK's programme is based upon the precautionary approach inherent in the convention. It states that 'it is appropriate to take action ahead of unequivocal evidence being established about the nature and possible effects of man-made climate change' .

Agenda 21, agreed at the 1992 Rio conference, recommends in relation to radioactive waste that states should not:

"promote or allow the storage or disposal of high-level, intermediate level and low-level radioactive wastes near the marine environment unless they determine that scientific evidence, consistent with the internationally agreed princi ples and guidelines, shows that such storage or disposal poses no unacceptable risk to people and the marine environment or does not interfere with other legitimate uses of the sea, making, in the process of consideration, appropri ate use of the concept of the precautionary approach."

Other Treaties

Although the original Vienna Convention of 1985 and its subsequent Protocol on Substances that Deplete the Ozone Layer, which was established in Montreal in September 1987, do not use explicitly precautionary language, the Protocol has since been amended to include this new terminology. Thus the June 1990 London Amendments to the Montreal Protocol state that:

"[The Parties to this Protocol are] determined to protect the ozone layer by taking precautionary measures to control equitably total global emissions of substances that deplete it, with the ultimate objective of their elimination on the basis of developments in scientific knowledge, taking into account technical and economic considerations and bearing in mind the developmental needs of developing countries."

The 1992 OSPAR Convention, replacing the Oslo and Paris Conventions, was adopted at a meeeting of the Oslo and Paris Commissions in Paris. The Preamble to this new convention states:

"Considering that the present Oslo and Paris Conventions do not adequately control some of the many sources of pollution, and that it is therefore justifiable to replace them with the present Convention, which addresses all sources of pollution of the marine environment and the adverse effects of human activities upon it, takes into account the precautionary principle and strengthens regional cooperation".

The Convention further provides in Article 2 that the Contracting Parties shall apply:-

"...the precautionary principle, by virtue of which preventive measures are to be taken when there are reasonable grounds for concern that substances or energy introduced, directly or indirectly, into the marine environment may bring about hazards to human health, harm living resources and marine ecosystems, damage amenities or interfere with other legitimate uses of the sea, even when there is no conclusive evidence of a causal relationship between the inputs and the effects".

The Convention has been signed but not yet ratified and is therefore not yet in force. The UK government has declared its intention to ratify when Parliamentary time can be found.

The Convention on the Protection and use of Transboundary Watercourses and International Lakes, which is not yet in force, refers specifically to the precautionary principle as a guiding principle underlying its operative measures:

"In taking the measures referred to in paragraph 1 and 2 of this article, the Parties shall be guided by the following principles:

(a) The precautionary principle, by virtue of which action to avoid the potential transboundary impact of the release of hazardous substances shall not be postponed on the ground that scientific research has not fully proved a causal link between those substances, on the one hand, and the potential transboundary impact, on the other hand..."

Precaution and Procedure in international law and organisation - some examples:

Under the current terms of the London Convention, certain substances cannot be dumped at sea (except in exceptional cases). These substances are listed in Annex I of the Convention. Annex II lists, although in an indeterminate fashion, a series of substances for which dumping was contingent upon the issue of a nationally-provided permit. National authorities can issue such permits "only after careful consideration of all the factors set forth in Annex III," which include the characteristics and composition of the matter to be dumped, the characteristics of the dumping site and dumping method, and other general considerations such as "the practical availability of alternative land-based methods of treatment, disposal or elimination, or of treatment to render the matter less harmful for dumping at sea."

This is at best only indirectly susceptible of a precautionary interpretation. An Annex II substance can be dumped merely on the basis of a "careful consideration" of a series of characteristics. Those characteristics are relatively open-ended; there are no specified forms, or parameters, of those characteristics that would lead to the proposed dumping being denied a permit. For instance, there are no criteria given for determining the "practical availability of ... treatment to render the matter less harmful for dumping at sea," nor is there any agreed commitment to do more than carefully consider such practical availability were it to exist.

After the Convention's Tenth Consultative Meeting in 1986, the Scientific Group on Dumping established an ad hoc Group of Experts on the Annexes, which after three meetings, produced a draft New Assessment Procedure (NAP) for consideration at the Fourteenth Consultative Meeting in 1991. In discussions on the adoption of the renamed Draft Waste Assessment Framework (WAF) at the Fifteenth Consultative Meeting of the Contracting Parties to the London Convention in November 1992, the Chairman of the Scientific Group noted that it was felt by some that the reverse listing approach, inclusion of a prior notification procedure, and additional scientific input to the action list would strengthen the WAF. Several delegations felt that a reverse listing approach in place of a prohibition list should be given consideration via future refinements of the WAF. However, since the WAF follows the current construction of the London Convention, it was decided that reverse listing should be included in discussions regarding amendments to the Convention. The Meeting agreed to request the Scientific Group to undertake the necessary scientific and technical assessment of a reverse listing approach in relation to the interpretation of Annexes I and II and taking into account relevant existing resolutions on radioactive wastes, industrial wastes, incineration at sea and the precautionary principle. The Meeting ultimately agreed to adopt the WAF on a provisional basis, in conjunction with the existing regulations, recommendations and resolutions of the London Convention, pending resolution of policy issues such as the reverse listing approach.

From the outset, one of the official "guiding principles" of the Group of Experts was:

> "that any new structure for the operational procedure of the Convention should reflect a precautionary approach to dumping."

And the introduction to the WAF confirms that:

> "In applying the WAF ... it is important that national authorities adopt a precautionary approach to the

> introduction of substances into the environment and actively pursue measures that will reduce contamination where there is reason to suspect that harmful effects may occur, even though stringent proof of a cause-effect relation may be lacking."

This kind of approach is evident, for instance, in the WAF's provisions for the assessment of alternatives to disposal of waste at sea. In place of a "careful consideration" of whether such alternatives are "practical", there is now a two stage process: first, a waste prevention audit, and, second, a comparison of waste management options. The former requires that "applications for permits should be refused and existing permits should be reviewed" if the "feasibility" of each of a number of techniques for waste prevention "have not been adequately addressed." These techniques include product reformulation, clean production technologies, process modification, input substitution, and on-site, closed-loop recycling. Waste management options are considered:

> "Applications to dispose of wastes at sea should demonstrate that consideration has been given to waste prevention at source ..... and to each element in a hierarchy of waste management options."

The hierarchy in "an order of increasing environmental impact" includes the waste prevention measures cited in the waste prevention audit above, off-site recycling, re-use, destruction of hazardous constituents, treatment to reduce or remove the hazard, and disposal into land, air and water. The framework concludes:

> "Generally speaking, a permit to dispose of wastes at sea should be refused if opportunities exist to recycle, re-use or treat the waste without undue risk to human health or incurring disproportionate costs.... The practical availabil ity of other means of disposal should be considered in the light of a comparative risk assessment involving both sea disposal and the alternatives."

Clearly, the WAF is an EIA of a new order. Proposed activities must demonstrate that they satisfy specific precautionary procedures. The precautionary impact of this type of EIA is thus more direct than indirect. A proto-polluter is required to demonstrate under the terms of the assessment procedure that certain specific regulatory standards are either in place or not needed even under the precautionary framework of the WAF.

Under the 1992 OSPAR Convention, the Parties (United Kingdom and France) wishing to retain the option of dumping low and intermediate level radioactive wastes at sea (which is otherwise prohibited under the Convention) will be required to report to the OSPAR Commission on, inter alia, "progress in establishing alternative land-based options and on the results of scientific studies which show that any potential dumping operations would not result in hazards to human health, harm to living resources or marine ecosystems, damage to amenities or interference with other legitimate uses of the sea".

Any regulatory measure will be directly precautionary if it seeks to limit specified environmental impacts whose consequences are uncertain, but which carry a non-negligible risk of being environmentally damaging. Particular activities are either prohibited or legally mandated. Several such measures have been mentioned above in relation to the WAF. The quantified restrictions on CFC production contained in the amended Montreal protocol are another example of directly precautionary measures, as would be any restrictions on CO_2 emissions authorised by the Climate Convention or its protocols.

Precautionary measures may not remain precautionary. Advances in scientific capability, for instance, can resolve the uncertainties that a specific precautionary measure was designed to address; in such a case, the measure is translated into a purely preventive strategy as the epistemological context of regulation is altered. Adjustments to moral context can have a similar effect. The commercial whaling moratorium, for instance, may have been instituted as a precautionary measure, but changing social mores may reinstitutionalise it as a straightforward moral imperative. D'Amato and Chopra (1991)

At the June 1993 Fifteenth Joint Meeting of the Oslo and Paris Commissions, a Recommendation concerning Increases in Radioactive Discharges from Nuclear Reprocessing Plants was adopted. Under the terms of the Recommendation, the Contracting Parties agree, inter alia, that a new or revised discharge authorisation for radioactive discharges from nuclearreprocessing installations should only be issues by national authorities if special consideration is given to "a full environmental impact assessment" and "the demonstration that the planned discharges are based upon the use of the Best Available Techniques and observe the precautionary principle".

Notably, the Recommendation relates to the commissioning of the THORP plant at Sellafield which will cause additional radioactive discharges from Sellafield into the Irish Sea, and thence into the remainder of the maritime area covered by the Paris Convention. However, the Recommendation is not binding and, notwithstanding that the UK had recently signed the new OSPAR Convention which endorses the precautionary principle, in an answer to a Parliamentary question in the UK House of Commons, the UK government has asserted that as the UK did not accept the recommendation, it would be taking no specific action as a result of it in relation to THORP. This suggests that even where the precautionary principle may be enshrined in an international agreement, implementation of these international obligations by contracting parties at national level may nevertheless be problematic. A particularly significant form of direct precaution is that urged in the Bamako Convention, namely "clean production methods, rather than the pursuit of a permissable emissions approach based on assimilative capacity assumptions." This cannot be said to be international practice because the convention is not in force, however it is a design for a genuinely precautionary procedure at the international level. The Convention further states that:

> "In this respect Parties shall promote clean production methods applicable to entire product life cycles including: raw material selection, extraction and processing; product conceptualization, design, manufacture and assemblage;

materials transport during all phases; industrial and house hold usage ... clean production shall not include "end-of-pipe" pollution controls such as filters and scrubbers ..."

Calls for clean production are predicated on the scientific inadequacies of emission standards based on assimilative capacity assessments of the environment in question. Assimilative capacity calculations require a predictive assessment of causal pathways within ecosystems; they therefore run counter to the inherent uncertainties of predictive science in areas of causal uncertainty and complexity, discussed earlier. Early criticisms of assimilative capacity calculations came from within the scientific community and tended to argue for the incorporation of a substantial margin of error into the determination of acceptable emission standards; levels of acceptability should be set by technical feasibility criteria - the use of "best available technology" - and therefore lower, and more precautionary than would otherwise have been the case. Sperling (1986)

Clean production takes these kinds of arguments further by taking account of "all of the material flows through society." It has been defined by an expert group convened by UNEP's Industry and Environment Office as: "the conceptual and procedural approach to production that demands all phases of the life-cycle of a product should be addressed with the objective of prevention or minimization of short and long-term risks to humans and to the environment." Baas, Hofman et al (1990)

Moreover, a legal commitment to clean production will contribute substantially to meeting the environmental imperative of integrated forms of pollution control. The Sienna Forum on International Law of the Environment (YB Int' Env. L. 1990) has noted that:

"The 'sector by sector' approach, adopted in concluding conventions, often dictated by the need to respond to specific incidents, involves the risk of losing sight of the need for an integrated approach to the prevention of pollution and the continuing deterioration of the environment."

Traditional Sources: from discourse to obligation

(a) Treaties

Article 38 of the Statute of the International Court of Justice cites as a source of international law, "international conventions, whether general or particular, establishing rules expressly recognized by the contesting states."

The treaties referred to above - climate change, biodiversity, European Union - create contractual obligations binding on those parties that ratify. They are therefore committed to adopting the precautionary principle as a general principle in fulfilling the objectives of the conventions. The practice of the conventions will determine the ultimate effect of that commitment. We now have some experience of precautionary practice as is evidenced by the examples cited above.

Of all the treaty references, arguably the most significant is that of the Treaty of European Union. This is because the principle will now attach itself to the interpretation of existing secondary legislation when applied to contemporary problems and be the preambular inspiration behind future legislation.Two further points are worth stressing. First, the language employed is of a "harder", binding type rather than a "softer", recommending type. Where Article 130r of the SEA stated principles of the latter type ("preventive action should be taken", "polluter should pay"), the Maastricht revision states simply that Community policy shall follow the precautionary principle.

Alternatively, it could be said that the consensus demonstrated by the 166 signatories to the climate change convention (now 63 ratifications) does add real authority to the claim that the precautionary principle has achieved some kind of status as a universal policy principle.

Of course, other treaty references such as OSPAR 1992 are not yet in force. However treaties which are signed and not ratified may nontheless provide evidence of the emergence of a rule of customary international law.

(b) Customary international law

Drawing partly from the above account of treaty developments, it may also be said that the evidence for the precautionary principle constituting a customary norm of international law is increasingly conclusive. Article 38 of the International Court of Justice cites "international custom, as evidence of a general practice accepted as law." Customary norms have been deemed by the Court to arise when state practice is extensive and virtually uniform, and regarded by states as legally obligatory. *(North Sea Continental Shelf cases)*

Consider, simply, the importance of the UN Conference on Environment and Development in contributing evidence in support of the emergence of a customary rule of law with universal application. The vast majority of world's leaders were represented at UNCED, the political declarations were therefore authorised at the highest possible level by the largest collection of leaders ever assembled, and the Conventions were signed by virtually all States. In the Rio Declaration on Environment and Development, which contains 27 principles to guide State and inter-State behaviour, and which was universally accepted at UNCED, the precautionary principle, is stated in mandatory terms.

During the discussions of the application of the precautionary principle at the Fourteenth Consultative Meeting of the Contracting Parties to the London Dumping Convention in November 1991, it was noted by several delegations that the precautionary principle had been adopted in several other international fora and incorporated into national environmental law and policy as such represented an increasingly accepted basis for environmental protection policy and a shift in emphasis in decision-making in favour of a bias towards safety and prevention of release of contamination.

Even the brief citations of explicit precautionary language above provides considerable evidence of the extension and uniformity of the precautionary principle. It should be stressed that this review is by no means comprehensive; precautionary measures are now contained, both explicitly and implicitly, in numerous interstate conventions, ministerial declarations, and reports and recommendations issued by international organizations, both governmental and otherwise. Some of these are binding in themselves, some are not, some would be if the agreements they are contained in were ratified. In generating a customary rule one is faced with a mixed bag of sources.

Opinio juris may be established in a variety of ways. Recent treaty developments provide prima facie evidence of an emergent sense of legal obligation to adhere to the precautionary principle. Significantly, those parties opposing the formal inclusion of the principle into the terms of the conventions noted above, have argued against that inclusion on grounds of redundancy. For instance, the United States submission to the London Dumping Convention's working group on the precautionary principle stated that: "It is largely because the Convention employs such an approach that it is unclear how the express adoption of a precautionary approach would change decision-making under the LDC." Hey (1991). The terms of opposition to the principle, in other words, can demonstrate the prevailing sense of obligation towards it.

State practice may itself constitute evidence of opinio juris. This is especially so in newly-developing areas of law; as states continue to endorse the precautionary principle, customary law can form instantaneously, precisely because there is no pre-existing relevant body of customary international law to be displaced. Bin Cheng (1965) (1983); Tunkin (1961); Kunz (1953) An informative precedent is provided by the development of rules governing space sovereignty. Christol (1962)

During the International Geophysical Year (IGY) (1957-1958), the urgent need for internationally-collaborative research efforts became widely-recognised. Expectations that the scientific community should not miss out on the chance for extended scientific investigation of phenomena unique to the period, and the lack of a pre-existing customary law of outer-space, allowed for the instant development of a new body of international customary law. The rule that national sovereignty over air space does not extend as far as the minimum altitude required for planetary orbit, grew directly from the cooperative endeavours of the IGY. The analogy with current international environmental developments is obvious enough; the precautionary principle may be seen as emerging in response to uniform expectations surrounding the need for international collaboration, expectations generated by a rapidly growing awareness of environmental degradation and its transnational genesis.

Alternatively, the instantaneous nature of these developments may be exaggerated; norms of precaution are evident well before the principle's international articulation in the late 1980s. As early as 1972, Kirgis (1972) argues that in a transnational context United States practice, "after having indicated some reluctance to consider unproven damage, has now evolved into a rather clear recognition of a duty to take account of it, and even to abstain from proposed action if the damage could be serious and if available safeguards do not give substantial assurance of safety."

Towards genuine international law?

Transnational identities point towards the development of a body of law that addresses problems of global interdependence directly, rather than indirectly through the medium of state sovereignty. International environmental law has already partially dispensed with that medium; the expansive role of transnational epistemic communities in the construction and implementation of particular regional environmental regimes has been convincingly demonstrated. Cameron and Wade-Gery (1992). These closely self-identifying groups of policy-makers and scientists have acted directly in response to their perception of a transnational environmental interest, and thus begun a conceptual redefinition of sovereignty.

Because the precautionary principle arises from, and reciprocally stimulates, global epistemic communities, it constitutes a move towards a similar redefinition at the global level. In as much as it represents a growing transnational interest in the protection of the environment as an end in itself, it serves the development of the law of an international society, the society of all societies, and no longer the international law of the society of independent sovereign states. Allott (1990) has stressed that it is a particular:

> "consciousness which makes possible, which legitimates, which naturalizes, the way in which we conceive of interna tional society and international law."

The precautionary principle represents the beginnings of a change in this consciousness; the extent of the uncertainties it seeks to resolve, and the transnational identities consequently generated, threaten the adequacy of international law and policy developed on the basis of existing conceptions of sovereignty. Hence a reconceptualization of international society and law becomes possible. To quote Allott again:

> "When law becomes not merely the multilateralization of individual purpose but the universalization of social pur pose, it transcends self-interest and becomes the self-creating of a society."

This, he argues, is a genuine international society, contrasting with what he terms the "phantom international society" which has been generated by a "partial social process... conceived as the interacting of the governmental public realms of the state-societies as units of willing and acting, mathematical points with location but without extension..."

These reconceptualizations are obviously only at an incipient stage, but they hold out the promise of international law that will function as the law of an actual international society: one that is not conceived of as a community of states with separate interests, but one that is increasingly and transnationally concerned with the protection of its entire environment.

Conclusion

The precautionary principle is a general principle which binds state parties to the international conventions which give expression to it. It is a principle of international environmental law. There remains debate about whether it is yet a principle of customary international law binding on all states. In that debate I feel comfortable in arguing that it is, whether I am persuasive, others must judge.

Allott, P. 1990. Eunomia: New Order for a New World. Oxford University Press.

Baas, Hofman, Huisingh, Huisingh, Koppert & Neumann. 1990. Protection of the North Sea: Time for Clean Production.

Bin Cheng. 1965. United Nations Resolutions on Outer Space: Instant International Customary Law. 5 Indian Journal of International Law 23.

Bin Cheng. 1983. Custom: The Future of General State Practice in a Divided World, in

Johnston and MacDonald. The Structure and Process of International Law 513.

Birnie, P. and Boyle, A. . International Law and the Protection of theEnvironment. .Oxford 1992.

Bodansky, D. 1991. Proceedings of the American Society of International Law.

Cameron, J. The precautionary principle - core meaning, constitutional framework and procedures for implementation. Conference paper. Institute of Environmental Studies, University of New South Wales, to be published in 1994.

Cameron, J. and Abouchar, J. 1991. The precautionary principle: A fundamental principle of law and policy for the protection of the global environment. BCInt'l CLR VolXIV, No1.

Cameron, J. and Wade-Gery, W. Addressing uncertainty, law policy and the development of the precautionary principle.

CSERGE Working Paper GEC 92-42. To be published by the European Science Foundation Programme on Environment, Science and Society, in Environmental Policy Instruments, Prof. Bruno Dente, ed.

Christol, C. 1962. The International Law of Outer Space.

Climate Change: The UK Programme : United Kingdom's Report under the Framework Convention on Climate Change (Cm 2427) January 1994.

Convention for the Protection and Development of the Marine Environment of the Wider Caribbean Region. Article 12. 24 March 1983 The Cartagena Agreement.

Convention for the Regulation of Antarctic Mineral Resources Activities text. 27 I.L.M. 859 1988.

Convention on the Prevention of Marine Pollution by Dumping of Wastes and Other Matter. 1972. 11 ILM 1294 1972.

Convention on the Regulation of Antarctic Mineral Resource Activities. 1988. Article 4.

D'Amato & Chopra. 1991. Whales: their emerging right to life, 85 American Journal of International Law 21.

de La Fayette, L. Review of Freestone & Ijlstra (eds). 1991. The North Sea: Perspectives on Regional Environmental Cooperation. Graham & Trotman 1990. Netherlands International Law Review, Vol. 38.

Final Ministerial Declaration of the Second World Climate Conference. 1990

Fourteenth Consultative Meeting of the London Dumping Convention. Comments on the Secretariat Paper submitted by the United States to the LDC 14/INF.23. 4 November 1991.

Freestone, D. 1991. International Law and Sea Level Rise, Ch.7, in Freestone & Churchill (eds).International Law and Global Climate Change 1991. Graham & Trotman/Martinus Nijhoff.
Freestone, D. The Precautionary Principle, Ch.2 in Freestone & Churchill (eds.), International Law and Global Climate Change. 1991. Graham & Trotman/Martinus Nijhoff.

Gundling, L. 1990. The Status in International Law of the Precautionary Principle, International Journal of Estuarine and Coastal Law, Vol. V, 23.

Handl, G. 1990. Environmental Security and Global Change: the Challenge to International Law, in Handl (ed.) 1 Yb. Int'l Env.L.

Hey, E. The Precautionary Approach and the LDC prepared for the Secretariat of the LDC, August 1991. LDC 14/4. 4 September 1991.

London Dumping Convention. 14/INF.15.

Kunz. 1953. The Nature of Customary International Law, 47 American Journal of International Law 662 666.

Ministerial Meeting of the Oslo and Paris Commissions - Outcome (Paris, 21-22 September 1992), submitted by the Oslo and Paris Commissions Secretariat to the Fifteenth Consultative Meeting. LDC 15/INF.11. 2 October 1992.

Montreal Protocol on Substances that Deplete the Ozone Layer, Adjustments and Amendments. 1991. 30 International Legal Materials.

Montreal Protocol on Substances that Deplete the Ozone Layer, Decision IV/5 and Annex IV, Report of the Fourth Meeting of the Parties ot the UNEP/Ozl.Pro.4/15, 25 November 1992.

Montreal Protocol on Substances that Deplete the Ozone Layer, Preamble, paragraph 6, as amended at the Second Meeting of the Parties to the Montreal Protocol, London 27-29 June 1990, Doc. UNEP/Oz.L.Pro2/3, Annex II, p 25.

Montreal Protocol on Substances that Deplete the Ozone Layer, Preamble, paragraph 6, as amended at the Second Meeting of the Parties to the Montreal Protocol, London 27-29 June 1990, reproduced in 1 Yb. Int'l. Env.L..

Nollkaemper, A. 1991. The Precautionary Principle in International Environmental Law: What's New Under the Sun? Marine Pollution Bulletin. Volume 22, No. 3, March.

Nordic Convention on the Protection of the Environment, Stockholm, 19 February 1974, 13 ILM 591 (1974). Article 3.1991. Sections E.16-E.19.

North Sea Continental Shelf Cases (West Germany v. Netherlands; West Germany v. Denmark), 1969 I.C.J. 3, 43-44.

OECD Secretariat Report, The Role of Uncertainty in Decision-Making in the Area of Environmental Protection, ENV/EC/ECO(91)12, made available to Parties to the London Dumping Convention as Dealing with uncertainty. LDC 14/INF.9, 10 October 1991.

O'Riordan, T. 1992. The Precaution Principle in Environmental Management, Centre for Social Economic Research on the Global Environment, GEC 92-03.

OSCOM Decision 89/1. 14 June 1989.

Oslo Commission Procedures and Decisions Manual, pp C 3/86-E, 1/10/-8/10: pp C A/86-E, 1/2-2/2; and pp C 8/89, 1/5-5/5.

Preamble to the WAF. Annex 4 to LC 15/16 and Annex to LDC.2/Circ 266.

.

Report of the Fifteenth Consultative Meeting. LC 15/16. 3 December 1992.

Report of the Fifteenth Consultative Meeting. 9-13 November 1992. LC 15/16 3 December 1992. Paragraphs 5.2-5.18.

Report of the Fourteenth Consultative Meeting. 25-29 November 1991. Paragraphs 4.1-4.19 and Annex 2 of the LDC 14/16 30 December 1991.

UN Secretary-General Report to the General Assembly at its 46th Session. Doc. A/46/156, 19 April 1991.

Second International Conference on the Protection of the North Sea, London. 24-25 November 1987. Ministerial Declaration issued by the Department of the Environment of the United Kingdom. April 1988.

Sperling, K.R. 1986. Protection of the North Sea: Balance and Prospects. Marine Pollution Bulletin. Vol. 17, No. 6.

Statute of the International Court of Justice. Article 38.1.

Treaty of Rome. Article 130r section 2, as amended by the Single European Act, O.J., 1987. L.169.

Treaty of Rome, Title XVI. Article 130r section 2, as amended by Title II of the Treaty on European Union signed in Maastricht on February 7, 1992.

Tunkin. 1961. Remarks on the Juridical Nature of Customary Norms of International Law, 49 California Law Review 419.

United Nations Framework Convention on Climate Change. 1992.

United Nations General Assembly Resolution 7 (XXXVII) World Charter for Nature 1982. Article 11(c).

von Moltke, K. 1988. The Vorsorgenprinzip in West German Policy. Royal Commission on the Environment. 12th Report. Appendix 3. Legislative references of the Vorsorgenprinzip include Bundesimmissionsschutzgestz (Federal Emission Control Act); the Atomgesetz 9 (Nuclear Energy Act). Article 7, note 2, no 3. and the Gestz uber die Umweltvertraglichkeitsprufung (Environmental Impact Assessment Act).

Part V

The Future

Chapter 16

Seeping Through the Pores

By Timothy O'Riordan and James Cameron

We ended the introductory chapter with the view that day to day behaviour by individuals and households the world over is an amalgam of precaution and nonprecaution. Can we honestly equate a greater commitment to precaution with a shift towards a more sustainable existence? We do not believe that the precautionary principle is either sufficiently well-defined nor properly mature as a practical concept to make such a judgement. Giving the earth space to breathe is part of the strong sustainability criterion outlined by modern environmental economists (see Turner, 1993, 17-20). So, too, is the protection of critical life support processes, namely those that truly keep the earth as a viable totality. Both of these are cardinal concepts of precaution. But we lack the scientific understanding and the sense of preciousness about these mysterious keystone processes adequately to generate any kind of responsive and anticipatory safeguarding device. And we are still many miles away from an ethic, let alone a mechanism, to fund those individuals and nation states whose formerly legitimate development opportunities have to be stalled in the name of safeguarding critically vulnerable life support processes for the earth as a whole.

Finding the mechanisms is troublesome enough. More problematic is the search for a meaningful relationship between precaution, sustainable development and global citizenship. All these ideas are so befuddled with contrary ideologies and inconsistent interpretations that they have become metaphors for a global power play between the forces of what might broadly be called humanity, and those that fall under the imperative of capitalism. The swirl of contradictory ambivalence between these two not wholly incompatible motives for the pursuit of happiness and wealth leave these great environmental themes in limbo. The precautionary principle is caught in a net of conflict, not entirely of its own making. Ironically, it is because it is so closely connected to dramatic happenings in the worlds of science, diplomacy, economics, ethics and the law that it has gained some political prominence.

But humanism and capitalism need not work at cross purposes. So there is room for the precautionary principle to seep through the pores of social change. There will be no "big bang" of collective environmental enlightenment. Indeed, to aim at such an objective would be both foolhardy and inevitably counterproductive. We offer a number of small steps through which a more clearly identifiable practice of precaution might evolve, bearing in mind that in every human culture there must, and should, be great variations in both interpretation and in practice.

Guiding behaviour

The most likely combination for guiding behaviour away from potential environmental damage towards more far-seeing sustaining action remains collectively accepted regulation and innovative use of economic incentives. The regulatory format wil have to be transnational, backed by regimes that buttress its purpose and its authority. The complicated legal and political apparatus underlying regional and global agreements needs to be streamlined to shrug off its tendency toward excessive bureaucracy and cumbersome administrative procedures. Sadly all the signs are in the opposite direction. It is not easy to see a reversal of the trend without a greater sense of trust and collective commitment to the objectives of shared action. Perhaps the very weightiness of time-consuming administrative and political preparation for complicated conventions will encourage the emergence of smaller, more fleet of foot networks of diplomats and interest group representatives who more readily might charge themselves with a common purpose.

As to the matter of the reconstitution of market subsidies that distort prices in favour of malpractice and exploitation, and their substitution for environmental taxes, permit trading arrangements and secondary markets in resource rights and waste discharges, will the theory has been developed, but the practice remains tardy (see Turner et al., 1994). As David Pearce suggests, economists are ambivalent about precaution as a device for allocating prices and environmental values, partly because of its bias in favour of preventive costs over uncertain future gains. Ironically, the use of market prices alone will not promote the cause of precaution. Such prices require political weighting to give them "bite" over current consumption patterns. This moves the process of pricing away from "pure" economics into the arenas of politics, ethics, diplomacy and the law. This in turn requires a precaution-sensitised citizenry for its success. And this in turn again, requires radical transformations of the current roles for education and the media.

Envisioning futures

With the advent of computerised virtual reality, and the growing sophistication of graphics software, it is possible to visualise arrangements while individuals can create their own global futures, in such matters as atmospheric warming, ozone depletion and species loss. Equally more significant is the same exercise at the local level of Local Agenda 21s. Here the scope is for a variant of a simulation game through which players can scan assumptions about future states, test the robustness of the science, and pick out futures that explicitly take into account such moral concerns as burden sharing, intergenerational fairness, intrinsic natural rights and the safeguarding of ecological space. This computer programming could be used in the schools, on specialised TV channels with "voting" procedures built in, or through the local and national media. The software will need to be sophisticated enough to allow for uncertainty to be treated separately as data limitation, data variability and indeterminacy. This should allow players to recognise the significance of probability as applied to the exercise of civic responsibility via such devices as group-framed ethical weighting. Already this practice is being followed in embryonic form via sustainable development "round table" networks in Australia, New Zealand and Canada. Here groups of representatively selected citizens mediate their way to common positions over resource use, consumption patterns and landuse futures to prepare a common agenda for a sustainable transition. There is no reason in principle why various aspects of precaution, as outlined in Chapter 1, could not be slotted into this process.

Trading environmental space

There is much interest in the notion of joint implementation in global environmental management (see for example Brown and Adger, 1993 for a good summary, and Pearce and Bann, 1993 for some examples). Broadly speaking the idea is to allow parties to pool their responsibilities over long term environmental protection whereby one "buys" up the potential damage of the other as part of a commitment to sustainable development. Examples include private and public US agencies purchasing forest development to sequester CO_2, in exchange for builidng another coal fired electricity plant in the US. Similarly Norway has grant aided this manifestation of more electricity efficient light bulbs in Mexico, to offset its unwillingness and costliness of reducing its transport-based CO_2 emissions.

Into this arena could tread the precautionary principle. Ironically one role would be to ensure long term guarantees of compliance of the offset. This is no point, for instance, in planting a forest to absorb CO_2, only to see it cut down by vandals, desperate locals who want the land, or by insurance fraudsters and the like. So precaution, in the form of liability cover, would have to apply to the administrative aspects as well as to the content of such arrangements.

Such arrangements would require very sensitive handling. It is easy to level the charge that tradeable environmental space is yet another example of power playing by the rich who now want their ozone assimilation and biodiversity tourist spots having, in part, created the forces that are destroying the earth (Sachs, 1993 provides the most accessible summary of such views). But here is where the triple focus of international agreement and regulation, commonly based futures determination and trading mechanisms for ensuring environmental rights are safeguarded could be made to collaborate in a myriad of exciting ways.

All this suggests that precaution should is less likely to evolve in regulatory regimes where environmental considerations do not yet figure prominently. This applies particularly to financial markets, national income accounting, corporate profit analysis, domestic household budgets, the hierarchical professions where established customs die hard (the law, accountancy, medicine, academia), and the media. Similarly in governing systems where care is not prized, where consultation is not welcomed, and where public interpretations of danger at odds with expert judgement are not accepted, so the precautionary principle will be resisted and treated with suspicion. It follows that day to day behaviour by individuals and households the world over is an amalgam of precaution and non-precaution. The great challenge is slowly but steadily to shift that bias towards a greater acceptance of precaution in the spirit of collective self interest.

This may happen in a variety of ways:

(i) via innovation in the use of economic measures to guide behaviour away from potential environmental damage towards more far-seeing sustaining action. Already this is beginning to happen in the use of market subsidies and taxes, deposit refund schemes and secondary markets in resource rights and waste discharges.

(ii) via small steps in compensatory arrangements such as planning gain or environmental betterment, carbon "offsets" (purchasing CO_2 emissions from other parties or countries at lower cost than removing one's own CO_2 emissions) and tradeable property rights in ecologically diverse regions so as to purchase development elsewhere but keep the most biologically rich areas for the world to enjoy.

(iii) via increased use of local media to stimulate and support local initiatives geared to a more sustainable use of energy and resources. Each small collective action cumulates into participatory precaution. We are still at the threshold of the revolution in local sustainability partnerships.

(iv) by accepting that science is based, as most scientists know, on inadequate models and best guess predictions. This means much more emphasis on monitoring and observation - boring but necessary - and the painstaking build up of more robust indicators of ecological health or disease. It also will place much more attention on interdisciplinarity, especially the crossing of the bridge between natural sciences, eco nomic valuation and political power. Valuation is a function of power, monetary surrogates are only as acceptable as are tolerated by those who have to pay or to impose them. If more justice is to be sought then mediation and consensus formation become important means of linking the natural sciences to this social burden.

All this suggests that precaution should enter by stealth, not by force; by supportive adjustment, not by brazen entry; by enlightened self interest, not by magisterial command. Precaution should seep through the pores of social change and environmental emancipation stimulating this all important modulation as much as it is stimulated by it. Precaution will best evolve slowly, through acceptance and discussion, as attitudes to the rights of future generations and to a more vernacular role for science become more accommodating. In all walks of life and at all levels of government, precaution should proceed with purpose and with tenacity. As governing regimes recognise international and intergenerational obligations, as democratic governments lead and are pushed to accept that collective action, even if it means short term difficulties, will lead to a more just and habitable world, so precaution will take hold in all aspects of environmental management and budget making. The citizen, the consumer, the householder and the politician are all one and the same people. Therefore as the precautionary principle flowers into full bloom so the artificial distinctions that unnaturally separate their roles and their attendant views on the world will slowly melt into obscurity.

Brown, K. and Adger, N. 1993. Forests for International Offsets: Economic and Political Issues of Carbon Sequestration. CSERGE Working Paper GEC 93-15, University of East Anglia, Norwich and University College London.

Pearce, D.W. and Bann, C. 1993. North-South Transfers and the Capture of Global Environmental Value. CSERGE Working Paper GEC 93-24, University College London and University of East Anglia, Norwich.

Sachs, W. (ed) 1993. The Politics of Global Ecology. Zed Books, London.

Turner, R.K. (ed) 1993. Sustainable Environmental Economics and Management. Belhaven, London.

Turner, R.K., Pearce, D.W. and Bateman, I.J. 1994. Environmental Economics: An Introduction. Harvester Wheatsheaf, Hemel Hempstead.

INDEX

Abgaben, *48*
Ackerman and Stewart, *222, 224*
Act (1976), German Clean Air, *36*
Action Plans, *188*
Action Programme, first, *236*
fourth, *235*
fifth, *235-6*
Administrator, *219*
Advisory Committee on the Release to the Environment of Genetically Modified Organisms (ACRE), *130, 180-1*
Africa, *114*
Agenda 21, *192, 194, 267, 270*
Agg and Zabel, *77*
Alkali Act (1874), *241*
Allott, *282*
Alps, *114*
American media, *171*
Americans, the, *21*
Article 38, International Court of Justice, *279*
Asia, *160*
Association of Chambers of Commerce (DIHT), *49*
Association of German Industry (BDI), *41*
Atlantic, the, *112*
Atom Act (1955), *45*
Attfield, Robin, *66, 129, 159*
Australia, *201, 252 294*
Australian, study of power, *28*

Baas et al., *87, 277*
Balkan, *169*
Baltic, *69*
Bamako Convention, *276*
Barlow et al., *105*
BAT, *50, 153, 221-2, 276*
BATNEEC, *25, 50, 147, 153, 158, 180*
Bavarian Christian Social Union (CSU), *46*
Belsky, *207*
Benzene case, *216*
Bergen, *236*

Bergen Ministerial Declaration on Sustainable Development in the ECE Regions, *213, 232, 239*
Bin Cheng, *280*
Biodiversity Convention of the Rio (1992) UNCED Conference, *160, 269*
Birkeland, *80*
Birnie and Boyle, *263*
Bodansky, Dan, *22, 52, 106, 200, 264*
Boehmer-Christiansen, Sonja, *16, 27, 53, 56, 267*
Boehmer-Christiansen and Skea, *39*
Boehmer-Christiansen and Weidner, *47*
Boehmer-Christiansen et al., *32*
Boelens, *86*
Braer disaster, *168*
Brandt, Willy, *43*
Bremerhaven Workshop, *72*
Breyer, *219*
Britain, 32, 201, *229-30*
British, the, *23, 230*
British, government, *128, 192, 238-9, 242*
Isle, *85*
law, *178*
media, *171*
minister, *237*
regulator, *103*
White Paper (1990), *242*
Brown and Adger, *295*
Brown Parliament, *47*
Brundtland Report, *160, 163, 232*
Bund, *43*

Cabinet, 168
Cadée, *78*
Cameron, James, *24, 145, 200, 266*
Cameron and Abouchar, *154, 163, 267*
Cameron and Berg, *72*
Cameron and Wade-Gery, *267,281*
Campbell, *121*
Canada, *201, 294*
Canaries, *112*
Caughley and Lawton, *83*
Central Electricity Generating Board (CEGB), *121*

Central Government, *196*
CFC, *69, 90, 205, 212, 232, 236, 239-40, 275*
Chair, Victorian Environmental Protection Agency (EPA), *258*
Chamber of Manufacturers, Australian, *258*
Chambers 20th Century Dictionary, *75, 91*
Chancellor, *41*
Chapter 28, Agenda 21, *192*
Chernobyl, *62, 156*
Christian Democrats (CDU), *46*
Christol, *280*
Citizen Action Groups, *44*
Clean Air Act (1970), *204, 207, 213-4, 219, 221*
Clean Air Act (1974), *47*
Clean Air Act Amendments (1977), *207*
Clean Water Act, *204, 207, 213, 215, 219, 221-2, 224*
Climate Convention, *275*
Clover, Charles, *67, 129*
Club of Rome, *163*
Co_2, *14, 27, 242, 275, 295-6*
Colorado potato beetle, Leptinotarsa decemlineata, *83*
Collins, *123*
Commission, *28, 237*
Commission for Sustainable Development, *160*
Committee, *130, 181*
Committee of the Regions, *190*
Common Agricultural Policy (CAP), *48*
Common Burden Principle, *34*
Commonwealth, Australian, *253*
Commonwealth, Government, *202*
Community, *233*
Compendium of Ecologically Sustainable Development Recommendations (ESD), *257*
Congress, *211, 217-9*
Conservative, *24, 130*
Constitution, Australian, *253*
Continuous Plankton Recorder (CPR), *85*
Contracting Parties, *271*
Convention on the Protection and use of Transboundary Watercourses and International Lakes, *271*
Corbyn and Niland, *258*
Costanza, Robert and Cowell, Laura, *16, 68*
Council, *194, 237*

Council Resolutions, *235*
CSIRO, *257*

Daily Telegraph, the, *170*
D'Amato and Chopra, *275*
Danish coastline, *70*
Davies, James, *170*
Davies et al., *78*
Dayton, *79*
Dayton et al., *80*
DDT, *212*
De La Fayette, *265*
Delaney Admendment, *215*
Department of the Environment (DoE), *90, 128, 177, 180-1, 186, 240*
Department of the Environment Guide to Environmental Appraisal of Development Plans (1993), *186*
Department of Prime Minister and Cabinet, Australia, *257*
Department of Transport (DoT), *185*
Denmark, *184, 186, 197*
Dethlefsen and Thurberg, *75*
Dickson, *86*
Die Grunen, *47*
Directive 79/831, *237*
Directive 80/778, *237*
Directive 90/219, *237*
Directive 90/220, *237*
Directive, Contained use of GMOs, *176*
Directive, Deliberate Release into the Environment of GMOs, *176*
Directive, European Community, *141*
District of Columbia Court of Appeals, *213, 216, 221*
Dogger Bank, *73*
Dovers and Handmer, *259*
Dower, *161*
Downs, Anthony, *165*
Downs cycle, *165*
Drake, *258*
Dutch, *195*
Dutch coastline, *70*
Dutch Elm Disease, *175*
Dwyer, *204, 215, 219-20*

Earl of Caithness, *237*

Earth, *41, 92, 109-10, 114-6*
Earth Mother, *108*
East German Government, *44*
East Germany, *32*
EC Commissioner, *237*
EC Council Decision, *236*
EC Directives, *176*
EC Fifth Environmental Action Programme Declaration, *190*
EC Member States, *242*
Ecologically Sustainable Development (ESD), *252, 254, 257*
EC Treaty, *236*
EDF v. EPA, *216*
Eisma and Irion, *86*
Endangered Species Act, *210, 218*
England, *213*
English, *170*
Enquete Kommission, *39*
Environmental Impact Assessment (EIA), *25, 274*
Environmental Imperative, *235*
Environmental Protection Act(EPA) (1990), *178, 184, 241*
Environmental Protection Agency (EPA), USA, *204, 207, 210-1, 213-5, 219-22, 224*
Environment Correspondent, *170*
Environment Court, NSW, *256*
Environment Protection Bill, S. Australia (1993), *255*
Ethyl Corp., *214*
Ethiopia, *165*
EU Directive, *186*
EU Fifth Environmental Action Plan, *186*
EU Nitrates Directive, *90*
Europe, *28, 51, 114*
European, *171, 184, 186*
European Commission (EC), *23, 106, 176, 190, 229, 233*
European Community, *145, 230, 233*
European Council, Declaration at Dublin, *235-6*
European Union (EU), *23, 27, 107, 196-7, 200-1, 278*
Expected Utility (EU), *132-4*
Expected Value (EV), *132-4*
Express, the, *170*
Extension of Extension, *163*
Extension of Precaution, *163*
Far East, *162*

Farrier, David, *253*
Farrier, David and Fisher, Liz, *68*
Federal Administrative Appeals Tribunal, Australia, *256*
Federal Air Quality Protection Act (BImSchG), *45*
Federal Economic Affairs Ministry (BMWi), *41*
Federal Food, Drug and Cosmetics Act (FDCA), *210, 213*
Federal Government, *231*
Federal Government Umweltprogramm, *35*
Federal Health Ministry, *42*
Federal Insecticides, Fungicide and Rodenticide Act (FIFRA), *210-1, 213*
Federal Ministry for the Environment, *35*
Federal Water Pollution Control Act, *204*
Federal Water Pollution Control Act (1974), *217-8*
Federation, *32*
Filey Brig, Yorkshire, *72*
Financial Times, the, *170*
First North Sea Conference, *73*
First Principles, *238*
Firth of Forth, *72*
Fisher, Liz, *202*
Floistad, *123*
Flournoy, *215*
Föderung, *34*
Foreign Affairs Ministry, *36*
Fourteenth Consultative Meeting, *273*
Fourth Conference, *70*
France, *201, 275*
Fraunhofer Institutes, *52*
Free Democrats (FDP), *43*
Freedom of Access to Environmental Information Regulation, *197*
Freeman, *56*
Freestone, *265, 267*
French Revolution, *230*
Friedensvorsorge, *39*
Friends of the Earth (FoE), *128*
Friends of the Earth, Model Environmental Charter, *188*

Gaia, *108-11, 114-6*
Gaian, *113*
Gaines and Roughgarden, *81*
Gebot, *36-7*

Gefahrenabwehr, *36, 231*
Gemeinlast prinzip, *33*
Genetically Modified Organisms (GMO), *173-7, 179-82*
Genscher, Hans Dietrich, *43, 47*
Gerlach, *86*
German, *156, 167*
German, Bight, *72*
coastline, *70*
constitution, *40*
Council of Experts, *231*
experience, *27*
Federal Government, *35, 40, 230*
Guidelines, *231, 238*
Federal Minister, *48*
socio-legal tradition, *16*
state, *55*
Germany, *230, 236, 238, 240*
Gewerbeordnung (GWO), 41
Giant Burrowing Frog, *256*
Global Environmental Facility, *160*
Global Forum, *192*
Godfray and Blyth, *85*
Gordon-below-Franklin, *253*
Government, *169, 184, 229*
Greece, *201*
GreenNet, *193*
Green Party, *47*
Greenpeace, *121, 124, 128*
Greens, the, *46*
Gross National Product (GNP), *158*
Group of Experts on the Annexes, *272*
Guardian, the, *128, 170*
Gundling, Lothar, *264, 267*
Gunkel, *79*

Habermas, *167*
Hague, the, *240*
Haigh, Nigel, *23, 104, 145, 200, 234, 267*
Hampstead Heath, *183*
Hams, Tony, *130*
Handl, Gunther, *264, 267*

Hansen, *78*
Harcourt, *83*
Harding, Ronnie, *68, 201*
Harding and Fisher, *259*
Hartkopf, Dr. Gunter, *44*
Hassell, *84*
Health Ministry, *44*
Helicon pellucidum, *78*
Helsinki Commission (HELCOM), *70*
Herculean, *222*
Hey, *267, 280*
Hill, Julie, *28, 65, 103, 107, 130*
Hill, Octavia, *183*
H.M. Government, *174*
Hoogweg, Ducrotoy and Wettering, *75*
Houck, *221-3*
House, the, *207*
House of Commons, *276*
House of Lords, *237*
Huber, *212-3*
Hunt, Jane, *67-8*
Hutchingson, *80*

ICES Advisory Committee on Marine Pollution, *75*
Independent on Sunday, the, *170*
India, *163*
Industrial Union Department, AFL-CIO, *210, 213, 216*
Initiative of German Business for World-wide Precautionary Action to Protect the Climate, *49*
Institute of Environmental Studies, University New South Wales, *257*
Intergovernmental Agreement on the Environment (IGAE), *252-5, 257-8*
Interim Ministerial Meeting (IMM), *70*
Interior Ministry, *36, 46*
International Council for the Exploration of the Sea (ICES), *75*
International Geophysical Year (IGY), *280*
International Monetary Fund (IMF), *161*
Interparliamentary Working Group for Nature-Appropriate Economic Activities (IPA), *41*
Investionshilfen, *47*
Ireland, *201*

Irish Sea, *276*
Israeli-Palestinian, *65*
Israeli Prime Minister, *65*

Jackson, *87*
Jamieson, Dale, *162*
Japan, *206*
Japanese Knotwood, *175*
Jasanoff, *122-3*
Johnson, *34, 213*
Johnston and MacGarvin, *89*
Johnston and Simmonds, *123*

Kareiva, *84*
Kent, *72*
Kettle, Brett, *68*
Keynesianism, *47*
Kiechle, Herr, *48*
Kirgis, *281*
Kirkpatrick, *75*
Klimatpolitik, *39*
Koelke, *45*
Kohl, Helmut, *47*
Köhler and Pluta, *76*
Kooperation, *33*
Krönke, *73*
Kunz, *280*

Länder, *32, 40, 42*
Lancelot et al., *78*
Land and Environment Court, NSW, *256*
Langguth, *44*
Large Combustion Plant Ordinance (1983), *45*
Lascelles, David, *170*
Latin, *209*
Latin America, *160*
Latour, *123*
Law et al., *76*
Lawton, *84*
Leader of the Palestine Liberation Organisation, *65*
Lean, Geoffrey, *170*
Left, the, *40*

Levidow and Tait, *172*
Lewin, *81*
Local Agenda 21 (LA21), *184, 192-5, 197, 294*
Local Authority Associations, *192*
Local Government Act, NSW, *257*
Local Government Management Board (LGMB), *192-3*
London Amendment to the Montreal Protocol, *270*
London Dumping Convention (LDC), *88, 272, 279*
Lord Caithness, *229*
Lovelock, James, *13, 63*
Luftereinhaltungsgesetz, *41*

Maastricht Treaty, *23, 235, 237, 278*
MacGarvin, Malcolm, *63, 68, 87, 146*
MacGarvin and Johnston, *75*
Maddox, Bronwen, *170*
Mail, the, *170*
Major, Mr. John, *169, 269*
Malaysian delegation, *162*
Mann and Lazier, *80*
Marine Mammal Protection Act, *210*
Mars, *109*
Marxist, *56*
Mathiessen et al., *76*
Matthews, *77*
Mayntz et al., *44*
Mazur, *124*
McCarthy, Mike, *170*
McDonnell, Gavin, *68*
McGowan and Walker, *80*
McIntyre and Pearce, *75*
Mediterranean, *201*
Menge and Sutherland, *79*
Mesarovich and Pestel, *163*
Mexico, *295*
Minimata, *206*
Ministerialbürokratie, *44*
Ministerial Declarations, *70, 267*
Ministerial North Sea Conference, *70*
Ministerial Statement of Conclusions, Interim Ministerial Meeting, *86*

Minister of State for the Environment, *229*
Ministers, *232*
Ministry of Agriculture, Fisheries and Food (MAFF), *124*
Mixed Function Oxidase (MFO), *76*
Montreal, *270*
Montreal Protocol, *275*
Morphet, Janice, *130*
Morphet et al., *195*
Muller, *32, 43*
Myers, *12*
Mytilus californianus, *80*

NAAQS, *220*
Narjes, *50*
National Environmental Policy Act (NEPA), (1970), *207*
National Parks and Wildlife Act, *256*
National Strategy, Australian, *257*
National Strategy for Ecologically Sustainable Development (ESD), *256*
Natur,
Nature's Capital, *146*
natürlichen Lebensgrundlagen, *32*
Netherlands, *184, 195*
New Assessment Procedure (NAP), *272*
Newly Industrialising Countries (NIC), *161*
New Scientist, the, *229*
New South Wales Environmental Protection Act, *255*
New South Wales Government, *255*
Newtonian, *63-4*
New Zealand, *294*
Nirmalakhandan and Speece, *75*
Nohrstedt, *167*
Nollkaemper, *267*
Non-governmental Organisations (NGO), *51, 121, 124*
Nordic Council Conference on Pollution of the North Sea, *267*
Nordic countries, *266*
Nord-Rhein-Westfalen, *41*
North America, *32, 43, 51*
North American, *114, 203*
North East Atlantic, *69, 233*
North East River Purification Board, *90*

North Sea, *63, 69, 119, 168, 231-3, 239*
North Sea Conference, *205*
North Sea Conference, Third, *240*
North Sea Interim Ministerial Meeting, *74*
North Sea Ministerial Conference, *119*
North Sea Ministerial Declarations, *89*
North Sea Quality Status Report, *77*
North Sea Task Force, *77, 123*
Norway, *295*
Norwegian Government, *232*
Not Entailing Excessive Cost (NEEC), *153, 158*
Not-in-my-back-yard (NIMBY), *141*
NO_x, *53*
NRDC v. EPA, *219, 221*

Observer, the, *170*
Operophtera brumata, *83*
Organisation for Economic Cooperation and Development (OECD), *12, 175, 233*
O'Riordan, *56, 156, 158-60, 163*
OSHA, *215-6*
Oslo and Paris Commissions (OSCOM and PARCOM), *70*
OSPARCOM, *86, 270, 275-6, 278*
Oxfordshire, *83*

Pacific Rim, *161*
Paine, *80*
Parfit, Derek, *155*
Paris Convention (PARCOM), *74, 276*
Parliament, *229, 237*
Parliamentary, *271*
Partnerships for Change, *192*
PCB, *69, 90*
Pearce, David, *21, 62, 107, 128, 138, 180, 294*
Pearce and Bann, *295*
Pearce et al., *54*
Pedersen, *204*
Percival, *204, 215, 220, 222*
Percival et al., *206*
Perrings and Pearce, *146*
Peterman and M'Gongle, *89*
Peters, *79, 82*

Phaeocystis, *78*
Pisaster ochraceus, *80*
Planning and Compensation Act, *185*
Planning Policy Guidance (PPG), *186*
Pleistocene, *115*
Polluter Pays Principle (PPP), *235*
Portugal, *201*
Preamble, *269*
President, Local Government Association, *253*
Press Association, *170*
Prime Minister, *169*
Prime Minister, Australian, *253*
Price and Stevens, *92*
Principle 15, 267
Precautionary Principle (PP), *132, 145, 163, 229, 257*
Programmes, *235*
Prokuda, *256*
Protection of the Environment Administrative Act (POE), NSW (1991), *255*
Protocol on Substances that Deplete the Ozone Layer, *270*
Puget Sound, *80*

Quality Status Report, *86, 124*
Quantative Structure Activity Relationship (QSAR), *75-6*

Ramchandran and Pearce, *132, 145*
Reagan, *205*
Red List (U.K. DoE), *77*
Report, *160*
Report from the Government to the Federal Parliament on the Protection of Air Quality (1984), *36*
Research and Development (R&D), *48, 50*
Reserve Mining Co. v. EPA, *207*
Resources Editor, *170*
Rhine, *72*
Rio Conference, *13*
Rio Declaration, *240, 268*
Rio Declaration, Principle 15, *18*
Rio Declaration of Principles, *23*
Rio de Janiero, *12, 160, 162, 186, 192, 232-3, 267*
risk assessment (RA), *25*

Robinson, Brian, *258*
Rodgers, *212*
Rothschild, *82*
Roughgarden, *81*
Round Table, *194*
Royal Commission on Environmental Pollution, *176, 230, 240*
Royal Society Study Group on Risk, *134*
Ruckelshaus, *207*
Ruhr, *43*
Russian roulette, *208*
Ryan, Sean, *170*

Sachs, *295*
Salomons, *86*
Salzwedel and Preusker, *45*
Science, *124*
Scientific Group on Dumping, *272*
Second International Conference on the North Sea, *238, 265, 267*
Second World Climate Conference Ministerial Declaration, *212*
Second World War, *40*
Secretary of State, *185*
Sellafield, *121-2, 276*
Shetlands, *72*
Shoalhaven Council, *256*
Sienna Forum on International Law of the Environment, *277*
Simberloff, *78*
Simmons, *12, 15*
Single European Act (SEA), *233, 236, 278*
Single European Act Articles, *234*
SO_2. *53*
Social Democratic Administration, *36*
Social Democratic Party (SPD), *43*
Sofortprogramme, *43*
Solaster dawsoni, *80*
Sorge, *38*
Sorgfaltspflicht, *38*
Southern North Sea, *201*
Spain, *201*
Special Working Groups (SWG), *194*
Sperling, *70, 277*
Staat, *40*
Staatsziel, *32*

Stand der Tecknik, *42, 45, 52*
State of the Environment, *188*
State of the Environment Reports, *188*
State Premiers, Australian, *253*
States, the, *202, 233*
States, Australian, *253*
Statute, International Court of Justice, *262, 278*
Stebbing, *69, 75*
Stebbing et al., *73, 76*
Stein, Mr. Justice, *256, 259*
Stewart, Alan, *255*
Stockholm Conference (1972), *43*
Strauch, *258*
Strauss, Franz-Josef, *47*
Strong et al., *84*
sub-Saharan Africa, *160*
Summit, *168*
Supreme Court, *218*
Sun, the, *170*
Sunderman, *77*

Tait and Levidow, *172-3*
Territory Chief Ministers, Australia, *253*
Thames estuary, *72*
Thermal Oxide Reprocessing Plant (THORP), *276*
Third Conference, *265*
Third Reich, *40*
Third World, *160-1*
This Common Inheritance: Britain's Environmental Strategy, *238*
Tickell, Sir Crispin, *113*
Times, the, *170*
Treaty of European Union, *268, 278*
Treaty of Maastricht, *229, 233*
Treaty of Rome, *233*
Tunkin, *280*
Turner, *19, 292*
Turner et al., *12, 20, 294*
TVA v. Hill, *218*
Tyne estuary, *72*

Umweltpolitik, *40*
Umweltschutz, *31-2*
Underwood, *78, 81*
Underwood and Denley, *79, 81*
United Kingdom (UK), *134, 141, 175-6, 180, 185-6, 190, 193, 195, 232, 275*
United Kingdom, Department of the Environment, *72*
Government, *176, 242, 269*
Strategy for Sustainable Development (1993), *174, 190*
United Nations Conference on Environment and Development (UNCED), *12, 130, 232-3, 252, 265-6, 268-9, 279*
United Nations Economic Commission for Europe, *232*
United Nations Environment Programme (UNEP), *12, 205*
United Nations Environment Programme (UNEP) Governing Council, *88*
United Nations Framework Convention on Climate Change, *18, 201, 209, 266*
United Nations Framework Convention on Desertification, *66*
United Nations Secretary General, *267*
United States of America (USA), *123, 140-1, 201, 204-7, 209, 212-3, 215, 217-8, 223, 280-1*
United States, administrative law, *22*
environmental law, *106*
Supreme Court, *216*
Universities, *195*

van Putten and Jackson, *204, 217*
Varley et al., *83*
Venus, *109*
Verbot, *37*
Verein Deutscher Ingineure (VDI), *41*
Verhutung, *39*
Vernon, *53*
Verursacher, *34, 48*
Verursacherprinzip, *33*
Vienna Convention, *270*
Volkswirtschaft, *34*
von Moltke, Konrad, *31, 39, 230-1*
Vorgbeuge, *39*
Vorsicht, *39*

Vorsorge, *34-5*
Vorsorgeprinzip, *16, 31, 33, 230-1*

Wadden Sea, *70*
Waldegrave, Mr., *229*
Waldsterben, *36, 45*
Wales, *175*
Warner, Sir Frederick, *66, 129, 134*
Waste Assessment Framework (WAF), *273, 275*
Water Licensing and Water Administration Acts, NSW, *255*
West, the, *162*
West German, *40, 267*
West Germany, *54*
Wey, *35-6, 44*
White Paper (1990), *24, 238-9*
Wicke, *54*
Willingness to Accept (WTA), *138*
Willingness to Pay (WTP), *138*
Wilson and Crouch, *208*
Wirtschaftliche Vertretbarkeit, *33*
Wooton, *82*
World Bank, *161*
World Resources Institute, *12*
Worldwatch Institute, *12*
Wynne, Brian, *65-6, 68, 91, 117-8*
Wynne, Brian and Mayer, Sue, *53, 68, 229*

NO ENTRIES FOR X

Yellow-bellied Glider, *256*
Yeo, Mr., *74*
Young, Michael, *257, 259*
Ythan, *90*

NO ENTRIES FOR Z